THE SOUP BOOK

THE SOUP BOOK

More than 120 superb soups, ranging from chilled, smooth and
chunky vegetable soups to sustaining poultry, meat and fish
gumbos, broths, chowders and rouilles

Beautifully illustrated with more than 450 photographs showing
how to make each step-by-step recipe, along with complete
nutritional information for every dish

Edited by Anne Sheasby

southwater

This edition is published by Southwater

Southwater is an imprint of Anness Publishing Ltd
Hermes House, 88 89 Blackfriars Road, London SE1 8HA
tel. 020 7401 2077; fax 020 7633 9499
www.southwaterbooks.com; www.annesspublishing.com

If you like the images in this book and would like to investigate using them for publishing, promotions or advertising, please visit our website www.practicalpictures.com for more information.

© Anness Publishing Ltd 2007

UK agent: The Manning Partnership Ltd, 6 The Old Dairy, Melcombe Road, Bath BA2 3LR
tel. 01225 478444; fax 01225 478440; sales@manning-partnership.co.uk
UK distributor: Grantham Book Services Ltd, Isaac Newton Way, Alma Park Industrial Estate, Grantham, Lincs NG31 9SD; tel. 01476 541080; fax 01476 541061; orders@gbs.tbs-ltd.co.uk
North American agent/distributor: National Book Network, 4501 Forbes Boulevard, Suite 200, Lanham, MD 20706; tel. 301 459 3366; fax 301 429 5746; www.nbnbooks.com
Australian agent/distributor: Pan Macmillan Australia, Level 18, St Martins Tower, 31 Market St, Sydney, NSW 2000; tel. 1300 135 113; fax 1300 135 103; customer.service@macmillan.com.au
New Zealand agent/distributor: David Bateman Ltd, 30 Tarndale Grove, Off Bush Road, Albany, Auckland; tel. (09) 415 7664; fax (09) 415 8892

Publisher: Joanna Lorenz
Senior Editorial Manager: Conor Kilgallon
Project Editors: Felicity Forster, Molly Perham, Lucy Doncaster and Elizabeth Woodland
Designer: Nigel Partridge
Cover Designer: Nigel Partridge
Production Manager: Steve Lang

Previously published as part of a larger volume, *The New Book of Soups*

10 9 8 7 6 5 4 3 2 1

NOTES
Bracketed terms are intended for American readers.

For all recipes, quantities are given in both metric and imperial measures and, where appropriate, in standard cups and spoons. Follow one set, but not a mixture, because they are not interchangeable.

Standard spoon and cup measures are level. 1 tsp = 5ml, 1 tbsp = 15ml, 1 cup = 250ml/8fl oz.

Australian standard tablespoons are 20ml. Australian readers should use 3 tsp in place of 1 tbsp for measuring small quantities of gelatine, flour, salt, etc.

American pints are 16fl oz/2 cups. American readers should use 20fl oz/2.5 cups in place of 1 pint when measuring liquids.

Electric oven temperatures in this book are for conventional ovens. When using a fan oven, the temperature will probably need to be reduced by about 10–20°C/20–40°F. Since ovens vary, you should check with your manufacturer's instruction book for guidance.

The nutritional analysis given for each recipe is calculated per portion (i.e. serving or item), unless otherwise stated. If the recipe gives a range, such as Serves 4–6, then the nutritional analysis will be for the smaller portion size, i.e. 6 servings. Measurements for sodium do not include salt added to taste.

Medium (US large) eggs are used unless otherwise stated.

Front cover shows Beef and Barley Soup – for recipe, see page 150

ETHICAL TRADING POLICY
Because of our ongoing ecological investment programme, you, as our customer, can have the pleasure and reassurance of knowing that a tree is being cultivated on your behalf to naturally replace the materials used to make the book you are holding. For further information about this scheme, go to www.annesspublishing.com/trees.

CONTENTS

INTRODUCTION

Soups are very versatile and can be made using many different ingredients. One of the great things about soup is that you can put a selection of fresh, raw and sometimes cooked ingredients into a pan with some well-flavoured stock, let the mixture bubble away for a short while, and within no time at all you have created a delicious, flavourful, home-made soup with very little effort.

Many soups are quick and easy to make and simply combine a few key ingredients with added flavourings, such as herbs or spices, whereas other soups – perhaps those ideal for a special occasion or a more substantial meal – may require a little more preparation. Some soups make ideal starters to a meal, and they are always a popular choice, while others are substantial enough to be meals in themselves, served with plenty of fresh crusty bread as an accompaniment. There are light and refreshing soups that are chilled, ideal for summer dining *al fresco*, and rich and creamy soups, perfect for meals shared with family and friends. Whichever kind you choose, it is well worth the effort to create fresh and flavourful soups in your own kitchen.

An essential ingredient in most soups is a good well-flavoured stock, preferably home-made. Stock (bouillon) cubes and stock powder save time, but it is hard to beat the flavour and quality of home-made stocks, and they are relatively easy and inexpensive to make. Once you have a good basic stock, whether it is vegetable, fish, meat or chicken stock, there is a huge range of soups that you can create in your

Above: Tom Yam Gung with Tofu is a famous Thai speciality.

kitchen. However, remember that your stock will only be as good as the quality of ingredients used to make it – you cannot produce a good, tasty stock from old, limp, past-their-best vegetables! If you are really short of time, you could choose one of the chilled fresh stock products available from some supermarkets and delicatessens.

Very little specialist equipment is needed to make soups, although you will find that a food processor or blender is invaluable and will save time and effort when you want to purée soup mixtures before serving – although pressing the soup through a sieve (strainer) or using a hand-held blender are perfectly good alternatives. You will probably already have in your kitchen a good-quality, heavy-based pan, a sharp knife and chopping board, and a vegetable peeler.

The addition of an attractive garnish, perhaps a sprinkling of chopped fresh herbs, some vegetables cut in julienne strips, or a swirl of cream added at the last minute, will enhance even the simplest of soups. Soups may be served on their own or topped with a few crunchy croûtons or grilled croûtes.

Left: Meatballs in Pasta Soup with Basil makes a substantial main course.

Soups feature in every cuisine around the world – whether they are called gumbos, potages, broth, chowders or consommées. Now that once-unfamiliar ingredients are readily available in specialist food shops and many supermarkets, there is absolutely no reason why you cannot make these in your own home.

In summer, choose from light and refreshing soups such as French Vichyssoise, Chilled Avocado with Cumin from Spain, or Mexican Chilled Coconut Soup. Smooth vegetable soups include Irish Parsnip Soup, Caribbean Peanut and Potato Soup, or velvety Pumpkin Soup with Rice from Morocco. Chunky vegetable, legume, pasta and noodle soups are ideal winter warmers. You could try classic Russian Borscht with *Kvas* and Soured Cream, Tuscan Bean Soup or North African Spiced Soup. Pasta and noodle soups range from Borlotti Bean and Pasta Soup and Avgolemono with Pasta to more exotic choices, such as Malaysian Prawn Laksa and Udon Noodles with Egg Broth and Ginger.

Soups made with chicken, meat, fish or shellfish are full of nourishment and make a complete meal served with

Below: Kale, Chorizo and Potato Soup is for those who enjoy hot and spicy food.

Above: Irish Country Soup is a hearty dish traditionally served with Soda Bread.

slices or chunks of fresh crusty bread or bread rolls, served warm or cold. Here the choice is wide and varied – from traditional Irish Country Soup and Lobster Bisque to the more unusual and exotic Smoked Haddock Chowder, Vermouth Soup with Seared Scallops, Rocket Oil and Caviar, or Scallop and Jerusalem Artichoke Soup.

Each recipe in this book has easy-to-follow step-by-step instructions and a beautiful colour photograph to show the finished dish. Few dishes give more all-round pleasure than a good home-made soup, and in this wonderful collection of recipes the world of soups is yours to explore.

VEGETABLES

Using vegetables offers the cook an infinite number of culinary possibilities, including creating a wide range of delicious and flavourful soups. The choice of vegetables is immense, and the growing demand for organic produce has led to pesticide-free vegetables becoming widely available. Vegetables are an essential component of a healthy diet and have countless nutritional benefits. They are at their most nutritious when freshly picked.

Carrots

The best carrots are not restricted to the cold winter months – summer welcomes the slender, sweet new crop, often sold with their feathery tops. Look for firm, smooth carrots – the smaller they are, the sweeter they taste. Carrots should be prepared just before use to preserve their valuable nutrients. They are delicious in Carrot and Orange Soup, as well as being an important ingredient in many other soups and in home-made stock. Raw carrots, cut into thin julienne strips, make an unusual and attractive garnish.

Right: Carrots give soup a sweet flavour, and add colour too.

Beetroot

Beetroot is the key ingredient in the classic Russian Borscht. It also combines well with other flavours, for example in Beetroot Soup with Mascarpone Brioche, which is a light and refreshing choice, or the more substantial Fragrant Beetroot and Vegetable Soup with Spiced Lamb Kubbeh. If cooking beetroot whole, wash carefully in order not to damage the skin or the nutrients and colour will leach out. Trim the stalks to about 2.5cm (1in) above the root. Small beetroots are sweeter and more tender than the larger ones.

Below: Celeriac is bumpy with a patchy brown/white skin.

Celeriac

Strictly speaking, celeriac is a root vegetable, as it is the root of certain kinds of celery. It has a similar but less pronounced flavour than celery, but when cooked it is more akin to potatoes. It is used in soups such as Celeriac Soup with Cabbage, Bacon and Herbs.

Swedes

The globe-shaped swede (rutabaga) has pale orange-coloured flesh with a delicate sweet flavour. Trim off the thick peel, then treat in the same way as other root vegetables. For soups, swede is usually peeled and diced, then cooked with other vegetables and stock until tender. It may be finely chopped and used in chunky vegetable soups, or cooked with stock and other ingredients, then puréed to create a smooth soup.

Left: Beetroot's deep ruby-red colour adds a vibrant hue to soups. It is a classic ingredient of the Russian soup Borscht.

Above: Parsnips are best used in the winter months and make good, hearty, warming soups.

Parsnips

These winter root vegetables have a sweet, creamy flavour and are a delicious element in many soups. Parsnips are best purchased after the first frost of the year, as the cold converts their starches into sugar, enhancing their sweetness. Scrub well before use and peel only if the skin is tough. Avoid large roots, which can be rather woody.

Turnips

Turnips have many health-giving qualities, and small turnips with their green tops intact are especially nutritious. Their crisp, ivory flesh, which is enclosed in white, green and pink-tinged skin, has a pleasant, slightly peppery flavour, the intensity of which depends on their size and the time of harvesting. Turnips add a lovely flavour and substance to vegetable-based soups, for example Russian Spinach and Root Vegetable Soup.

Jerusalem artichokes

This small, knobbly tuber has a sweet, nutty flavour. Peeling can be fiddly, although scrubbing and trimming is usually sufficient. Store in the refrigerator for up to one week. Use in the same way as potatoes – they make good, creamy soups.

Potatoes

There are thousands of potato varieties, and many lend themselves to particular cooking methods. Main crop potatoes, such as Estima and Maris Piper, and sweet potatoes (preferably the orange-fleshed variety which have a better flavour than the cream-fleshed type) are ideal for using in soups. Potatoes are also good (especially when mashed or puréed) as a thickener for some soups. Discard any potatoes with green patches. Vitamins and minerals are stored in, or just beneath, the skin, so it is best to use potatoes unpeeled.

Buying and storing root vegetables

Seek out bright, firm, unwrinkled root vegetables and tubers, which do not have soft patches. When possible, choose organically grown produce, and buy in small quantities to ensure freshness. Store root vegetables in a cool, dark place.

Broccoli

This nutritious vegetable should be a regular part of everyone's diet. Two types are commonly available: purple-sprouting, which has fine, leafy stems and a delicate head, and calabrese, the more substantial green variety with a lightly budded top

Above: Trim the stalks from broccoli and divide it into florets. The stems of young broccoli can be sliced and used, too.

and thick stalk. Choose broccoli that has bright, compact florets. Yellowing florets, a limp woody stalk and a pungent smell are an indication of overmaturity. Broccoli adds flavour and texture as well as a lovely colour to soups. Once cooked, it is often puréed to create an attractive green-coloured soup. It is a versatile vegetable and combines well in soups with other ingredients.

Cauliflower

The cream-coloured compact florets, or curds, should be encased in large, bright green leaves. There are also varieties with purple or green florets. Raw or cooked cauliflower has a mild flavour and is delicious when combined with other ingredients to make tasty soups such as Curried Cauliflower Soup or Cream of Cauliflower.

Cabbage

There are several different varieties of cabbage, and one of the best to use in soups is Savoy, which has substantial, crinkly leaves with a strong flavour. Firm red and white cabbages are also good for soups as they retain their texture.

Left: Cauliflower can be used either raw or cooked.

Spinach

This dark green leaf is a superb source of cancer-fighting antioxidants. It contains about four times more beta carotene than broccoli. It is also rich in fibre, which can help to lower harmful levels of LDL cholesterol in the body, reducing the risk of heart disease and stroke. Spinach does contain iron but not in such a rich supply as was once thought. It also contains oxalic acid, which inhibits the absorption of iron and calcium in the body. However, eating spinach with a vitamin C-rich food will increase absorption. Spinach also contains vitamins C and B6, calcium, potassium, folate, thiamine and zinc. Spinach and other leafy green vegetables are ideal shredded and added to soups or cooked in them and then puréed to create flavourful, nutritious dishes with a lovely deep green colour, ideal for swirling cream into just before serving.

Pumpkins

These are native to America, where they are traditionally eaten at Thanksgiving. Small pumpkins have sweeter, less fibrous flesh than the larger ones. Pumpkin can be used in smooth soups such as Pumpkin Soup with Rice. Squash, such as the butternut variety, makes an alternative to pumpkin – Roasted Garlic and Butternut Squash Soup with Tomato Salsa will waken up the taste buds.

Right: Making soup is a good way of using up a glut of courgettes in the autumn.

Below: Fresh, crisp cucumbers are excellent in chilled soups.

Above: Corn works particularly well in creamy fish-based soups.

Courgettes

The most widely available summer squash, courgettes (zucchini) have most flavour when they are small and young. Standard courgettes, as well as baby courgettes, may be used on their own or with other ingredients, such as mint and yogurt, to create delicious soups. They are a key ingredient in Greek Aubergine and Courgette Soup, served with tzatziki.

Cucumbers

The Chinese say food should be enjoyed for its texture as well as for its flavour; cucumbers have a unique texture and refreshing, cool taste. Varieties include English cucumbers, ridged cucumbers, gherkins and kirbys. Cucumbers are ideal for chilled soups such as Cucumber and Yogurt Soup with Salsa and Chilled Cucumber and Prawn Soup.

Corn

There are several varieties of corn – the kind we eat on the cobs is sweetcorn (corn). Baby corn cobs are picked when immature and are cooked and eaten whole. Corn and baby corn, as well as canned or frozen sweetcorn kernels, are all used in creative soup recipes such as Corn and Potato Chowder or Corn and Red Chilli Chowder.

Fennel

Florence fennel is closely related to the herb and spice of the same name. The short, fat bulbs have a similar texture to celery and are topped wtih edible feathery fronds. Fennel has a mild aniseed flavour, which is most potent when eaten raw. Cooking tempers the flavour, giving it a delicious sweetness. Fennel marries wonderfully with fish in Bourride of Red Mullet and Fennel.

Tomatoes

There are dozens of varieties to choose from, which vary in colour, shape and size. The egg-shaped plum tomato is perfect for many types of cooking, including soups, as it has a rich flavour and a high proportion of flesh to seeds – but it must be used when fully ripe. Too often, store-bought tomatoes are bland

and tasteless because they have been picked too young. Vine-ripened and cherry tomatoes, together with large beefsteak tomatoes, have good flavour and are also good for soups. Sun-dried tomatoes add a rich intensity to soups. Genetically engineered tomatoes are now sold in some countries; check the label. If tomatoes are cooked with their skins on, you will find that the soup may need puréeing and straining to remove skins and seeds.

Peeling and seeding tomatoes

Tomato seeds can give soups a bitter flavour. Removing them and the tomato skins will also give a smoother result, which is preferable for many soups.

1 Immerse the tomato in boiling water and leave for about 30 seconds – the base of each tomato can be slashed to make peeling easier.

2 Lift out the tomato with a slotted spoon, rinse in cold water to cool slightly, and then peel off the skin.

3 Cut the tomato in half, then scoop out the seeds with a teaspoon and remove the hard core. Dice or coarsely chop the flesh according to the recipe.

Buying and storing tomatoes

When buying tomatoes, look for deep-red fruit with a firm, yielding flesh. Tomatoes that are grown and sold locally will have the best flavour. Farmers' markets are a good place to buy vegetables, or you could grow your own. To improve the flavour of a slightly hard tomato, leave it to ripen fully at room temperature. It is best to avoid refrigeration because this stops the ripening process and adversely affects the taste and texture of the tomato.

Peppers

In spite of their name, (bell) peppers have nothing to do with the spice pepper used as a seasoning. They are actually members of the capsicum family and are called sweet peppers, bell peppers and even bull-nose peppers. The colour of the pepper tells you something about its flavour. Green peppers are the least mature and have a fresh "raw" flavour. Red peppers are ripened green peppers and are distinctly sweeter. Yellow/orange peppers taste more or less like red peppers, although perhaps slightly less sweet. Peppers add a lovely flavour and colour to soups such as Gazpacho or Chilled Tomato and Sweet Pepper Soup.

Right: Peppers add wonderful colours to soups – red, green, yellow and orange.

Above: Puréed avocados make soups really creamy.

Chillies

Native to America, this member of the capsicum family is extensively used in many cuisines, including Mexican, Indian, Thai, South American and African. There are more than 200 different varieties, and they add a fiery spiciness to soups.

Avocados

Strictly a fruit rather than a vegetable, the avocado has been known by many names – butter pear and alligator pear to name but two. There are four varieties: Hass, the purple-black small bumpy avocado, the Ettinger and Fuerte, which are pear-shaped and have smooth green skin, and the Nabal, which is rounder in shape. The black-coloured Hass has golden-yellow flesh, while green avocados have pale green to yellow flesh. Avocados can be used to make tempting soups such as Avocado and Lime Soup with a Green Chilli Salsa.

Right: Aubergine is delicious in minestrone soups.

Aubergines

The dark purple, glossy-skinned aubergine (eggplant) is the most familiar variety, although it is the small, ivory white egg-shaped variety that has inspired its American name. There is also the bright green pea aubergine that is used in Asian cooking, and a pale-purple Chinese aubergine. Creamy Aubergine Soup with Mozzarella and Gremolata is a delicious soup that will impress your dinner party guests.

Celery

Celery has a sharp and savoury flavour, which makes it excellent for soups and stocks. The tangy, astringent flavour and crunchy texture of celery contrasts well with the other ingredients. Most supermarkets sell both green and white celery (when celery grows naturally the stalks are green; banking up earth against the shoots makes it pale and white). Look for celery with fresh-looking leaves, and avoid any that have outer stalks missing.

Onions

Every cuisine in the world includes onions in one form or another. They are an essential flavouring, offering a range of taste sensations, from the sweet and juicy red onion and powerfully pungent white onion to the light and fresh spring onion (scallion). Pearl onions and shallots are the babies of the family. Shallots and leeks can be used in place of onions in many recipes, while spring onions may be used as a flavouring or garnish.

Buying and storing onions

When buying, choose onions that have dry, papery skins and are heavy for their size. They will keep for 1–2 months in a cool, dark place.

Garlic

An ingredient that everyone who does any cooking at all will need, garlic is a bulb that is available in many varieties. Their papery skins can be white, pink or purple. Colour makes no difference to taste, but the attraction of the large purple bulbs is that they make a beautiful display in the kitchen. As a general rule, the smaller the garlic bulb, the stronger it is likely to be. If stored in a cool, dry place and not in the refrigerator, garlic will keep for up to eight weeks.

Leeks

Like onions and garlic, leeks have a long history and are versatile, having their own distinct, subtle flavour. They are less pungent than onions, but are still therapeutically beneficial. Excellent in soups, leeks add delicious flavour and texture to many recipes. A classic combination of leeks and potatoes produces the popular soup Vichyssoise, which can be served hot or cold as a light starter. Commercially grown leeks are usually about 25cm (10in) long, but you may occasionally see baby leeks, which are very mild and tender and can also be used in soups. Try winter soups such as Chicken, Leek and Celery Soup or Irish Leek and Blue Cheese Soup.

Above: Garlic is used in meat and vegetable soups.

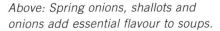

Above: Spring onions, shallots and onions add essential flavour to soups.

Above: Shiitake mushrooms are popular in Japanese soups.

Mushrooms

The most common cultivated variety of mushroom is actually one type in various stages of maturity. The button (white) mushroom is the youngest and has, as its name suggests, a tight, white, button-like cap. It has a mild flavour. Cap mushrooms are slightly more mature and larger in size, while the flat field (portabello) mushroom is the largest and has dark, open gills. Flat mushrooms have the most prominent flavour. Mushrooms are a useful ingredient in many soups, and add flavour and texture, as well as colour (especially the brown cap/chestnut [cremini] or field mushrooms). Fresh and dried wild mushrooms also add delicious taste to some soup recipes, such as Wild Mushroom with Soft Polenta.

Several varieties of wild mushroom are now available in supermarkets, for example oyster and shiitake. Oyster mushrooms are ear-shaped fungi that grow on rotting wood. Cap, gills and stem are all the same colour, which can be greyish brown, pink or yellow. They are now widely cultivated, although they are generally thought of as wild mushrooms. Delicious in both flavour and texture, they are softer than button (white) mushrooms when cooked but seem more substantial, having more of a "bite" to them.

Shiitake mushrooms are Japanese fungi from the variety of tree mushrooms (called *take* in Japan, the *shii* being the hardwood tree from which they are harvested). They have a meaty, slightly acid flavour and a distinct slippery texture. Try them in Shiitake Mushroom Laksa.

Buying and storing mushrooms

Buy mushrooms that smell and look fresh. Avoid ones with damp, slimy patches and any that are discoloured. Store in a paper bag in the refrigerator for up to 4 days. Wipe mushrooms with damp kitchen paper before use but never wash or soak them.

Rocket

Usually thought of as a salad vegetable, rocket is actually a herb with a strong peppery taste that adds flavour and colour to soups such as Leek, Potato and Rocket Soup.

Sorrel

Another salad vegetable that is a herb, sorrel has a refreshing, sharp flavour. In soups it is good mixed with other herbs and green leaves, as in Sorrel, Spinach and Dill Soup. Salad leaves are best when they are very fresh, and do not keep well. Avoid leaves that are wilted or discoloured. Store in the refrigerator for 3–4 days.

Above: Rocket gives soups a strong, peppery flavour.

Above: Fresh sorrel mixes well with other herbs.

Cleaning leeks

Leeks need meticulous cleaning to remove any grit and earth that may hide between the layers of leaves. This method will ensure that the very last tiny piece of grit will be washed away.

1 Trim off the root, them trim the top of the green part and discard. Remove any tough or damaged outer leaves.

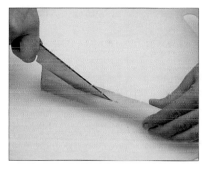

2 Slash the green part of the leek into quarters and rinse the entire leek well under cold running water, separating the layers to remove any hidden dirt or grit. Slice or leave whole, depending on the recipe.

LEGUMES

Pulses, lentils and peas provide the cook with a diverse range of flavours and textures, and they are a great addition to soups. They have long been a staple food in the Middle East, South America, India and the Mediterranean. Low in fat and high in complex carbohydrates, vitamins and minerals, legumes are also an important source of protein for vegetarians, matching animal-based sources when eaten with cereals.

PULSES

The edible seeds from plants belonging to the legume family, pulses are packed with protein, vitamins, minerals and fibre, and are low in fat. For the cook, their ability to absorb the flavours of other foods means that pulses can be used as the base for an infinite number of dishes, and many are ideal in soups.

Red kidney beans

These are dark red-brown kidney-shaped beans that keep their shape and colour when cooked. They are excellent in soups as well as many other dishes. Raw kidney beans contain a substance that cannot be digested and which may cause food poisoning if the toxins are not extracted. It is therefore essential that you fast-boil red kidney beans for 15 minutes before use.

Above: Dried broad beans can be used when fresh ones are not in season.

Broad beans

Usually eaten in their fresh form, broad (fava) beans change in colour from green to brown when dried, making them difficult to recognize. The outer skin can be very tough and chewy, and some people prefer to remove it after cooking. Broad beans add delicious flavour to soups – try Broad Bean, Minestrone or Catalan Potato Broad Bean Soup.

Cannellini beans

These small, white, kidney-shaped beans – sometimes called white kidney beans – have a soft, creamy texture when cooked and are popular in Italian cooking. They can be used in place of haricot (navy) beans and make a tasty addition to soups such as Pasta, Bean and Vegetable Soup.

Chickpeas

Also known as garbanzo beans, robust and hearty chickpeas have a delicious nutty flavour and creamy texture. They need lengthy cooking and are much

Left: Cannellini beans give soups a velvety and creamy texture, as well as extra fibre.

Cooking kidney beans

Most types of beans, with the exception of aduki beans and mung beans, require soaking for 5–6 hours or overnight and then boiling rapidly for 10–15 minutes to remove any harmful toxins. This is particularly important for kidney beans, which can cause serious food poisoning if not treated in this way.

1 Put the beans in a sieve (strainer) or colander and wash them well under cold running water.

2 Place the washed beans in a large bowl that allows plenty of room for expansion. Cover with cold water and leave to soak overnight or for 8–12 hours, then drain and rinse.

3 Place the beans in a large pan and cover with fresh cold water. Bring to the boil and boil rapidly for 10–15 minutes, then reduce the heat and simmer for 1–1½ hours until tender.

4 Drain and use as required.

used in Middle Eastern cooking, including soups such as Chickpea and Lentil Soup with Honey Buns and North African Spiced Soup.

Soya beans

These small, oval beans contain all the nutritional properties of animal products but without the disadvantages. They are extremely dense and need to be soaked for up to 12 hours before cooking. They combine well with robust ingredients such as garlic, herbs and spices, and they make a healthy addition to soups. Soya beans are also used to make tofu, tempeh, textured vegetable protein (TVP), flour and the different versions of soy sauce. Tofu is widely used in Asian soups – try Thai Hot and Sweet Vegetable and Tofu Soup, which uses tofu as an ingredient.

Buying and storing beans

Below: Chickpeas add heartiness to soups.

Look for plump, shiny beans with unbroken skins. Beans toughen with age so, although they will keep for up to a year in a cool, dry place, it is best to buy them in small quantities from stores with a regular turnover of stock. Avoid any beans that look dusty or dirty or smell musty, and store them in an airtight container in a cool, dark and dry place.

LENTILS AND PEAS

These are among our oldest foods. Lentils are hard even when fresh, so they are always sold dried. Unlike other pulses, they do not need soaking before being cooked.

Red lentils

Bright orange-coloured red split lentils, sometimes known as Egyptian lentils, are the most familiar variety. They cook in just 20 minutes, disintegrating into a thick purée. They are ideal for thickening soups. Try creative recipes such as Thai-style Lentil and Coconut Soup, or Spiced Lentil Soup with Parsley Cream.

Puy lentils

These tiny, dark blue-green lentils are superior in taste and texture to other varieties and are great added to soups.

Green and brown lentils

Sometimes referred to as continental lentils, these pulses

Right: Soya beans vary in colour from creamy-yellow through brown to black.

Above, from top: Red lentils and puy lentils make excellent thickeners for soup.

retain their disc shape when cooked. They take longer to cook than split lentils – about 40–45 minutes – and are ideal for adding to warming soups.

Peas

Dried peas come from the field pea, not the garden pea, which is eaten fresh. Unlike lentils, peas are soft when young and require drying. They are available whole or split; the latter have a sweeter flavour and cook more quickly. Like split lentils, split peas do not hold their shape when cooked, making them perfect for soups. They take about 45 minutes to cook. Dried peas require soaking overnight before use.

Buying and storing lentils and peas

Although lentils and peas can be kept for up to a year, they toughen with time. Buy from stores with a fast turnover of stock and store in airtight containers in a cool, dark place.

MEAT AND POULTRY

Packed with high-quality protein, meat is an excellent food and is used in a variety of soup recipes. Careful rearing means leaner animals and hence healthier cuts of meat, making it perfectly possible to follow current dietary advice while still enjoying meat and poultry. Nowadays we are spoilt for choice with all the types and cuts of meat available. Most butchers and many supermarkets with fresh meat counters are only too happy to advise you on the best cuts of meat to use for all your recipes, including soups.

Chicken

The stock from cooking chicken makes an ideal basis for many delicious soups. If you can, choose corn-fed, free-range or organic birds for the best flavour. Cuts used in soups include breasts, legs and thighs. Boneless thighs or breasts are a good buy.

Duck

There isn't much meat on a duck, so buy big rather than small birds or choose duck breasts. Although leaner than it used to be, duck is still a fatty meat, so remove as much of the fat as possible before cooking. Duck goes well with oranges, and Duck Broth with Orange Spiced Dumplings is a delicious recipe. Lean duck can be used instead of chicken in some soups.

Below, from left: Corn-fed, free-range and organic chickens give the best flavour for chicken stocks.

Turkey

A turkey isn't just for Christmas – today's smaller birds are perfect for soups. Try recipes such as Chinese Chicken and Chilli Soup, or Chicken, Leek and Celery Soup, using turkey in place of chicken.

Bacon

Used in soups to add flavour, bacon can be bought sliced, in lardons (thin strips or dice), or in a piece. It is available smoked or unsmoked (green), and in different cuts – back (lean) or streaky (fatty). Bacon is a key ingredient in Irish Kidney and Bacon Soup, and Bacon Broth.

Pancetta

Pancetta is belly of pork that is cured with salt and spices, and it is eaten either raw in very thin slices, or cut more thickly and used in cooking. It can be substituted for bacon in soup recipes. Try it in the delicious Bacon and Chickpea Soup with Tortilla Chips.

Above: Bacon and pancetta can be used interchangeably.

Beef, lamb and pork

Some soup recipes call for the addition of beef, lamb or pork. These not only bring flavour to a dish, but also make a valuable contribution in terms of nutrition, since they are a source of high-quality protein. When making soup, the best cuts of beef, lamb and pork to choose are steak, chops or fillet, although other cuts such as pork belly, neck of lamb and minced beef, lamb or pork are also used, so be guided by the recipe or ask your butcher for advice. Meat bones are also used for making stocks.

Kidneys

Lamb, pork and ox (beef) kidney may all be used in soups. Ox kidney has the strongest flavour.

FISH

Fish is one of the quickest and easiest foods to cook, and makes an ideal ingredient for soups. As well as being delicious to eat, it is also very nutritious and a great source of easily digestible protein as well as other important nutrients such as B vitamins. White fish such as skinless cod, haddock and monkfish are naturally low in fat. Oily fish such as salmon, trout and mackerel are rich in omega-3 fats, which are beneficial to health, and we are actively encouraged to eat oily fish at least once a week. Oily fish are also a good source of all the B vitamins as well as vitamins A and D.

TYPES OF FISH

We have access to a wide range of fresh sea fish, as well as river and lake fish, some caught from our local shores and others imported from further afield. Although some fish is seasonal, many varieties are available all year round from good fishmongers, supermarkets and town markets.

Both white fish, such as haddock, cod, monkfish and mullet, and oily fish, such as mackerel and salmon, are used as an ingredient in creative soup recipes. Smoked fish such as smoked haddock or smoked cod are also used to create flavourful soups.

Whichever type of fish you are using as an ingredient in your soup, it is always best to buy firm, fresh fish.

Below. Cod blends well with cream or milk to make delicious fish chowders.

Round sea fish

This is a large group of fish that includes cod, haddock, whiting and mackerel, as well as more exotic varieties such as John Dory (or porgy), red mullet or snapper and parrot fish. These fish have a rounded body shape with eyes at each side of the head, and swim with the dorsal fin uppermost. These fish are normally sold whole or in fillets, cutlets or steaks.

Flat sea fish

Plaice, dabs, turbot, sole and skate are common examples of flat sea fish. Flat fish swim on their sides and have both eyes on top of their head. They usually have a white (blind) side and a darker upper surface, which is coloured to camouflage them within their local habitat. Flat fish are usually sold whole or filleted.

Freshwater fish

Freshwater fish may live in freshwater rivers or lakes and include varieties such as salmon, trout and pike. They are usually sold whole or in fillets, steaks or cutlets.

Above: Trout makes a tasty alternative to the more usual clam chowder.

Smoked fish

Fish is usually smoked by one of two methods: hot smoke or cold smoke. Typical examples of smoked fish include haddock, cod, salmon, mackerel, trout and kippers (smoked herrings).

Below: Smoked haddock is sold whole, as fillets (shown here) or thinly sliced.

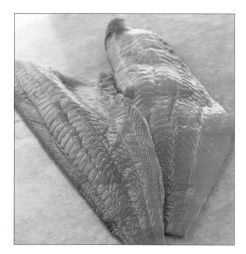

SHELLFISH

We are fortunate to have a good selection of fresh and frozen shellfish available all year round, either shellfish caught off our local shores, or varieties caught further afield and imported. Many shellfish and crustaceans have wonderfully exotic names and almost all shellfish is considered edible, from clams to razor-shells, sea snails and small scallops. Shellfish is at its best when eaten fresh and in season. Frozen shellfish is also available and is a good substitute if fresh is not available.

SHRIMPS AND PRAWNS

There are many varieties of shrimps and prawns, which are known collectively as shrimp in the United States. The smallest are tiny pink or brown shrimp. Next in size come the pink prawns with a delicate flavour. Then there are the larger variety of prawn, which turn bright red when they are cooked. They are highly prized for their fine, strong flavour. Best, and most expensive of all, are large succulent king prawns (jumbo shrimp) which have a superb flavour and texture. Similar to these is the cicala, which resembles a small, flat lobster. Shrimp and prawns can be used in a variety of different tasty soups such as Prawn and Egg-knot Soup, and Wonton and Prawn Tail Soup.

Buying shrimps and prawns

Shrimps and prawns should have bright shells that feel firm; if they look limp or smell of ammonia, do not buy them.

CRUSTACEANS AND MOLLUSCS

Crustaceans range from crabs and lobsters to bright orange crawfish. Squid and cuttlefish are molluscs – their shells are located inside their bodies.

Crab

There are dozens of varieties of crab, ranging from the large common crab to tiny shore crabs that are good only for making soup. All kinds of crabmeat, both fresh and canned, can be used in creative soup recipes. Try recipes such as Crab, Coconut and Coriander Soup, or Chinese Crab and Corn Soup.

Scallops

Scallops are available almost all year round, but are best in winter when the roes are full and firm. Always try to buy them with their delicious coral, although this is not always possible. You can buy them shelled, which saves the effort of cleaning them. But if you clean them yourself, the beard and all dark coloured parts must be removed before

Below: The common or brown crab contains plenty of tasty meat.

Peeling and deveining raw prawns

Raw prawns and large shrimps are often peeled before cooking. Raw prawns must have their intestinal tracts removed before cooking, a process called "de-veining". It is not necessary to de-vein shrimps.

1 Pull off the head and legs from each prawn or shrimp, then carefully peel off the body shell. Leave on the tail "fan" if you wish.

2 To remove the intestinal vein from prawns, make a shallow incision down the centre of the curved back of the prawn using a small sharp knife, cutting all the way from the tail to the head.

3 Pick out the thin black vein that runs the length of the prawn with the tip of the knife and discard.

Cleaning and preparing squid

Before you start, rinse the squid under cold running water.

1 Holding the body firmly in one hand, grasp the tentacles at the base with the other, and gently but firmly pull the head away from the body. As you do this the soft yellowish entrails will come away.

2 Use a sharp knife to cut off the tentacles from the head of the squid. Reserve the tentacles but discard the hard beak in the middle. Remove and reserve the ink sac, then discard the head.

3 Peel the membrane away from the body. Pull out the "quill". Wash the body under cold running water. Cut the body, flaps and tentacles to the required size.

they are cooked and eaten. Frozen scallops have little or no taste. Scallops are an ingredient in exotic soups such as Seafood Chowder, Vermouth Soup with Seared Scallops, and Scallop and Jerusalem Artichoke Soup.

Lobsters

These are the ultimate luxury seafood. Their flesh has a delicious flavour and makes wonderful soups. Lobsters must be bought live or freshly boiled. Try the luxurious, velvety Lobster Bisque topped with double (heavy) cream to really appreciate this superior seafood.

Squid and cuttlefish

These molluscs are indistinguishable in taste, but cuttlefish have a larger head and a wider body with stubbier tentacles. Once the bone has been removed, cuttlefish are very tender. The shell of a squid is nothing more than a long, thin, transparent quill. Both squid and cuttlefish have ten tentacles. Squid is more commonly used in soup recipes. Small squid and cuttlefish should be cooked briefly, just until they turn opaque, or they will become rubbery and tough. Larger specimens need long, slow cooking to make them tender, making them ideal for use in some soups. Try delicious Coconut and Seafood Soup.

Mussels

These shellfish have a smooth texture and sweet flavour. Both whole and shelled mussels may be used in soups, and they also make an attractive garnish, cooked and served in their open shells. Try flavourful soups such as Saffron-flavoured Mussel Soup.

Clams

There are many different types of clam, ranging from the tiny smooth-shelled variety to long, thin razor shells and the large Venus clams with beautiful ridged shells. All have a sweet flavour and a slightly chewy texture. Because they vary so much in size, it is best to ask the fishmonger how many clams you will need for a particular soup or be guided by the recipe. Try tempting recipes such as Clam Chowder or Chilli Clam Broth.

Buying and storing shellfish

When buying fresh shellfish such as scallops, mussels, clams and oysters, look for those with tightly closed shells. They are still alive when sold fresh, and any sign of an open shell may indicate that they are far from fresh. A sharp tap on the shell may persuade the shellfish to close up, but otherwise, avoid it. When buying cooked shellfish such as crab, lobster and prawns (shrimp), make sure the shells are intact. They should feel quite heavy and have a fresh, agreeable smell.

Once purchased, keep fresh shellfish chilled, and store in the refrigerator, covered with a damp cloth, until it is ready to use. As a general rule, fresh shellfish, as well as frozen (defrosted) shellfish, is best eaten on the day you purchase it or used within 24 hours – your fishmonger will be able to advise you more on the length of time recommended for storing shellfish.

Right: Queen scallops are smaller and cheaper than the larger king scallops, but have the same flavour.

PASTA AND NOODLES

The wide range of fresh and dried pasta available to us today ensures that you have plenty of choice when it comes to selecting which pasta to cook. Pasta is a nutritious food and plays an important part in a healthy, well-balanced diet. It is low in fat and provides a good source of carbohydrate. Pasta, especially small shapes such as stellette or pastina, is ideal for use in soups and is an important ingredient in recipes such as Pasta, Bean and Vegetable Soup.

SOUP PASTA

These tiny shapes, of which there are hundreds of different varieties, are mostly made from plain durum wheat pasta, although you may find them made with egg and even flavoured with carrot or spinach.

Types of soup pasta

Teeny-weeny pasta shapes are called pastina in Italian, and there are literally hundreds of different ones to choose from. In Italy they are always served in broths and clear soups, and are regarded almost as nursery food because they are so often served for children's meals.

Shapes of pastina vary enormously, and seem to get more and more fanciful as the market demands. The smallest and most plain

pasta per minestre (pasta for soups) is like tiny grains. Some look like rice and are in fact called *risi* or *risoni*, while others are more like barley and are called *orzi*. Fregola, from Sardinia, looks like couscous, and has a similar nutty texture and flavour. Semi di melone is like melon seeds, as its name suggests, while acini de pepe or peperini is named after peppercorns, which it resembles in shape and size if not in colour. Coralline, grattini and occhi are three more very popular tiny pasta shapes.

The next size up are the ones that are most popular with children. These include alfabeti and alfabetini (alphabet shapes), stelline and stellette (stars), rotellini (tiny wagon wheels) and anellini, which can be tiny rings, sometimes with ridges that make them look very pretty, or larger hoops. Ditali are similar to anellini but slightly thicker, while tubettini are thicker still.

Another category of *pasta per minestre* consists of slightly larger shapes, more like miniature versions of familiar types of short pasta. Their

names end in "ine", "ette" or "etti", denoting that they are the diminutive forms. These include conchigliette (little shells), farfalline and farfallette (little bows), funghetti (little mushrooms), lumachine (little snails), quadretti and quadrettini (little squares), orecchiettini (little ears), renette (like baby penne) and tubetti (little tubes). The size of these varies: the smaller ones are for use in clear broths, while the larger ones are more often used in making thicker soups.

Buying and storing soup pasta

The quality of pasta varies tremendously – choose good-quality Italian brands made from 100 per cent durum wheat, and buy fresh pasta from an Italian delicatessen rather than pre-packed fresh pasta from the supermarket.

Dried pasta will keep almost indefinitely in the store cupboard, but if you keep it in a storage jar, it is a good idea to use it all up before adding any from a new packet.

Fresh pasta is usually sold loose and is best cooked the same day, but can be kept in the refrigerator for a day or two. Fresh pasta from a supermarket is likely to be packed in plastic packs and bags and will keep for 3–4 days in the refrigerator. Fresh pasta freezes well and should be cooked from frozen. Convenient packs of supermarket pasta have the advantage of being easy to store in the freezer.

Left: Tiny soup pasta is available in hundreds of different shapes.

NOODLES

The fast food of the East, noodles can be made from wheat flour, rice, mung bean flour or buckwheat flour. Noodles can be used in a variety of flavourful soup recipes. Try some tasty soups such as Soba Noodles in Hot Soup with Tempura, Thai Cellophane Noodle Soup, Chiang Mai Noodle Soup, or Tokyo-style Ramen Noodles in Soup.

Wheat noodles

These are available in two types: plain and egg. Plain noodles are made from strong flour and water; they can be flat or round and come in various thicknesses. Egg noodles are more common than the wheat variety, and are sold both fresh and dried. The Chinese types are available in various thicknesses. Very fine egg noodles, which resemble vermicelli, are usually sold in individual coils. More substantial wholewheat egg noodles are widely available from larger supermarkets.

Udon and ramen are types of Japanese noodles. Udon noodles are thick and can be round or flat. They are available fresh, pre-cooked or dried. Wholewheat udon noodles have a more robust flavour. Ramen egg noodles are sold in coils and in Japan are often cooked and served with an accompanying broth.

Above:
Egg noodles add flavour and texture to Chinese soups.

Rice noodles

These very fine, delicate noodles are made from rice and are opaque-white in colour. Like wheat noodles, they come in various widths, from the very thin strands known as rice vermicelli, which are popular in Thailand and southern China, to the thicker rice sticks, which are used more in Vietnam and Malaysia.

Cellophane noodles

Made from mung beans, cellophane noodles are translucent and do not need to be boiled; they are simply soaked in boiling water for 10–15 minutes. They have a fantastic texture, which they retain when cooked, never becoming soggy.

Buckwheat noodles

Soba are the best-known type of buckwheat noodles. They are a much darker colour than wheat noodles – almost brownish-grey. In Japan they are traditionally used in soups.

Left: Rice noodles form the basis of many Asian soup recipes.

Below: Cellophane noodles do not need to be boiled.

Buying and storing noodles

Dried noodles are readily available in supermarkets. Packets of fresh noodles are found in the chiller cabinets of Asian stores and some supermarkets. They must be stored in the refrigerator or freezer. Dried noodles will keep for many months in an airtight container in a cool, dry place.

HERBS AND SPICES

Herbs, the aromatic and fragrant plants that we use to add flavour and colour to our dishes, have been cultivated all over the world for centuries. The majority of herbs are familiar as culinary herbs, but many are also good for medicinal and cosmetic purposes. In cookery, herbs are chosen mainly for their flavouring and seasoning properties as well as adding colour and texture to dishes. Herbs, both fresh and dried, add delicious flavour and aroma to a whole variety of dishes, including many hot and chilled soups.

HERBS

Herbs can make a significant difference to the flavour and aroma of a soup, and they can enliven the simplest of dishes.

Basil

This delicate aromatic herb is widely used in Italian and Thai cooking. The leaves bruise easily, so they are best used whole or torn, rather than cut with a knife.

Bay

These dark-green, glossy leaves are best left to dry for a few days before use. They have a robust, spicy flavour and are an essential ingredient in home-made stocks and for a bouquet garni.

Coriander

Warm and spicy, coriander (cilantro) looks similar to flat leaf parsley but its taste is completely different.

Dill

The mild yet distinctive, aniseed flavour of dill makes a good addition to soups, for example in Sorrel, Spinach and Dill Soup.

Kaffir lime leaves

These glossy green leaves are commonly used in Asian cuisines, lending a citrus flavour to soups. They are available fresh from Asian stores, or dried from large supermarkets.

Mint

Mint, a popular herb, has deep green leaves with an unmistakable strong and tangy scent and flavour. It is used in soup recipes such as Iced Melon Soup with Sorbet.

Oregano

This is a wild variety of marjoram with a robust flavour. It goes well with tomato-based soups.

Parsley

There are two types of parsley: flat leaf and curly. Both taste relatively similar, but the flat leaf variety is preferable in cooked dishes. Parsley is an excellent source of vitamin C, iron and calcium.

Above: Tarragon goes well with chicken and shellfish.

Above: Indian-style soups use spicy coriander.

Tarragon

This small, perennial plant bears slim green leaves, and its distinctive taste is said to be a cross between aniseed and mint. It marries well with chicken and shellfish in soups.

Thyme

This robustly flavoured aromatic herb is good in tomato-based soups, as well as soups containing lentils and beans. It is also an essential ingredient in a classic bouquet garni.

Buying and storing herbs

Fresh herbs are widely available, sold loose, in packets or growing in pots. Place stems in a jar half-filled with water and cover with a plastic bag. Sealed with an elastic band, the herbs should keep for about a week.

Right: Basil is an important herb in Italian cooking.

SPICES

Highly revered for thousands of years, spices – the seeds, fruit, pods, bark and buds of plants – add flavour, colour and interest to the most unassuming of ingredients, while the evocative aroma of spices stimulates the appetite. Spices add delicious flavour to many soup recipes.

Chillies

Chillies are available fresh as well as in dried, powdered and flaked form. Dried chillies tend to be hotter than fresh, and this is certainly true of chilli flakes, which contain both the seeds and the flesh. The best pure chilli powders do not contain added ingredients, such as onion and garlic. All types of chilli may be used in a variety of soup recipes.

Coriander

Alongside cumin, ground coriander is a key ingredient in Indian curry powders and garam masala, and in northern Europe the ivory-coloured seeds are used as a pickling spice. Coriander seeds have a sweet, earthy, burnt-orange flavour that is more pronounced than the fresh leaves. The ready-ground powder rapidly loses its flavour and aroma, so it is best to buy whole seeds, which are easily ground in a mortar using a pestle, or in a coffee grinder. Before grinding, lightly dry-roast the seeds in a frying pan to enhance their flavour. Coriander adds delicious flavour and warmth to soups.

Cumin

Cumin is a familiar component of Indian, Mexican, North African and Middle Eastern cooking and is added to soups to give a delicious flavour and aroma. The seeds have a robust aroma and slightly bitter taste, which is tempered by dry-roasting. Black cumin seeds are milder and sweeter. Ground cumin can be harsh, so it is best to buy the whole seeds and grind them just before use to be sure of a fresh flavour.

Ginger

Fresh root ginger is spicy, peppery and fragrant, and adds a hot, yet refreshing, flavour to soups such as the Japanese Miso Broth with Spring Onions and Tofu. When buying ginger, look for firm, thin-skinned and unblemished roots and avoid withered, woody looking roots as these are likely to be dry and fibrous.

Left: Lemon grass stalks are essential in many Asian soup recipes.

Left: Cumin adds taste and aroma.

Lemon grass

This long fibrous stalk has a fragrant citrus aroma and flavour when cut. It is familiar in South-east Asian cooking and may be used as an ingredient in soups from this region. To use, remove the tough, woody outer layers, trim the root, then cut off the lower 5cm (2in) and slice or pound in a mortar using a pestle. Bottled chopped lemon grass and lemon grass purée are also available.

Pepper

Undoubtedly the oldest, most widely used spice in the world, pepper is a versatile seasoning and is invaluable for soups, because it not only adds flavour of its own to a dish, but also brings out the flavour of the other ingredients.

Saffron

The world's most expensive spice is made from the dried stigmas of *Crocus salivus*. Only a tiny amount of this bright orange spice is needed to add a wonderful colour and delicate flavour to fish and shellfish soups.

Salt

It is usually best to leave the seasoning of stocks and soups until the last minute, just before serving. Add salt a little bit at a time, until you have the seasoned flavour you require.

Above: Pink, black and white peppercorns bring out the flavour of your chosen soup ingredients.

Buying and storing spices

Always buy spices in small quantities from a store with a regular turnover. Store in airtight jars in a cool place.

OTHER FLAVOURINGS

There are many other flavourings that are used to add depth to soups – for example, olive oil, flavoured oils and vinegars, alcohol, chilli sauce, pesto and soy sauce, as well as more exotic flavourings such as dashi or fish sauce. Many add that important final touch or richness to a soup, contributing an important element to the overall character. Listed below are some of the flavourings used in this book.

Oils and vinegars

Flavoured oils and vinegars are brilliant for splashing into finished soups to pack an extra punch. Consider chilli oil for a super-fiery flavour in a spicy soup, or basil or rocket oil to enliven a fish or Mediterranean-style soup. Infuse virgin olive oil with chillies, roasted whole garlic cloves, whole spices, woody herbs or citrus peel instead of buying flavoured oil. Flavour and colour oil with soft aromatic herbs such as basil. Vinegar adds bite to some soups, so look out for the many types available, including wine vinegars, balsamic vinegar, sherry vinegar and fruit-flavoured vinegars, such as raspberry.

Left: Balsamic vinegar is used in Italian soups.

Alcohol

Add to soups in moderation. The golden rule is to simmer the soup for a few minutes to cook off the strong alcohol, leaving the flavour. White wine, Pernod and vermouth work very well with creamy fish soups.

Flavoured creams

These provide a wonderful way to introduce contrasting flavour to a finished soup. Crème fraîche or whipped double (heavy) cream can be transformed by adding a purée of fresh herbs, grilled (bell) peppers or sun-dried tomatoes. Infused saffron and pesto can also be added.

Flavoured butters

Flavoured butters can be spread on warm bread to accompany a soup, or added to each bowl just before serving. Flavourings range from herbs and spices to shellfish.

Coconut milk

Buy this in cans or long-life cartons, or make it yourself at home. Put 225g/8oz/ 2²/3 cups desiccated (dry unsweetened shredded) coconut into a food processor, add 450ml/³/4 pint/ scant 2 cups boiling water and process for about 30 seconds. Leave to cool slightly, then transfer to a sieve (strainer) lined with muslin (cheesecloth) placed over a bowl and gather the ends of the cloth. Twist to extract the liquid.

Left: Raspberry vinegar adds colour.

Above: Chilli sauces add heat and flavour to soups.

Pesto and pistou

Pesto and pistou are closely related, the latter hailing from southern France, where it is stirred into a rich vegetable soup. Both are made by mixing crushed garlic, basil and olive oil, and pesto also contains pine nuts and Parmesan cheese. Stir into soup to add flavour and colour.

Chilli sauce

For those who like very hot food, chilli sauce can be offered at the table, or a dash can be added to flavour soups during cooking or to individual servings of soup.

Soy sauce

Made from fermented soya beans, soy sauce is one of Asia's most important contributions to the global pantry. There are three types of Chinese soy sauce on the market: light, dark and regular. As a rule, light soy sauce is used for soups. It is the initial extraction, like the first pressing of virgin olive oil. It has the most delicate flavour and is light brown in colour with a "beany" fragrance.

There are several different types of Japanese soy sauce, too. Usukuchi soy sauce is light in colour and tastes less salty than the Chinese light soy. Tamari is dark and thick with a strong flavour, and is even less salty than the light type. Shoyu is a full-flavoured sauce that is aged for up to two years. In between, there is the very popular Kikkoman, a brand name for the equivalent of the Chinese regular soy sauce – neither too weak nor too strong.

The Indonesian kecap manis is thick and black, with a powerful aroma but a surprisingly sweet taste.

Soy sauce is used as a flavouring in Japanese soups such as Clear Soup with Seafood Sticks, and Sapporo-style Ramen Noodles in Soup.

Fish sauce

Fish sauce is an essential seasoning for Thai and Vietnamese cooking, in the same way that soy sauce is important to the Chinese and the Japanese. In Vietnam it is often made using shrimp, but in Thailand the sauce is more often made using salted, fermented fish.

All types of fish sauce have a pungent flavour and aroma and are very salty. Thai *nam pla* has a slightly stronger flavour and aroma than the Vietnamese or Chinese versions. The colour of fish sauce can vary considerably; lighter-coloured sauces are considered to be better than darker versions. Fish sauce is used as a seasoning in some soup recipes such as Coconut and Seafood Soup, and Thai Pumpkin and Coconut Soup.

Shrimp paste

Known in Malaysia as *blachan*, this is an essential ingredient in many South-east Asian dishes, including soups. It is made from tiny shrimps that have been salted, dried, pounded and then left to ferment in the hot humid conditions until the aroma is very pungent. The colour of the paste can be anything from oyster pink to purplish brown, depending upon the type of shrimp and the precise process used. It is compressed and sold in block form or packed in tiny tubs or jars. The moment you unwrap it, the smell of rotten fish is quite overpowering, but this vanishes during cooking. Shrimp paste adds depth and pungency to a soup, for example in Balinese Vegetable Soup, a popular dish served on beans.

Miso

Many Japanese start the day with a bowl of miso soup for breakfast. Miso is one of the oldest traditional ingredients. Boiled *daizu* (soya beans) are crushed, then mixed with a culture called *koji*, which is made with wheat and rice, barley or beans. The fermented mixture is allowed to mature for up to three years. Numerous kinds and brands of miso are available in supermarkets. They are categorized into three basic grades according to strength of flavour and colour: shiro-miso (white, light and made with rice). aka-miso (red, medium and made with barley), and kuro-miso (black, strong and made with soya beans). Miso is quite salty and has a strong fermented bean flavour. Try it in Miso Broth with Spring Onions and Tofu.

Mirin

This amber-coloured, heavily sweetened sake is used only in cooking. It is one of Japan's ancient sake and is made from *shochu* (distilled sake). There is a synthetically made, cheap mirin-like liquid available called mirin-fuhmi (mirin flavouring), as opposed to hon-mirin (real mirin). Hon-mirin has an alcohol content of 14 per cent, whereas mirin-fuhmi is only 1 per cent. Both are available in bottles of 300ml/^{1}/$_2$ pint/1^1/$_4$ cups or 600ml/1 pint/2^1/$_2$ cups from Asian stores and good supermarkets. Mirin has a syrupy texture and adds a mild sweetness to soups.

Left: Thai fish sauce adds a strong, salty flavour to soups.

EQUIPMENT AND TECHNIQUES

One advantage of making your own soups is that you won't need any specialist equipment to try a wide range of tasty recipes. You will need basic equipment such as good knives and a chopping board or two, as well as a good-quality heavy-based pan and utensils such as wooden spoons etc. One additional piece of equipment that is very useful in soup-making is a food processor or blender, to enable you to purée cooked soups, if you wish. However, if you don't have one of these, many of the soups that require puréeing can simply be hand-pressed to make them smooth.

Heavy-based pan

For making soups you should choose a good-quality heavy-based pan. A good pan that conducts and holds heat well allows the vegetables to cook for longer before browning, so that they can be softened without changing colour. If you are health-conscious, choose a good-quality non-stick pan, and

Right: There are many different types of vegetable peeler.

Below: Using a balloon whisk.

you may be able to slightly reduce the amount of butter or oil used to sauté the vegetables.

Vegetable peelers

The quickest way to peel vegetables is to use a swivel peeler. For example, trim off the top and end of a carrot, then hold the carrot in one hand and run the peeler away from you down its length, turning the carrot as you work. Use a julienne peeler to cut vegetables such as carrots and courgettes into thin julienne strips. Use julienne strips of vegetables in recipes or as an attractive garnish for chilled or cooked hot soups.

Wooden spoon

Use a wooden spoon to stir soups. This will not damage the base of the pan (important if the pan is non-stick). However, wood absorbs flavours, so wash and dry the spoon well after use, and don't leave the spoon in the soup while it is cooking.

Below: Using a wooden mushroom or champignon.

Chopping an onion

Use a small knife to trim the root end of the onion and remove the skin with the tough layer underneath. Cut the onion in half. Place the cut side down on a chopping board and use a large sharp knife to slice down through the onion without cutting through its root. Slice horizontally through the onion. Finally, cut down across all the original cuts and the onion will fall apart into fine dice.

Whisk

A balloon whisk is useful when making some soups, for quickly incorporating ingredients such as eggs and cream, which could curdle, or flour mixtures that can form lumps. Steady the pan or bowl with one hand and, holding the whisk in the other hand, make quick flicking movements.

Wooden mushroom

A wooden mushroom (or champignon), which looks like a large, flat toadstool, is useful for pressing ingredients through a fine sieve (strainer) to give a smooth purée. The back of a large spoon or ladle can also be used.

Blender

A hand-held blender is brilliant, as it allows you to blend the soup directly in the pan. Controlling the speed is easy, to give the required consistency. Be careful when using a hand-held blender in a non-stick pan, and be sure not to let the blender touch the base or sides of the pan because it will cause damage to the surface.

Chopping fresh herbs

Rinse and thoroughly dry the herbs and remove the leaves from the stalks, if necessary (this is essential when chopping herbs such as rosemary, which has very tough, woody stalks. Place the herbs on a chopping board and, using a knife or other sharp tool, cut the herbs into small pieces (as finely or as coarsely as you wish), holding the tip of the blade against the chopping board and rocking the blade back and forth.

Alternatively, you can use a mezzaluna ("half-moon" in Italian). This is a curved crescent-shaped blade attached to two handles, which rocks back and forth over the herbs to chop them. It is good for chopping a lot of herbs at once.

Above: Cream of Mushroom Soup with Crostini, made smooth and creamy using a food processor or blender.

Mouli-legume

A more traditional method is to use a mouli-legume, a cooking instrument from France that is a cross between a sieve (strainer) and a food mill. It sits over a bowl and has a blade to press the food through two fine sieves. The blade is turned by hand to push the soup through the sieves, leaving all the fibres and solids behind. A mouli-legume can grind food quickly into a coarse or fine texture.

Electric food processor and blender

The most common items of equipment for puréeing soups are food processors and free-standing blenders. Both types of machine are quick and efficient, but the food processor does not produce as smooth a result as a conventional blender, and for some recipes the soup will need to be strained afterwards. Food processors can also be used for finely chopping and slicing vegetables for salsas and garnishes.

Below: Using a mouli-legume.

Below: Using a hand-held blender.

Below: Using a food processor.

MAKING STOCKS

Fresh stocks are indispensable for creating good home-made soups. They add a depth of flavour that plain water just cannot achieve. Although many supermarkets now sell tubs of fresh stock, these may be expensive, especially if you need large quantities. Making your own is surprisingly easy and much more economical, particularly if you can use leftovers.

Home-made stocks aren't just cheaper, they are also a lot tastier, and they are much more nutritious too, precisely because they are made with fresh, natural ingredients. You can, of course, use stock (bouillon) cubes, granules or bouillon powder, but be sure to check the seasoning as these tend to be particularly high in salt.

Use the appropriate stock for the soup you are making. Onion soup, for example, is improved with a good beef stock. Be careful to use a vegetable stock, though, if you are catering for vegetarians. Recipes are given here for vegetable stock, fish stock, chicken stock, meat stock and basic stocks for Chinese and Japanese cooking.

Freezing stock

A good idea for keen and regular soup makers is to freeze portions of concentrated home-made stock in plastic freezer bags, or ice-cube trays, so you always have a supply at your disposal whenever you need some. Frozen stock can be stored in the freezer for up to three months (fish stock for up to 2 months). Ensure that you label each stock carefully for easy identification later.

Vegetable stock

Use this versatile stock as the basis for all vegetarian soups. It may also be used for meat, poultry or fish soups.

MAKES 2.5 LITRES/4½ PINTS/10 CUPS

INGREDIENTS
  2 leeks, roughly chopped
  3 celery sticks, roughly chopped
  1 large onion, unpeeled, roughly
    chopped
  2 pieces fresh root ginger, chopped
  1 yellow (bell) pepper, chopped
  1 parsnip, chopped
  mushroom stalks
  tomato peelings
  45ml/3 tbsp light soy sauce
  3 bay leaves
  a bunch of parsley stalks
  3 sprigs of fresh thyme
  1 sprig of fresh rosemary
  10ml/2 tsp salt
  freshly ground black pepper
  3.5 litres/6 pints/15 cups cold water

1 Put all the ingredients into a stockpot or large pan. Bring slowly to the boil, then lower the heat and simmer for 30 minutes, stirring from time to time.

2 Allow to cool. Strain, then discard the vegetables. The stock is ready to use.

Fish stock

Fish stock is much quicker to make than poultry or meat stock. Ask your fishmonger for heads, bones and trimmings from white fish. Lobster or crab shell pieces (taken after boiling lobster or crab and scooping out the meat) can also be used in place of fish trimmings to make a tasty fish stock, together with the other flavourings listed.

MAKES 1 LITRE/1¾ PINTS/4 CUPS

INGREDIENTS
  675g/1½lb heads, bones and
    trimmings from white fish
  1 onion, sliced
  2 celery sticks with leaves,
    chopped
  1 carrot, sliced
  ½ lemon, sliced (optional)
  1 bay leaf
  a few sprigs of fresh parsley
  6 black peppercorns
  1.35 litres/2¼ pints/6 cups
    cold water
  150ml/¼ pint/⅔ cup dry
    white wine

1 Rinse the fish heads, bones and trimmings well under cold running water. Put in a stockpot or large pan with the vegetables and lemon, if using, the herbs, peppercorns, water and wine. Bring to the boil, skimming the surface frequently, then reduce the heat and simmer for 25 minutes.

2 Strain the stock without pressing down on the ingredients in the sieve (strainer). If not using immediately, leave to cool and then refrigerate. Use within 2 days.

Chicken stock

A good home-made poultry stock is invaluable in the kitchen. If poultry giblets are available, add them (except the livers) with the wings. Once made, chicken stock can be kept in an airtight container in the refrigerator for 3–4 days, or frozen for longer storage (up to 3 months).

MAKES ABOUT 2.5 LITRES/4½ PINTS/
10 CUPS

INGREDIENTS
    1.2–1.3kg/2½–3lb chicken or turkey
    (wings, backs and necks)
    2 onions, unpeeled, quartered
    1 tbsp olive oil
    4 litres// pints/16 cups
    cold water
    2 carrots, roughly chopped
    2 celery sticks, with leaves if
    possible, roughly chopped
    a small handful of parsley stalks
    a few sprigs of fresh thyme or
    5ml/1 tsp dried
    1 or 2 bay leaves
    10 black peppercorns,
    lightly crushed

1 Combine the poultry wings, backs and necks in a stockpot or large pan with the onion quarters and the oil.

2 Cook over a moderate heat, stirring occasionally, until the poultry and onions are lightly and evenly browned.

Right: Moroccan Chicken Soup with Charmoula Butter uses a good-quality home-made stock for a rich flavour.

3 Add the water and stir well to mix in the sediment on the bottom of the pan. Bring to the boil and skim off any impurities as they rise to the surface of the stock.

4 Add the chopped carrots and celery, fresh parsley, thyme, bay leaf and black peppercorns. Partly cover the stockpot and simmer the stock for 3 hours.

5 Strain the stock through a sieve (strainer) into a bowl. Discard the chicken bones and the vegetables. Leave the stock to cool, then chill in the refrigerator for an hour.

6 When cold, carefully remove the layer of fat that will have set on the surface. The stock is now ready to use in your chosen soup recipe.

Meat stock

The most delicious meat soups rely on a good home-made stock for success. A stock (bouillon) cube will do if you have no time to make your own, but fresh home-made stock will give a much better flavour and basis for soups, so it's well worth spending a little time making your own. Once it is made, meat stock can be kept in the refrigerator for up to 4 days, or frozen for up to 3 months.

MAKES ABOUT 2 LITRES/3½ PINTS/8 CUPS

INGREDIENTS
  1.8kg/4lb beef bones, such as
    shin, leg, neck and shank, or
    veal or lamb bones, cut into
    6cm/2½ in pieces
  2 onions, unpeeled, quartered
  2 carrots, roughly chopped
  2 celery sticks, with leaves if
    possible, roughly chopped
  2 tomatoes, coarsely chopped
  4.5 litres/7½ pints/18¾ cups
    cold water
  a handful of parsley stalks
  few sprigs of fresh thyme or
    5ml/1 tsp dried
  2 bay leaves
  10 black peppercorns, lightly crushed

1 Preheat the oven to 230°C/450°F/ Gas 8. Put the bones in a roasting pan or casserole dish and roast, turning occasionally, for 30 minutes, until they start to brown.

2 Add the onions, carrots, celery and tomatoes and baste with the fat in the pan. Roast for a further 20–30 minutes until the bones are well browned. Stir and baste occasionally.

3 Transfer the bones and roasted vegetables to a stockpot or large pan. Spoon off the fat from the roasting pan. Add a little of the water to the roasting pan or casserole and bring to the boil on top of the stove, stirring well to scrape up any browned bits. Pour this liquid into the stockpot.

4 Add the remaining water to the pot. Bring just to the boil, skimming frequently to remove all the foam from the surface. Add the parsley, thyme, bay leaves and peppercorns.

5 Partly cover the stockpot and simmer the beef stock for 4–6 hours. The bones and vegetables should always be covered with enough liquid, so top up with a little boiling water from time to time if necessary.

6 Strain the stock through a colander, then skim as much fat as possible from the surface. If possible, cool the stock and then refrigerate it; the fat will rise to the top and set in a layer that can be removed easily.

Stock for Chinese cooking

This stock is an excellent basis for soup-making, and is ideal for Asian soups. Refrigerate the stock when cool – it will keep for up to 4 days. Alternatively, it can be frozen in small containers for up to 3 months and defrosted when required.

MAKES 2.5 LITRES/4½ PINTS/11 CUPS

INGREDIENTS
  675g/1½lb chicken portions
  675g/1½lb pork spareribs
  3.75 litres/6½ pints/15 cups
    cold water
  3–4 pieces fresh root ginger,
    unpeeled, crushed
  3–4 spring onions (scallions),
    each tied into a knot
  45–60ml/3–4 tbsp Chinese rice wine
    or dry sherry

Below: Roast Lamb Shanks in Barley Broth.

1 Use a sharp knife to trim off any excess fat from the chicken and spareribs, then chop them into small pieces.

2 Place the chicken and sparerib pieces into a stockpot or large pan with the cold water. Add the crushed fresh root ginger and the spring onions tied in knots.

3 Bring the stock to the boil and skim off the froth. Reduce the heat and simmer over a gentle heat, uncovered, for 2–3 hours.

4 Strain the stock, discarding the pork, chicken, ginger and spring onion knots. Add the Chinese rice wine or dry sherry and return to the boil. Simmer for 2–3 minutes.

Above: Kombu seaweed is used in Japanese stocks.

Stock for Japanese cooking

Dashi is the stock that gives the characteristically Japanese flavour to many dishes. Known as Ichiban-dashi, it is used for delicately flavoured dishes, including soups. Of course instant stock is available in all Japanese supermarkets, either in granule form, in concentrate or even in a tea-bag style. Follow the instructions on the packet.

MAKES ABOUT 800ML/1⅓ PINTS/3½ CUPS

INGREDIENTS
  10g/¼oz dried kombu seaweed
  10–15g/¼–½oz dried bonito flakes

1 Wipe the kombu seaweed with a damp cloth and cut two slits in it with scissors, so that it flavours the stock effectively.

2 Soak the kombu in 900ml/1½ pints/ 3¾ cups cold water for 30–60 minutes.

3 Heat the kombu in its soaking water in a pan over a moderate heat. Just before the water boils, remove the seaweed. Add the bonito flakes and bring to the boil over a high heat, then remove the pan from the heat.

4 Leave the stock until all the bonito flakes have sunk to the bottom of the pan. Line a sieve (strainer) with kitchen paper or muslin (cheesecloth) and place it over a large mixing bowl, then gently strain the stock. Use as required or cool and refrigerate for up to 2 days.

Left: A Chinese-style soup made delicous with pork and prawn dumplings.

THICKENING SOUPS

Many soups do not need any thickening ingredients added, as the puréed soup is thick enough. Vegetables such as potatoes, onions and carrots, once cooked and puréed in a soup, will often help to thicken the soup sufficiently. If your soup does need thickening, try one of the methods below.

Beurre manié

This smooth flour and butter paste is used to thicken soups at the end of the cooking time. Equal quantities of plain flour and butter are kneaded together, then a small knob of the paste is added to the soup and whisked until it is fully incorporated before adding the next. The soup is brought to the boil and simmered for about 1 minute, until thickened and to avoid a raw flour flavour. A similarly useful paste can be made using flour and cream.

Cream

Double (heavy) cream can be used to thicken a fine soup. It is added towards the end of cooking, then the soup is brought to the boil and simmered gently for a few minutes until the soup is slightly reduced and thickened.

Ground almonds

Ground almonds can be used as a thickener in soups, and they add extra flavour as well as texture to the soup. The delicate flavour of almonds blends particularly well with fish- and chicken-based soups. However, ground almonds

Below: Making beurre manié.

Above: Adding ground almonds.

do not thicken soup in the same way that ingredients such as flour and cornflour (cornstarch) do, to make a thick, smooth soup. Instead they add body, texture, flavour and richness.

Cornflour or arrowroot

These fine flours are mixed with a little cold water (about double the volume of the dry ingredient) to make a smooth, thick, but runny paste. Stir the paste into the hot soup and simmer, stirring, until thickened. Cornflour (cornstarch) takes about 3 minutes to thicken completely and lose its raw flavour. Arrowroot achieves maximum thickness on boiling and tends to become slightly thinner if it is allowed to simmer for any length of time, so this is usually

Below: Mixing cornflour with water.

Above: Adding breadcrumbs.

avoided. Cornflour gives an opaque result, but arrowroot becomes clear when it boils, so it is useful for thickening clear liquids and soups.

Breadcrumbs

The more rustic approach is to use fresh white breadcrumbs to thicken soup. They can be toasted in oil before being stirred into a simmering soup, or added directly to a finished dish.

Eggs

Beaten eggs, egg yolks, or a mixture of eggs and a little cream can be used to enrich and slightly thicken a smooth soup. Whisk into the hot soup, but do not allow it to boil once they are added or it will curdle.

Below: Whisking in beaten eggs.

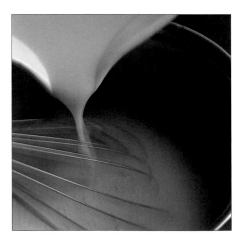

GARNISHES

Garnishes should look attractive, be edible, complement the flavour of the soup and add that final finishing touch. Some typical ones include sprinkling the soup with chopped herbs or stirring them into it just before serving, or topping thick, rich soups with a fresh herb sprig or two for an attractive garnish. Croûtons, made from either plain or flavoured bread, add appeal and crunch to many soups. Below are some typical garnishes, as well as a few tips for some more unusual ones.

Swirled cream

A swirl of cream is the classic finish for many soups, such as a smooth tomato soup and Vichyssoise. This garnish gives a professional finish to your soup, although the technique is simplicity itself.

1 Transfer the cream into a jug with a good pouring lip. Pour a swirl on to the surface of each bowl of soup.

2 Draw the tip of a fine skewer quickly backwards and forwards through the cream to create a delicate pattern. Serve the soup immediately.

Above: Toasted croûtes with cheese.

Herbs

Adding a handful of chopped fresh herbs to a bowl of soup just before serving can make a good soup look great. A bundle of chives makes a dainty garnish. Cut 5–6 chives to about 6cm/2½in long and tie them in a bundle using another length of chive.

Fried croûtons

This classic garnish adds texture as well as flavour to soups. To make croûtons, cut bread into small cubes and fry in a little oil. Toss the bread continuously so that the cubes are golden all over, then drain on kitchen paper.

Grilled croûtes

Topped with grilled cheese, croûtes not only look good, but taste great in all sorts of soups. To make them, toast small slices of baguette on both sides. If you like, you can rub the toast with a cut clove of garlic, then top with grated Cheddar or Parmesan, a crumbled blue cheese, such as Stilton, or a slice of goat's (chèvre) cheese. Grill (broil) briefly until the cheese is beginning to melt.

Crisp-fried shallots

Finely sliced shallots make a quick garnish for smooth lentil and vegetable soups. Cut them crossways into rings, then shallow fry in hot oil until crisp.

Above: Making vegetable julienne.

Crisps

Try shop-bought thick-cut crisps (US potato chips) or tortilla chips; alternatively, make your own vegetable crisps (chips) Wafer-thin slices of fresh raw beetroot (beet), pumpkin and parsnip can all be deep-fried in hot oil for a few moments to produce delicious and unusual crisps.

Vegetable julienne

An effective way of preparing ingredients for adding a splash of colour to soup is to cut them into julienne strips. Shreds of spring onions (scallions) or red and green chillies make great garnishes.

Below: Diced tomatoes, onions and coriander make an attractive garnish.

LIGHT AND REFRESHING SOUPS

What could be a better way of starting a meal on a warm

summer evening than a bowl of refreshing soup, served al

fresco with a bottle of chilled white wine? In this section

there are light and cooling recipes, such as Chilled Coconut

Soup, and Chilled Avocado Soup with Cumin, as well as more

unusual dishes, such as Beetroot Soup with Mascarpone

Brioche, and Iced Tomato and Vodka Soup. Or for an

international flavour, try Tom Yam Gung with Tofu.

CHILLED AVOCADO SOUP <u>WITH</u> CUMIN

ANDALUSIA IS HOME TO BOTH AVOCADOS AND GAZPACHO, SO IT IS NOT SURPRISING THAT THIS CHILLED AVOCADO SOUP, WHICH IS ALSO KNOWN AS GREEN GAZPACHO, WAS INVENTED THERE. IN SPAIN, THIS DELICIOUSLY MILD, CREAMY SOUP IS KNOWN AS SOPA DE AGUACATE.

SERVES 4

INGREDIENTS
  3 ripe avocados
  1 bunch spring onions (scallions),
    white parts only, trimmed and
    roughly chopped
  2 garlic cloves, chopped
  juice of 1 lemon
  1.5ml/¼ tsp ground cumin
  1.5ml/¼ tsp paprika
  450ml/¾ pint/scant 2 cups fresh
    chicken stock, cooled and all
    fat skimmed off
  300ml/½ pint/1¼ cups iced water
  salt and ground black pepper
  roughly chopped fresh flat leaf
    parsley, to garnish

1 Starting half a day ahead, put the flesh of one avocado in a food processor or blender. Add the spring onions, garlic and lemon juice and purée until smooth. Add the second avocado and purée, then the third, with the spices and seasoning. Purée until smooth.

2 Gradually add the chicken stock. Pour the soup into a metal bowl and chill.

3 To serve, stir in the iced water, then season to taste with plenty of salt and black pepper. Garnish with chopped parsley and serve immediately.

Energy 242Kcal/1001kJ; Protein 2.8g; Carbohydrate 3g, of which sugars 1.3g; Fat 24.2g, of which saturates 5.2g; Cholesterol 0mg; Calcium 22mg; Fibre 4.6g; Sodium 9mg.

CUCUMBER AND SALMON SOUP WITH SALSA

CHARRED SALMON BRINGS A HINT OF HEAT TO THE REFRESHING FLAVOURS OF THIS CHILLED SOUP.
GOOD-LOOKING AND BEAUTIFULLY LIGHT, IT MAKES THE PERFECT OPENER FOR AN AL FRESCO MEAL.

SERVES 4

INGREDIENTS
    3 medium cucumbers
    300ml/½ pint/1¼ cups Greek
      (US strained plain) yogurt
    250ml/8fl oz/1 cup vegetable
      stock, chilled
    120ml/4fl oz/½ cup crème fraîche
    15ml/1 tbsp chopped fresh chervil
    15ml/1 tbsp chopped fresh chives
    15ml/1 tbsp chopped fresh
      flat leaf parsley
    1 small fresh red chilli, seeded and
      very finely chopped
    a little oil, for brushing
    225g/8oz salmon fillet, skinned and
      cut into eight thin slices
    salt and ground black pepper
    fresh chervil or chives, to garnish

4 Brush a griddle or frying pan with oil and heat until very hot. Add the salmon slices and sear them for 1–2 minutes, then turn over carefully and sear the other side until tender and charred.

5 Ladle the chilled soup into soup bowls. Top each portion with two slices of salmon, then pile a portion of salsa in the centre. Garnish with the chervil or chives and serve.

1 Peel two of the cucumbers and halve them lengthways. Scoop out and discard the seeds, then roughly chop the flesh. Purée the chopped flesh in a food processor or blender.

2 Add the yogurt, stock, crème fraîche, chervil, chives and seasoning, and process until smooth. Pour the mixture into a bowl, cover and chill.

3 Peel, halve and seed the remaining cucumber. Cut the flesh into small neat dice. Mix with the chopped parsley and chilli in a bowl. Cover the salsa and chill until required.

Energy 314Kcal/1299kJ; Protein 17.8g; Carbohydrate 3.9g, of which sugars 3.7g; Fat 26.1g, of which saturates 13.1g; Cholesterol 62mg; Calcium 183mg; Fibre 1.2g; Sodium 92mg.

ICED TOMATO AND VODKA SOUP

THIS FRESH-FLAVOURED SOUP PACKS A PUNCH LIKE A FROZEN BLOODY MARY. IT IS DELICIOUS SERVED AS AN IMPRESSIVE FIRST COURSE FOR A SUMMER'S DINNER PARTY WITH SUN-DRIED TOMATO BREAD.

SERVES 4

INGREDIENTS
   450g/1lb ripe, well-flavoured
      tomatoes, halved or
      roughly chopped
   600ml/1 pint/2½ cups jellied beef
      stock or consommé
   1 small red onion, halved
   2 celery sticks, cut into large pieces
   1 garlic clove, roughly chopped
   15ml/1 tbsp tomato purée (paste)
   10ml/2 tsp lemon juice
   10ml/2 tsp Worcestershire sauce
   a handful of small fresh basil leaves
   30ml/2 tbsp vodka
   salt and ground black pepper
   crushed ice, 4 small celery sticks and
      sun-dried tomato bread, to serve

1 Put the halved or chopped tomatoes, jellied stock or consommé, onion and celery in a blender or food processor. Add the garlic, then spoon in the tomato purée. Pulse until all the vegetables are finely chopped, then process to a smooth paste.

2 Press the mixture through a sieve (strainer) into a large bowl and stir in the lemon juice, Worcestershire sauce, basil leaves and vodka.

3 Add salt and pepper to taste. Cover and chill. Serve the soup with a little crushed ice and place a celery stick in each bowl.

COOK'S TIPS
• Canned beef consommé is ideal for this recipe, but vegetable stock, for vegetarians, will work well too.
• If you or your guests are fond of celery, you can stand more celery sticks in a jug (pitcher) of iced water on the table for people to help themselves. The celery sticks can be used as additional edible stirrers and taste delicious after being dipped into the soup.
• Making your own sun-dried tomato bread is easy and is bound to impress your guests. If you don't have time, however, look out for tomato-flavoured ciabatta or focaccia.

Energy 46Kcal/194kJ; Protein 1.3g; Carbohydrate 5.5g, of which sugars 5.2g; Fat 0.4g, of which saturates 0.1g; Cholesterol 0mg; Calcium 22mg; Fibre 1.6g; Sodium 44mg.

BEETROOT SOUP WITH MASCARPONE BRIOCHE

ALTHOUGH IT SOUNDS QUITE COMPLEX, THIS SOUP IS ACTUALLY RIDICULOUSLY EASY TO MAKE. THE SWEET, EARTHY FLAVOUR OF FRESH, COOKED BEETROOT IS COMBINED WITH ZESTY ORANGE.

SERVES 4

INGREDIENTS

350g/12oz cooked beetroot (beet),
  roughly chopped
grated rind and juice of 1 orange
600ml/1 pint/2½ cups unsweetened
  cranberry juice
450ml/¾ pint/scant 2 cups Greek
  (US strained plain) yogurt
a little Tabasco sauce
4 slices brioche
60ml/4 tbsp mascarpone
salt and ground black pepper
fresh mint sprigs and cooked
  cranberries, to garnish

1 Purée the beetroot with the orange rind and juice, half the cranberry juice and the yogurt in a food processor or blender until smooth.

2 Press the purée through a sieve (strainer) into a clean bowl. Stir in the remaining cranberry juice and the Tabasco sauce. Season with salt and black pepper to taste. Chill the soup in the refrigerator for at least 2 hours.

3 Preheat the grill (broiler). Using a large pastry cutter, stamp a round out of each slice of brioche.

COOK'S TIP
If the combination of cranberry and orange is a little tart, add a pinch or two of caster (superfine) sugar to the soup, according to taste.

4 Arrange the brioche rounds on a grill (broiler) rack and toast until golden. Ladle the soup into bowls and top each with brioche and mascarpone. Garnish with mint and cranberries.

Energy 404Kcal/1695kJ; Protein 13.5g; Carbohydrate 53.5g, of which sugars 17.2g; Fat 16.6g, of which saturates 7.2g; Cholesterol 13mg; Calcium 237mg; Fibre 1.7g; Sodium 264mg.

CHILLED COCONUT SOUP

*REFRESHING, COOLING AND NOT TOO FILLING, THIS SOUP IS THE PERFECT ANTIDOTE TO HOT
WEATHER. EXCELLENT FOR SERVING AFTER AN APPETIZER, IT WILL REFRESH THE PALATE.*

SERVES 6

INGREDIENTS

1.2 litres/2 pints/5 cups milk
225g/8oz/2⅔ cups desiccated
   (dry unsweetened shredded)
   coconut
400ml/14fl oz/1⅔ cups
   coconut milk
400ml/14fl oz/1⅔ cups
   chicken stock
200ml/7fl oz/scant 1 cup double
   (heavy) cream
2.5ml/½ tsp salt
2.5ml/½ tsp ground white
   pepper
5ml/1 tsp caster (superfine) sugar
small bunch of fresh coriander
   (cilantro)

1 Pour the milk into a large pan. Bring
it to the boil, stir in the coconut, lower
the heat and allow to simmer for 30
minutes. Spoon the mixture into a food
processor and process until smooth.
This may take a while – up to
5 minutes – so pause frequently and
scrape down the sides of the bowl.

2 Rinse the pan to remove any coconut
that remains, pour in the processed
mixture and add the coconut milk. Stir
in the chicken stock (home-made, if
possible, which gives a better flavour
than a stock [bouillon] cube), cream,
salt, pepper and sugar. Bring to the
boil, stirring occasionally, then lower
the heat and cook for 10 minutes.

3 Reserve a few coriander leaves to
garnish, then chop the rest finely and
stir into the soup. Pour the soup into a
large bowl, let it cool, then cover and
put into the refrigerator until chilled.
Just before serving, taste the soup and
adjust the seasoning, as chilling will
alter the taste. Serve in chilled bowls,
garnished with the coriander leaves.

Energy 499Kcal/2068kJ; Protein 9.6g; Carbohydrate 15.6g, of which sugars 15.6g; Fat 44.8g, of which saturates 33.4g; Cholesterol 58mg; Calcium 284mg; Fibre 5.1g; Sodium 341mg.

TOM YAM GUNG <u>WITH</u> TOFU

ONE OF THE MOST REFRESHING AND HEALTHY SOUPS, THIS FRAGRANT DISH IS A FAMOUS THAI SPECIALITY, AND WOULD MAKE AN IDEAL LIGHT LUNCH OR SUPPER.

SERVES 4

INGREDIENTS

30ml/2 tbsp groundnut (peanut) oil
300g/11oz firm tofu, cut into small bitesize pieces
1.2 litres/2 pints/5 cups good vegetable stock
15ml/1 tbsp Thai chilli jam (nam pick pow)
grated rind of 1 kaffir lime
1 shallot, finely sliced
1 garlic clove, peeled and finely chopped
2 kaffir lime leaves, shredded
3 red chillies, seeded and shredded
1 lemon grass stalk, finely chopped
6 shiitake mushrooms, thinly sliced
4 spring onions (scallions), shredded
45ml/3 tbsp Thai fish sauce (nam pla)
45ml/3 tbsp lime juice
5ml/1 tsp caster (superfine) sugar
45ml/3 tbsp chopped fresh coriander (cilantro) leaves
salt and ground black pepper

1 Heat the oil in a wok and fry the tofu for 4–5 minutes until golden, turning occasionally to brown on all sides. Use a slotted spoon to remove the tofu and set aside. Tip the oil from the wok into a large, heavy-based pan.

COOK'S TIP
Kaffir lime leaves have a distinct citrus flavour. Fresh leaves can be bought from Asian shops, and some supermarkets sell them dried. Thai fish sauce (nam pla) and chilli jam (nam pick pow) are available from some supermarkets.

2 Add the stock, chilli jam, kaffir lime rind, shallot, garlic, lime leaves, two-thirds of the chillies and the lemon grass to the pan. Bring to the boil and simmer for 20 minutes.

3 Strain the stock into a clean pan. Stir in the remaining chilli, the shiitake mushrooms, spring onions, fish sauce, lime juice and sugar. Simmer for 3 minutes. Add the fried tofu and heat through for 1 minute. Mix in the chopped coriander and season to taste. Serve at once in warmed bowls.

Energy 122Kcal/506kJ; Protein 7.1g; Carbohydrate 3.6g, of which sugars 2.9g, Fat 8.9g, of which saturates 1.5g; Cholesterol 0mg; Calcium 395mg; Fibre 0.7g; Sodium 273mg.

AVGOLEMONO

THIS IS A GREAT FAVOURITE IN GREECE AND IS A FINE EXAMPLE OF HOW A FEW INGREDIENTS CAN MAKE A MARVELLOUS DISH IF CAREFULLY CHOSEN AND COOKED. IT IS ESSENTIAL TO USE A WELL-FLAVOURED STOCK. ADD AS LITTLE OR AS MUCH RICE AS YOU LIKE.

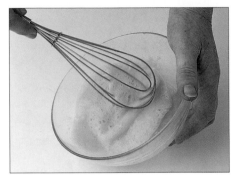

2 Whisk the egg yolks in a bowl, then add about 30ml/2 tbsp of the lemon juice, whisking constantly until the mixture is smooth and bubbly. Add a ladleful of soup and whisk again.

3 Remove the soup from the heat and slowly add the egg mixture, whisking all the time. The soup will turn a pretty lemon colour and will thicken slightly.

4 Taste and add more lemon juice if necessary. Stir in the parsley. Serve at once, without reheating, garnished with lemon slices and parsley sprigs.

SERVES 4

INGREDIENTS

900ml/1½ pints/3¾ cups chicken
   stock, preferably home-made
50g/2oz/generous ⅓ cup long
   grain rice
3 egg yolks
30–60ml/2–4 tbsp lemon juice
30ml/2 tbsp finely chopped fresh
   parsley
salt and freshly ground black pepper
lemon slices and parsley sprigs,
   to garnish

1 Pour the stock into a pan, bring to simmering point, then add the drained rice. Half cover and cook for about 12 minutes until the rice is just tender. Season with salt and pepper.

COOK'S TIP
The trick here is to add the egg mixture to the soup without it curdling. Avoid whisking the mixture into boiling liquid. It is safest to remove the soup from the heat entirely and then whisk in the mixture in a slow but steady stream. Do not reheat as curdling would be almost inevitable.

Energy 96Kcal/404kJ; Protein 3.3g; Carbohydrate 10.9g, of which sugars 0.2g; Fat 4.7g, of which saturates 1.2g; Cholesterol 151mg; Calcium 39mg; Fibre 0.4g; Sodium 10mg.

PEA SOUP <u>WITH</u> PROSCIUTTO

THIS SIMPLE SOUP IS QUICK AND EASY TO PREPARE. IT HAS A DELICIOUSLY SMOOTH AND CREAMY TEXTURE, WHILE MAKING A VERY LIGHT AND REFRESHING DISH. USING FROZEN PEAS CUTS OUT THE LABOUR INVOLVED IN SHELLING FRESH PEAS, WITHOUT COMPROMISING THE FLAVOUR.

SERVES 6

INGREDIENTS
    25g/1oz/2 tbsp butter
    1 leek, sliced
    1 garlic clove, crushed
    450g/1lb/4 cups frozen petits pois
        (baby peas)
    1.2 litres/2 pints/5 cups
        vegetable stock
    small bunch of fresh chives,
        coarsely chopped
    300ml/½ pint/1¼ cups double
        (heavy) cream
    90ml/6 tbsp Greek (US strained
        plain) yogurt
    4 slices prosciutto, roughly chopped
    salt and ground black pepper
    fresh chives, to garnish

1 Melt the butter in a pan. Add the leek and garlic, cover and cook gently for 4–5 minutes, until softened.

2 Stir in the petits pois, vegetable stock and chives. Bring slowly to the boil, then simmer for 5 minutes. Set aside to cool slightly.

3 Process the soup in a food processor or blender until smooth. Pour into a bowl, stir in the cream and season to taste with salt and black pepper. Chill in the refrigerator for at least 2 hours.

4 When ready to serve, ladle the soup into bowls and add a spoonful of Greek yogurt to the centre of each bowl. Scatter the chopped prosciutto over the top of the soup and garnish with chives before serving.

COOK'S TIP
For a clever and attractive garnish, cut five lengths of chive to about 6cm/2½ in long, then use another chive to tie them together. Lay a bundle of chives on top of each bowl of soup.

Energy 378Kcal/1561kJ; Protein 9.7g; Carbohydrate 10.6g, of which sugars 3.7g, Fat 33.5g, of which saturates 20g; Cholesterol 85mg; Calcium 71mg; Fibre 4.2g; Sodium 198mg.

SORREL, SPINACH AND DILL SOUP

THE WARM FLAVOUR OF HORSERADISH AND THE ANISEED FLAVOUR OF DILL MELD WITH SORREL AND SPINACH TO MAKE THIS UNUSUAL RUSSIAN SOUP. AN EXCELLENT SUMMER SOUP, SERVED CHILLED.

SERVES 6

INGREDIENTS

25g/1oz/2 tbsp butter
225g/8oz sorrel, stalks
   removed
225g/8oz young spinach,
   stalks removed
25g/1oz fresh horseradish,
   grated
750ml/1¼ pints/3 cups cider
1 pickled cucumber,
   finely chopped
30ml/2 tbsp chopped fresh dill
225g/8oz cooked fish, such
   as pike, perch or salmon, skinned
   and boned
salt and ground black pepper
sprig of dill, to garnish

1 Melt the butter in a large pan. Add the prepared sorrel and spinach leaves together with the grated fresh horseradish.

2 Cover the pan and allow to cook gently for 3–4 minutes, or until the sorrel and spinach leaves have wilted.

3 Tip into a food processor or blender and process to a fine purée (paste). Ladle into a tureen or bowl and stir in the cider, cucumber and dill.

4 Chop the fish into bitesize pieces. Add to the soup, then season well. Chill for at least 3 hours before serving, garnished with a sprig of dill.

Energy 156Kcal/653kJ; Protein 11.4g; Carbohydrate 4.8g, of which sugars 4.7g; Fat 6.6g, of which saturates 2.8g; Cholesterol 19mg; Calcium 201mg; Fibre 1.9g; Sodium 324mg.

EGG <u>AND</u> CHEESE SOUP

IN THIS CLASSIC ROMAN SOUP, EGGS AND CHEESE ARE BEATEN INTO HOT SOUP, PRODUCING THE SLIGHTLY SCRAMBLED TEXTURE THAT IS CHARACTERISTIC OF THIS DISH.

SERVES 6

INGREDIENTS

3 eggs
45ml/3 tbsp fine semolina
90ml/6 tbsp freshly grated
  Parmesan cheese
pinch of nutmeg
1.5 litres/2½ pints/6¼ cups cold
  meat or chicken stock
salt and ground black pepper
12 rounds of country bread or
  ciabatta, to serve

COOK'S TIP
Once added to the hot soup, the egg will begin to cook and the soup will become less smooth. Try not to overcook the soup at this stage because it may cause the egg to curdle.

1 Beat the eggs in a bowl, then beat in the semolina and the cheese. Add the nutmeg and beat in 250ml/8fl oz/ 1 cup of the meat or chicken stock. Pour the mixture into a measuring jug (pitcher).

2 Pour the remaining stock into a large pan and bring to a gentle simmer, stirring occasionally.

3 A few minutes before you are ready to serve the soup, whisk the egg mixture into the hot stock. Raise the heat slightly, and bring it barely to the boil. Season and cook for 3–4 minutes.

4 To serve, toast the rounds of country bread or ciabatta, place two in each soup plate and ladle on the hot soup. Serve immediately.

Energy 245Kcal/1030kJ; Protein 14.1g; Carbohydrate 27.5g, of which sugars 1.3g; Fat 9.4g, of which saturates 4.1g; Cholesterol 110mg; Calcium 246mg; Fibre 1.1g; Sodium 424mg.

CHILLED CUCUMBER AND PRAWN SOUP

IF YOU'VE NEVER SERVED A CHILLED SOUP BEFORE, THIS IS THE ONE TO TRY. IT IS DELICIOUSLY LIGHT, AND MAKES A PERFECT COOL AND REFRESHING MEAL IN THE SUMMER.

2 Stir in the milk, bring almost to boiling point, then lower the heat and simmer for 5 minutes. Tip the soup into a blender or food processor and purée until very smooth. Season to taste.

3 Pour the soup into a large bowl and leave to cool. When cool, stir in the prawns, chopped herbs and cream. Cover, transfer to the refrigerator and chill for at least 2 hours.

4 To serve, ladle the soup into four individual bowls, top each portion with a dollop of crème fraîche, if using, and place a prawn over the edge of each dish. Scatter over a little extra chopped dill and tuck two or three chives under the prawns on the edge of the bowls to garnish. Serve at once.

SERVES 4

INGREDIENTS
  25g/1oz/2 tbsp butter
  2 shallots, finely chopped
  2 garlic cloves, crushed
  1 cucumber, peeled, seeded
    and diced
  300ml/½ pint/1¼ cups milk
  225g/8oz cooked peeled prawns
    (shrimp)
  15ml/1 tbsp each finely chopped
    fresh mint, dill, chives and chervil
  300ml/½ pint/1¼ cups
    whipping cream
  salt and ground white pepper
For the garnish
  30ml/2 tbsp crème fraîche (optional)
  4 large, cooked prawns, peeled with
    tail intact
  fresh dill and chives

1 Melt the butter in a pan and cook the shallots and garlic over a low heat until soft but not coloured. Add the cucumber and cook gently, stirring frequently, until tender.

COOK'S TIP
If you prefer hot soup, reheat it gently until hot but not boiling. Do not boil, or the delicate flavour will be spoilt.

VARIATION
If you like, you can use other cooked shellfish in place of the peeled prawns (shrimp) – try fresh, frozen or canned crab meat or cooked, flaked salmon.

Energy 412Kcal/1704kJ; Protein 14.2g; Carbohydrate 6g, of which sugars 6g; Fat 37g, of which saturates 23g; Cholesterol 206mg; Calcium 184mg; Fibre 0.2g; Sodium 197mg.

TOMATO AND PEACH JUS WITH PRAWNS

AMERICAN-STYLE SOUPS, MADE FROM THE CLEAR JUICES EXTRACTED FROM VEGETABLES OR FRUITS AND REFERRED TO AS "WATER" SOUPS BY CHEFS, PROVIDE THE INSPIRATION FOR THIS RECIPE.

SERVES 6

INGREDIENTS

1.5kg/3–3½lb ripe peaches
1.2kg/2½lb beef tomatoes
30ml/2 tbsp white wine vinegar
1 lemon grass stalk, crushed
  and chopped
2.5cm/1in fresh root ginger, grated
1 bay leaf
150ml/¼ pint/⅔ cup water
18 tiger prawns (shrimp), shelled
  with tails on and de-veined
olive oil, for brushing
salt and ground black pepper
fresh coriander (cilantro) leaves and
  2 vine-ripened tomatoes, peeled,
  seeded and diced, to garnish

1 Peel the tomatoes and peaches and cut into chunks. Put into a food processor and purée them. Stir in the vinegar and seasoning.

2 Line a large bowl with muslin (cheesecloth). Pour the purée into the bowl, gather up the ends of the muslin and tie tightly. Suspend over the bowl and leave at room temperature for 3 hours or until about 1.2 litres/2 pints/ 5 cups juice have drained through.

3 Meanwhile, put the lemon grass, ginger and bay leaf into a pan with the water, and simmer for 5–6 minutes. Set aside to cool.

4 When the mixture is cool, strain into the tomato and peach juice and chill in the refrigerator for at least 4 hours.

5 Using a sharp knife, slit the prawns down their curved sides, cutting about three-quarters of the way through and keeping their tails intact. Open the prawns out flat.

6 Heat a griddle or frying pan and brush with a little oil. Sear the prawns for 1–2 minutes on each side, until tender and slightly charred. Pat dry on kitchen paper to remove any remaining oil. Cool, but do not chill.

7 When ready to serve, ladle the soup into bowls and place three prawns in each portion.

8 Add some torn coriander leaves and diced tomato to each bowl, to garnish.

Energy 188Kcal/797kJ; Protein 12.7g; Carbohydrate 25.2g, of which sugars 25.2g; Fat 4.8g, of which saturates 0.8g; Cholesterol 98mg; Calcium 71mg; Fibre 5.8g; Sodium 116mg.

SMOOTH VEGETABLE SOUPS

A bowl of smooth and creamy vegetable soup served with some crusty bread makes an excellent light lunch at any time of the year. Choose whichever vegetables are fresh and in season — tomatoes and herbs in the summer, pumpkins and squash for the autumn, leeks and root vegetables during the winter months. In this section you will find simple Creamy Heart of Palm Soup and Mushroom Soup alongside more exotic dishes such as Peanut and Potato Soup and Curried Parsnip Soup with Croûtons.

CURRIED PARSNIP SOUP <u>WITH</u> CROÛTONS

THE MILD SWEETNESS OF PARSNIPS AND MANGO CHUTNEY IS GIVEN AN EXCITING LIFT WITH A BLEND OF SPICES IN THIS SIMPLE SOUP GARNISHED WITH NAAN CROÛTONS.

SERVES 4

INGREDIENTS
30ml/2 tbsp olive oil
1 onion, chopped
1 garlic clove, crushed
1 small green chilli, seeded and
  finely chopped
15ml/1 tbsp grated fresh
  root ginger
5 large parsnips, diced
5ml/1 tsp cumin seeds
5ml/1 tsp ground coriander
2.5ml/½ tsp ground turmeric
30ml/2 tbsp mango chutney
1.2 litres/2 pints/5 cups water
juice of 1 lime
salt and ground black pepper
60ml/4 tbsp natural (plain) yogurt
  and mango chutney, to serve
chopped fresh coriander (cilantro),
  to garnish (optional)

For the sesame naan croûtons
  45ml/3 tbsp olive oil
  1 large naan
  15ml/1 tbsp sesame seeds

1 Heat the oil in a large pan and add the onion, garlic, chilli and ginger. Cook for 4–5 minutes, until the onion has softened. Add the parsnips and cook for 2–3 minutes. Sprinkle in the cumin seeds, coriander and turmeric and cook for 1 minute, stirring constantly.

2 Add the chutney and the water. Season well and bring to the boil. Reduce the heat and simmer for 15 minutes, until the parsnips are soft.

3 Cool the soup slightly, then process it in a food processor or blender until smooth, and return it to the saucepan. Stir in the lime juice.

4 For the naan croûtons, cut the naan into small dice. Heat the oil in a large frying pan and cook until golden all over. Remove from the heat and drain off any excess oil. Add the sesame seeds and return to the heat for 30 seconds, until the seeds are golden.

5 Ladle the soup into bowls. Add a little yogurt and top with mango chutney and naan croûtons.

Energy 189Kcal/792kJ; Protein 4g; Carbohydrate 26.6g, of which sugars 15.5g; Fat 8.2g, of which saturates 1.2g; Cholesterol 0mg; Calcium 101mg; Fibre 7.5g; Sodium 110mg.

CREAM OF MUSHROOM SOUP WITH CROSTINI

CLASSIC CREAM OF MUSHROOM SOUP IS STILL A FIRM FAVOURITE, ESPECIALLY WITH THE ADDITION OF LUXURIOUSLY CRISP AND GARLICKY MUSHROOM CROÛTES.

SERVES 6

INGREDIENTS
25g/1oz/2 tbsp butter
1 onion, chopped
1 garlic clove, chopped
450g/1lb/6 cups button (white), chestnut or brown cap mushrooms, roughly chopped
15ml/1 tbsp plain (all-purpose) flour
45ml/3 tbsp dry sherry
900ml/1½ pints/3¾ cups vegetable stock
150ml/¼ pint/⅔ cup double (heavy) cream
salt and ground black pepper
fresh chervil sprigs, to garnish

For the crostini
15ml/1 tbsp olive oil, plus extra for brushing
1 shallot, chopped
115g/4oz/1½ cups button (white) mushrooms, finely chopped
15ml/1 tbsp chopped fresh parsley
6 brown cap (cremini) mushrooms
6 slices baguette
1 small garlic clove
115g/4oz/1 cup soft goat's cheese

1 Melt the butter in a pan and cook the onion and garlic for 5 minutes. Stir in the mushrooms, cover and cook for 10 minutes, stirring occasionally.

2 Stir in the flour and cook for 1 minute. Stir in the sherry and stock and bring to the boil, then simmer for 15 minutes. Cool slightly, then purée the soup in a food processor or blender until smooth.

3 Meanwhile, prepare the crostini. Heat the oil in a small pan. Add the shallot and button mushrooms, and cook for 8–10 minutes, until softened. Drain well and transfer to a food processor. Add the parsley and process until finely chopped.

4 Preheat the grill (broiler). Brush the brown cap mushrooms with oil and cook for 5–6 minutes.

5 Toast the slices of baguette, rub with the garlic and put a spoonful of cheese on each. Top the grilled (broiled) mushrooms with the mushroom mixture and place on the crostini.

6 Return the soup to the pan and stir in the cream. Season, then reheat gently. Ladle the soup into six bowls. Float a crostini in the centre of each and garnish with chervil.

Energy 313Kcal/1305kJ; Protein 6.2g; Carbohydrate 26.8g, of which sugars 2.5g; Fat 20g, of which saturates 11g; Cholesterol 43mg; Calcium 75mg; Fibre 2.2g; Sodium 283mg.

CREAMY HEART OF PALM SOUP

THIS DELICATE SOUP HAS A LUXURIOUS, CREAMY, ALMOST VELVETY TEXTURE. THE SUBTLE YET DISTINCTIVE FLAVOUR OF THE PALM HEARTS IS LIKE NO OTHER, ALTHOUGH IT IS MILDLY REMINISCENT OF ARTICHOKES AND ASPARAGUS. SERVE WITH FRESH BREAD FOR A SATISFYING LUNCH.

SERVES 4

INGREDIENTS
  25g/1oz/2 tbsp butter
  10ml/2 tsp olive oil
  1 onion, finely chopped
  1 large leek, finely sliced
  15ml/1 tbsp plain (all-purpose) flour
  1 litre/1¾ pints/4 cups
    well-flavoured chicken stock
  350g/12oz potatoes, peeled
    and cubed
  2 x 400g/14oz cans hearts of palm,
    drained and sliced
  250ml/8fl oz/1 cup double
    (heavy) cream
  salt and ground black pepper
  cayenne pepper and chopped fresh
    chives, to garnish

1 Heat the butter and oil in a large pan over a low heat. Add the onion and leek and stir well until coated in butter. Cover and cook for 5 minutes until softened and translucent.

2 Sprinkle over the flour. Cook, stirring, for 1 minute.

3 Pour in the stock and add the potatoes. Bring to the boil, then lower the heat and simmer for 10 minutes. Stir in the hearts of palm and the cream, and simmer gently for 10 minutes.

4 Process in a blender or food processor until smooth. Return the soup to the pan and heat gently, adding a little water if necessary. The consistency should be thick but not too heavy. Season with salt and ground black pepper.

5 Ladle the soup into heated bowls and garnish each with a pinch of cayenne pepper and a scattering of fresh chives. Serve immediately.

VARIATION
For a richer, buttery flavour, add the flesh of a ripe avocado when blending.

Energy 486Kcal/2016kJ; Protein 4.9g; Carbohydrate 25.9g, of which sugars 3g; Fat 41.1g, of which saturates 24.4g; Cholesterol 99mg; Calcium 127mg; Fibre 3.7g; Sodium 97mg.

PEANUT AND POTATO SOUP

PEANUT SOUP IS A FIRM FAVOURITE THROUGHOUT CENTRAL AND SOUTH AMERICA, AND IS PARTICULARLY POPULAR IN BOLIVIA AND ECUADOR. AS IN MANY LATIN AMERICAN RECIPES, THE GROUND NUTS ARE USED AS A THICKENING AGENT, WITH UNEXPECTEDLY DELICIOUS RESULTS.

SERVES 6

INGREDIENTS
60ml/4 tbsp groundnut (peanut) oil
1 onion, finely chopped
2 garlic cloves, crushed
1 red (bell) pepper, seeded
  and chopped
250g/9oz potatoes, peeled and diced
2 fresh red chillies, seeded
  and chopped
200g/7oz canned chopped tomatoes
150g/5oz/1¼ cups unsalted peanuts
1.5 litres/2½ pints/6¼ cups beef stock
salt and ground black pepper
30ml/2 tbsp chopped fresh coriander
  (cilantro), to garnish

1 Heat the oil in a large heavy pan over a low heat. Stir in the onion and cook for 5 minutes, until beginning to soften. Add the garlic, pepper, potatoes, chillies and tomatoes. Stir well to coat the vegetables evenly in the oil, cover and cook for 5 minutes, until softened.

2 Meanwhile, toast the peanuts by gently cooking them in a large dry frying pan over a medium heat. Keep a close eye on them, moving the peanuts around the pan until they are evenly golden. Take care not to burn them.

COOK'S TIP
Replace the unsalted peanuts with peanut butter if you like. Use equal quantities of chunky and smooth peanut butter for the ideal texture.

3 Set 30ml/2 tbsp of the peanuts aside, to use as garnish. Transfer the remaining peanuts to a food processor and process until finely ground. Add the vegetables and process again until smooth.

4 Return the mixture to the pan and stir in the beef stock. Bring to the boil, then lower the heat and simmer for 10 minutes.

5 Pour the soup into heated bowls. Garnish with a generous scattering of coriander and the remaining peanuts.

Energy 260Kcal/1079kJ; Protein 8g; Carbohydrate 14.7g, of which sugars 6.2g; Fat 19.2g, of which saturates 3.6g; Cholesterol 0mg; Calcium 30mg; Fibre 3g; Sodium 20mg.

MUSHROOM SOUP

USING A MIXTURE OF PARIS BROWNS, FIELD AND BUTTON MUSHROOMS GIVES THIS SOUP TEXTURE AND CHARACTER. THIS MAKES A FLAVOURSOME LIGHT MEAL SERVED WITH FRESH CRUSTY BREAD.

SERVES 4–6 AS A LIGHT MEAL
OR 6–8 AS A SOUP COURSE

INGREDIENTS
20g/¾oz/1½ tbsp butter
15ml/1 tbsp oil
1 onion, roughly chopped
4 potatoes, about 250–350g/9–12oz,
   roughly chopped
350g/12oz mixed mushrooms, such
   as Paris Browns, field (portabello)
   and button (white), cleaned and
   roughly chopped
1 or 2 garlic cloves, crushed
150ml/¼ pint/⅔ cup white wine or
   dry (hard) cider
1.2 litres/2 pints/5 cups good
   chicken stock
bunch of fresh parsley, chopped
salt and ground black pepper
whipped or sour cream,
   to garnish

1 Heat the butter and oil in a large pan over medium heat. Add the chopped onion, turning it in the butter until well coated. Stir in the potatoes. Cover and sweat over a low heat for 5–10 minutes until softened but not browned.

2 Add the mushrooms, garlic and white wine or cider and stock. Season, bring to the boil and cook for 15 minutes, until all the ingredients are tender.

3 Put the mixture through a mouli-legume (food mill), using the coarse blade, or liquidize (blend). Return the soup to the rinsed pan, and add three-quarters of the parsley. Bring back to the boil, season, and garnish with cream and the remaining parsley.

GARLIC SOUP

THIS INTERESTING AND SURPRISINGLY SUBTLY FLAVOURED IRISH SOUP MAKES GOOD USE OF AN ANCIENT INGREDIENT THAT IS NOT ONLY DELICIOUS BUT ALSO BELIEVED TO HAVE HEALTH-GIVING PROPERTIES. IT CERTAINLY BRINGS A GREAT SENSE OF WELL-BEING AND IS A REAL TREAT FOR GARLIC-LOVERS. SERVE IT WITH SOME CRUSTY BREAD AS A REAL WINTER WARMER.

SERVES 8

INGREDIENTS
12 large garlic cloves, peeled
15ml/1 tbsp olive oil
15ml/1 tbsp melted butter
1 small onion, finely chopped
15g/½oz/2 tbsp plain
   (all-purpose) flour
15ml/1 tbsp white wine vinegar
1 litre/1¾ pints/4 cups good
   chicken stock
2 egg yolks, lightly beaten
bread croûtons, fried in butter,
   to serve

VARIATION
Grilled croûtes make a nice change in place of the croûtons. Toast small slices of baguette, top with grated Cheddar and grill (broil) until the cheese melts.

1 Crush the garlic. Put the oil and butter into a pan, add the garlic and onion, and cook them gently for 20 minutes, until soft but not brown.

2 Add the flour and stir to make a roux. Cook for a few minutes, then stir in the wine vinegar, stock and 1 litre/ 1¾ pints/4 cups water. Simmer for about 30 minutes.

3 When ready to serve the soup, whisk in the lightly beaten egg yolks. Put the croûtons into eight soup bowls and pour over the hot soup.

COOK'S TIP
When adding egg yolks to thicken a soup, reheat the soup gently but do not bring it back to the boil, otherwise the egg will curdle.

Top: Energy 155Kcal/648kJ; Protein 3.2g; Carbohydrate 13.6g, of which sugars 3.4g; Fat 7.6g, of which saturates 3.2g; Cholesterol 11mg; Calcium 23mg; Fibre 2.1g; Sodium 44mg.
Bottom: Energy 55Kcal/229kJ; Protein 1.6g; Carbohydrate 3.6g, of which sugars 0.6g; Fat 4g, of which saturates 1.3g; Cholesterol 53mg; Calcium 13mg; Fibre 0.4g; Sodium 11mg.

ITALIAN PEA AND BASIL SOUP

THE PUNGENT FLAVOUR OF BASIL LIFTS THIS APPETIZING ITALIAN SOUP, WHILE THE ONION AND GARLIC GIVE DEPTH. SERVE IT WITH GOOD CRUSTY BREAD TO ENJOY IT AT ITS BEST.

2 Add the peas and stock to the pan and bring to the boil. Reduce the heat, add the basil and seasoning, then simmer for 10 minutes.

3 Spoon the soup into a food processor or blender (you may have to do this in batches) and process until the soup is smooth.

4 Return the soup to the rinsed pan and reheat gently until piping hot. Ladle into warm bowls, sprinkle with shaved Parmesan and garnish with basil.

VARIATION
You can also use mint or a mixture of parsley, mint and chives in place of the basil, if you like.

SERVES 4

INGREDIENTS
  75ml/5 tbsp olive oil
  2 large onions, chopped
  1 celery stick, chopped
  1 carrot, chopped
  1 garlic clove, finely chopped
  400g/14oz/3½ cups frozen
    petits pois (baby peas)
  900ml/1½ pints/3¾ cups
    vegetable stock
  25g/1oz/1 cup fresh basil leaves,
    roughly torn, plus extra to garnish
  salt and ground black pepper
  shaved Parmesan cheese,
    to serve

1 Heat the oil in a large pan and add the onions, celery, carrot and garlic. Cover the pan and cook over a low heat for 45 minutes, or until the vegetables are soft, stirring occasionally to prevent the vegetables sticking.

Energy 261Kcal/1078kJ; Protein 8.8g; Carbohydrate 22.9g, of which sugars 10.9g; Fat 15.7g, of which saturates 2.3g; Cholesterol 0mg; Calcium 73mg; Fibre 7.3g; Sodium 16mg.

ASPARAGUS AND PEA SOUP WITH PARMESAN

THIS BRIGHT AND FLAVOURSOME SOUP USES EVERY INCH OF THE ASPARAGUS, INCLUDING THE WOODY ENDS, WHICH ARE USED FOR MAKING THE STOCK, WHILE THE TIPS MAKE AN ATTRACTIVE GARNISH.

SERVES 6

INGREDIENTS

   350g/12oz asparagus
   2 leeks
   1 bay leaf
   1 carrot, roughly chopped
   1 celery stick, chopped
   few stalks of fresh parsley
   1.75 litres/3 pints/7½ cups
     cold water
   25g/1oz/2 tbsp butter
   150g/5oz fresh garden peas
   15ml/1 tbsp chopped fresh parsley
   120ml/4fl oz/½ cup double
     (heavy) cream
   grated rind of ½ lemon
   salt and ground black pepper
   shavings of Parmesan cheese,
     to serve

1 Cut the woody ends from the asparagus, then set the spears aside. Roughly chop the woody ends and place them in a large pan. Cut off and chop the green parts of the leeks and add to the asparagus stalks with the bay leaf, carrot, celery, parsley stalks and the cold water. Bring to the boil and simmer for 30 minutes. Strain the stock and discard the vegetables.

2 Cut the tips off the asparagus and set aside, then cut the stems into short pieces. Chop the remainder of the leeks.

3 Melt the butter in a large pan and add the leeks. Cook for 3–4 minutes until softened, then add the asparagus stems, peas and chopped parsley. Pour in 1.2 litres/2 pints/5 cups of the asparagus stock. Bring to the boil, reduce the heat and cook for 6–8 minutes, until all the vegetables are tender. Season well.

4 Cool the soup slightly, then purée it in a food processor or blender until smooth. Press the purée through a very fine sieve into the rinsed pan. Stir in the cream and lemon rind.

5 Bring a small pan of water to the boil and cook the asparagus tips for about 2–3 minutes until just tender. Drain and refresh under cold water. Reheat the soup, but do not allow it to boil.

6 Ladle the soup into six warmed bowls and garnish with the asparagus tips. Serve immediately, with shavings of Parmesan cheese and plenty of ground black pepper.

VARIATION
For a lighter soup, you could replace the cream with low-fat milk, but the finished dish will not taste as rich.

IRISH POTATO SOUP

THIS MOST IRISH OF ALL SOUPS IS NOT ONLY EXCELLENT AS IT IS, BUT VERSATILE TOO, AS IT CAN BE USED AS A BASE FOR NUMEROUS OTHER SOUPS. USE A FLOURY POTATO, SUCH AS GOLDEN WONDER.

SERVES 6–8

INGREDIENTS

50g/2oz/¼ cup butter
2 large onions, peeled and
  finely chopped
675g/1½lb potatoes, diced
about 1.75 litres/3 pints/7½ cups
  hot chicken stock
sea salt and ground black pepper
a little milk, if necessary
chopped fresh chives, to garnish

1 Melt the butter in a large heavy pan and add the onions, turning them in the butter until well coated. Cover and leave to sweat over a very low heat for about 10 mintues.

2 Add the potatoes to the pan, and mix well with the butter and onions. Season with salt and pepper, cover and cook without colouring over a gentle heat for about 10 minutes. Add the stock, bring to the boil and simmer for 25 minutes, or until the vegetables are tender.

3 Remove from the heat and allow to cool slightly. Purée the soup in batches in a blender or food processor.

4 Reheat the soup over a low heat and adjust the seasoning. If the soup seems too thick, add a little extra stock or milk to achieve the right consistency.

5 Serve the soup very hot, sprinkled with chopped chives.

COOK'S TIP
The best potatoes to use in soups are the floury ones, because they cook more quickly and disintegrate easily. Choose varieties such as Golden Wonder, Maris Piper, Estima and King Edward.

Energy 167Kcal/699kJ; Protein 2.9g; Carbohydrate 23.5g, of which sugars 5.3g; Fat 7.5g, of which saturates 4.5g; Cholesterol 18mg; Calcium 26mg; Fibre 2.1g; Sodium 201mg.

ARTICHOKE SOUP WITH BRUSCHETTA

JERUSALEM ARTICHOKES ORIGINATE FROM NORTH AMERICA, YET LEND THEMSELVES BEAUTIFULLY TO THE METHODS AND FLAVOURS OF MEDITERRANEAN COOKING.

SERVES 6

INGREDIENTS
    squeeze of lemon juice
    450g/1lb Jerusalem artichokes
    65g/2½oz/5 tbsp butter
    175g/6oz potatoes, roughly diced
    1 small onion, chopped
    1 garlic clove, chopped
    1 celery stick, chopped
    1 small fennel bulb, halved, cored
      and chopped
    1.2 litres/2 pints/5 cups vegetable
      stock
    300ml/½ pint/1¼ cups double
      (heavy) cream
    pinch of freshly grated nutmeg
    salt and ground black pepper
    basil leaves, to garnish

For the artichoke and anchovy bruschetta
    6 thick slices French bread
    1 garlic clove
    50g/2oz/¼ cup unsalted butter
    400g/14oz can artichoke hearts,
      drained and halved
    45ml/3 tbsp tapenade
    9 salted anchovy fillets, halved
      lengthways

1 Prepare a large bowl of cold water with a squeeze of lemon juice added. Peel and dice the Jerusalem artichokes, adding them to the water as soon as each one is prepared. This will prevent them from discolouring.

2 Melt the butter in a large, heavy-based saucepan. Drain the artichokes and add to the pan with the potatoes, onion, garlic, celery and fennel. Stir well and cook for 10 minutes, stirring occasionally, until beginning to soften.

3 Pour in the stock and bring to the boil, then simmer for 10–15 minutes, until all the vegetables are softened. Cool the soup slightly, then process in a food processor or blender until smooth. Press it through a sieve (strainer) into a clean pan. Add the cream and nutmeg, and season well.

4 To make the bruschetta, lightly toast the French bread slices on both sides. Rub each slice with the garlic clove and set aside. Melt the butter in a small pan. Add the artichoke hearts and cook for 3–4 minutes, turning once.

5 Spread the tapenade on the toast and arrange pieces of artichoke heart on top. Top with anchovy fillets and garnish with basil leaves.

6 Reheat the artichoke soup without allowing it to boil, then ladle it into bowls. Serve the bruschetta with the soup.

Energy 790Kcal/3303kJ; Protein 14.3g; Carbohydrate 85.6g, of which sugars 16.4g; Fat 45.8g, of which saturates 27.3g; Cholesterol 111mg; Calcium 232mg; Fibre 7.6g; Sodium 1030mg.

CHUNKY VEGETABLE SOUPS

In this section you will find a collection of traditional

European dishes such as French Onion Soup with Gruyère

Croûtes, and Castilian Garlic Soup. You can also try more

exotic vegetable recipes such as Shiitake Mushroom Laksa, and

Balinese Vegetable Soup — you will find the ingredients are

readily available in many supermarkets allowing you to

dare to try something new.

TORTILLA TOMATO SOUP

THERE ARE SEVERAL TORTILLA SOUPS. THIS ONE IS AN AGUADA — OR LIQUID — VERSION, AND IS INTENDED FOR SERVING AS AN APPETIZER OR LIGHT MEAL. IT IS VERY EASY AND QUICK TO PREPARE, OR MAKE IT IN ADVANCE AND FRY THE TORTILLA STRIPS AS IT REHEATS. THE CRISP TORTILLA PIECES ADD INTEREST AND GIVE THE SOUP AN UNUSUAL TEXTURE.

SERVES 4

INGREDIENTS

4 corn tortillas
15ml/1 tbsp vegetable oil, plus extra
  for frying
1 small onion, chopped
2 garlic cloves, crushed
350g/12oz ripe plum tomatoes
400g/14oz can plum tomatoes, drained
1 litre/1¾ pints/4 cups chicken stock
small bunch of fresh coriander (cilantro)
50g/2oz/½ cup grated (shredded)
  mild Cheddar cheese
salt and ground black pepper

1 Using a sharp knife, cut each tortilla into four or five strips, each measuring about 2cm/¾in wide. Pour vegetable oil to a depth of 2cm/¾in into a frying pan. Heat until a small piece of tortilla, added to the oil, floats on the top and bubbles at the edges.

2 Add a few tortilla strips to the hot oil and fry until crisp and golden brown.

3 Remove the tortilla chips with a slotted spoon and drain on kitchen paper. Cook the remaining tortilla strips in the same way.

4 Heat the 15ml/1 tbsp vegetable oil in a large pan. Add the onion and garlic and cook over a medium heat for 2–3 minutes, until the onion is soft and translucent. Do not let the garlic turn brown or it will give the soup a bitter taste.

5 Skin the fresh tomatoes by plunging them into boiling water for 30 seconds, refreshing them in cold water, draining them and then peeling off the skins with a sharp knife.

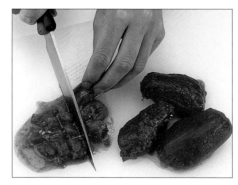

6 Chop the fresh and canned tomatoes and add them to the onion mixture. Pour in the chicken stock. Bring to the boil, then lower the heat and simmer for 10 minutes, until the liquid has reduced slightly. Stir the mixture occasionally.

7 Roughly chop or tear the coriander into pieces. Add it to the soup and season with salt and ground black pepper to taste.

8 Place a few of the crisp tortilla pieces in each of four large heated soup bowls. Ladle the soup on top. Sprinkle each portion with some of the grated mild Cheddar cheese and serve immediately.

COOK'S TIP
An easy way to chop fresh herbs is to put them in a mug and snip with a pair of scissors. Hold the scissors vertically with one hand on each handle and work the blades back and forth until the herbs are finely and evenly chopped. If you are using woody herbs, such as rosemary or thyme, remember to strip the leaves from the stalks before putting them in the mug. They are then ready to be chopped.

Energy 270Kcal/1135kJ; Protein 8.3g; Carbohydrate 36.9g, of which sugars 7.2g; Fat 10.7g, of which saturates 3.6g; Cholesterol 12mg; Calcium 164mg; Fibre 3.3g; Sodium 248mg.

FRENCH ONION SOUP
WITH GRUYÈRE CROÛTES

*THIS IS PERHAPS THE MOST FAMOUS OF ALL ONION SOUPS. TRADITIONALLY, IT WAS SERVED AS A
SUSTAINING EARLY MORNING MEAL TO THE PORTERS AND WORKERS OF LES HALLES MARKET IN PARIS.*

SERVES 6

INGREDIENTS

50g/2oz/¼ cup butter
15ml/1 tbsp olive oil
2kg/4½lb yellow onions, peeled
  and sliced
5ml/1 tsp chopped fresh thyme
5ml/1 tsp caster (superfine) sugar
15ml/1 tbsp sherry vinegar
1.5 litres/2½ pints/6¼ cups good
  beef, chicken or duck stock
25ml/1½ tbsp plain (all-purpose) flour
150ml/¼ pint/⅔ cup dry white wine
45ml/3 tbsp brandy
salt and ground black pepper
For the croûtes
6–12 thick slices day-old French
  stick or baguette, about 2.5cm/
  1in thick
1 garlic clove, halved
15ml/1 tbsp French mustard
115g/4oz/1 cup coarsely grated
  Gruyère cheese

1 Melt the butter with the oil in a large
pan. Add the onions and stir to coat
them in the fat. Cook over a medium
heat for 5–8 minutes, stirring once or
twice, until the onions begin to soften.
Stir in the thyme.

2 Reduce the heat to very low, cover
the pan and cook the onions for
20–30 minutes, stirring frequently, until
they are very soft and golden yellow.

4 Meanwhile, bring the stock to the
boil in another pan. Stir the flour
into the onions and cook for about
2 minutes, then gradually pour in the
hot stock. Add the wine and brandy and
season the soup to taste with salt and
pepper. Simmer for 10–15 minutes.

5 For the croûtes, preheat the oven to
150°C/300°F/Gas 2. Place the slices of
bread on a greased baking tray and bake
for 15–20 minutes, until dry and lightly
browned. Rub the bread with the cut
surface of the garlic and spread with
the mustard, then sprinkle the grated
Gruyère cheese over the slices.

3 Uncover the pan and increase the
heat slightly. Stir in the sugar and cook
for 5–10 minutes, until the onions start
to brown. Add the sherry vinegar and
increase the heat again, then continue
cooking, stirring frequently, until the
onions turn a deep, golden brown – this
could take up to 20 minutes.

COOK'S TIP
The long slow cooking of the onions
is the key to success with this soup.
If the onions brown too quickly the
soup will be bitter.

6 Preheat the grill (broiler) on the
hottest setting. Ladle the soup into a
large flameproof pan or six flameproof
bowls. Float the croûtes on the soup,
then grill until the cheese melts,
bubbles and browns. Serve immediately.

Energy 484Kcal/2030kJ; Protein 15.3g; Carbohydrate 67.2g, of which sugars 21.5g; Fat 15.1g, of which saturates 8.7g; Cholesterol 36mg; Calcium 314mg; Fibre 6.4g; Sodium 611mg.

GRANDFATHER'S SOUP

THIS TRADITIONAL EASTERN EUROPEAN SOUP DERIVES ITS NAME FROM THE FACT THAT IT IS EASILY DIGESTED AND THEREFORE THOUGHT TO BE SUITABLE FOR THE ELDERLY.

SERVES 4

INGREDIENTS
1 large onion, finely sliced
25g/1oz/2 tbsp butter
350g/12oz potatoes, peeled
  and diced
900ml/1½ pints/3¾ cups
  beef stock
1 bay leaf
salt and freshly ground
  black pepper
For the drop noodles
75g/3oz/⅔ cup self-raising
  (self-rising) flour
pinch of salt
15g/½oz/1 tbsp butter
15ml/1 tbsp chopped fresh parsley,
  plus a little extra to garnish
1 egg, beaten
chunks of bread, to serve

1 In a wide heavy-based pan, cook the onion gently in the butter for 10 minutes, or until it begins to soften and go golden brown.

2 Add the diced potatoes and cook for 2–3 minutes, then pour in the stock. Add the bay leaf, salt and pepper. Bring to the boil, then reduce the heat, cover and simmer for about 10 minutes.

3 To make the noodles, sift the flour and salt into a bowl and rub in the butter. Stir in the parsley, then add the egg and mix to a soft dough.

4 Drop half-teaspoonfuls of the dough into the simmering soup. Cover and simmer gently for a further 10 minutes. Ladle into warmed soup bowls, sprinkle over a little parsley, and serve.

Energy 239Kcal/1001kJ; Protein 5.5g; Carbohydrate 33.3g, of which sugars 5g; Fat 10.2g, of which saturates 5.7g; Cholesterol 69mg; Calcium 96mg; Fibre 2.3g; Sodium 157mg.

RUSSIAN BORSCHT

BEETROOT IS THE MAIN INGREDIENT OF BORSCHT, AND ITS FLAVOUR AND COLOUR DOMINATE THIS WELL-KNOWN SOUP. IT IS A CLASSIC OF BOTH RUSSIA AND POLAND.

SERVES 4–6

INGREDIENTS
  900g/2lb uncooked beetroot, peeled
  2 carrots, peeled
  2 celery sticks
  40g/1½oz/3 tbsp butter
  2 onions, sliced
  2 garlic cloves, crushed
  4 tomatoes, peeled, seeded
    and chopped
  1 bay leaf
  1 large parsley sprig
  2 cloves
  4 whole peppercorns
  1.2 litres/2 pints/5 cups beef or
    chicken stock
  150ml/¼ pint/⅔ cup beetroot *kvas*
    (see Cook's Tip) or the liquid from
    pickled beetroot
  salt and freshly ground black pepper
  soured cream, garnished with
    chopped fresh chives or sprigs of
    dill, to serve

1 Cut the beetroot, carrots and celery into thick strips. Melt the butter in a pan and cook the onions over a low heat for 5 minutes, stirring occasionally.

2 Add the beetroot, carrots and celery and cook for a further 5 minutes.

COOK'S TIP
Beetroot *kvas* adds an intense colour and a slight tartness. If unavailable, peel and grate 1 beetroot, add 150ml/¼ pint/⅔ cup stock and 10ml/2 tsp lemon juice. Bring to the boil, cover and leave for 30 minutes. Strain before using.

3 Add the crushed garlic and chopped tomatoes to the pan and cook, stirring, for 2 more minutes.

4 Place the bay leaf, parsley, cloves and peppercorns in a piece of muslin (cheesecloth) and tie with string.

5 Add the muslin bag to the pan with the stock. Bring to the boil, reduce the heat, cover and simmer for 1¼ hours, until the vegetables are tender. Discard the bag. Stir in the beetroot *kvas* and season. Ladle into bowls and serve with soured cream. Garnish with chives or dill.

Energy 125Kcal/532kJ; Protein 5.3g; Carbohydrate 26.2g, of which sugars 23.5g; Fat 0.7g, of which saturates 0.1g; Cholesterol 0mg; Calcium 71mg; Fibre 6.6g; Sodium 166mg.

HUNGARIAN CHERRY SOUP

SOUPS MADE FROM SEASONAL FRUITS ARE A FAVOURITE CENTRAL EUROPEAN TREAT, AND CHERRY SOUP IS ONE OF THE GLORIES OF THE HUNGARIAN TABLE. IT IS OFTEN SERVED AT THE START OF A DAIRY MEAL, SUCH AS AT THE FESTIVAL OF SHAVUOT WHEN DAIRY FOODS ARE TRADITIONALLY FEASTED UPON.

SERVES 6

INGREDIENTS

1kg/2¼lb fresh, frozen or canned
   sour cherries, such as Morello or
   Montmorency, pitted
250ml/8fl oz/1 cup water
175–250g/6–9oz/about 1 cup sugar,
   to taste
1–2 cinnamon sticks, each about
   5cm/2in long
750ml/1¼ pints/3 cups dry red wine
5ml/1 tsp almond essence (extract),
   or to taste
250ml/8fl oz/1 cup single
   (light) cream
250ml/8fl oz/1 cup sour cream or
   crème fraîche

1 Put the pitted cherries, water, sugar, cinnamon and wine in a large pan. Bring to the boil, reduce the heat and simmer for 20–30 minutes, until the cherries are tender. Remove from the heat and add the almond essence.

2 In a bowl, stir a few tablespoons of single cream into the sour cream or crème fraîche to thin it down, then stir in the rest until the mixture is smooth. Stir the mixture into the cherry soup, then chill until ready to serve.

Energy 518Kcal/2163kJ; Protein 4.1g; Carbohydrate 51.8g, of which sugars 51.7g; Fat 24.8g, of which saturates 16.4g; Cholesterol 70mg; Calcium 107mg; Fibre 1.5g; Sodium 34mg.

CASTILIAN GARLIC SOUP

THIS RICH, DARK GARLIC SOUP COMES FROM LA MANCHA IN CENTRAL SPAIN, AND IS SIMILAR TO PORTUGUESE GARLIC SOUP. THE REGION IS FAMOUS FOR ITS SUMMER SUNSHINE, AND THE LOCAL SOUP HAS A HARSH, STRONG TASTE TO MATCH THE CLIMATE.

SERVES 4

INGREDIENTS
   30ml/2 tbsp olive oil
   4 large garlic cloves, peeled
   4 slices stale country bread
   20ml/4 tbsp paprika
   1 litre/1¾ pints/4 cups
     beef stock
   1.5ml/¼ tsp ground cumin
   4 free-range (farm-fresh) eggs
   salt and ground black pepper
   chopped fresh parsley, to garnish

VARIATION
If you prefer, you can simply whisk
the eggs into the hot soup.

1 Preheat the oven to 230°C/450°F/ Gas 8. Heat the olive oil in a large pan. Add the whole peeled garlic cloves and cook until they are golden, then remove and set aside. Fry the slices of bread in the oil until golden, then set these aside.

2 Add 15ml/1 tbsp of the paprika to the pan, and fry for a few seconds. Stir in the beef stock, cumin and remaining paprika, then add the reserved garlic, crushing the cloves with the back of a wooden spoon. Season to taste, then cook for about 5 minutes.

3 Break up the slices of fried bread into bitesize pieces and stir them into the soup. Ladle the soup into four ovenproof bowls. Carefully break an egg into each bowl of soup and place in the oven for about 3 minutes, until the eggs are set. Sprinkle the soup with chopped fresh parsley and serve immediately.

Energy 202Kcal/843kJ; Protein 9.3g; Carbohydrate 15.3g, of which sugars 1.5g; Fat 12.2g, of which saturates 2.4g; Cholesterol 190mg; Calcium 69mg; Fibre 0.6g; Sodium 202mg.

BALINESE VEGETABLE SOUP

THE BALINESE BASE THIS POPULAR SOUP ON BEANS, BUT ANY SEASONAL VEGETABLES CAN BE ADDED OR SUBSTITUTED. THE RECIPE ALSO INCLUDES SHRIMP PASTE, WHICH IS KNOWN LOCALLY AS TERASI.

2 Finely grind the chopped garlic, macadamia nuts or almonds, shrimp paste (blachan) and the coriander seeds to a paste using a pestle and mortar or in a food processor.

SERVES 8

INGREDIENTS

225g/8oz green beans
1.2 litres/2 pints/5 cups lightly
    salted water
1 garlic clove, roughly
    chopped
2 macadamia nuts or 4 almonds,
    finely chopped
1cm/1/2in cube shrimp paste
    (blachan)
10–15ml/2–3 tsp coriander seeds,
    dry fried
30ml/2 tbsp vegetable oil
1 onion, finely sliced
400ml/14fl oz can coconut milk
2 bay leaves
225g/8oz/4 cups beansprouts
8 thin lemon wedges
30ml/2 tbsp lemon juice
salt and ground black pepper

1 Top and tail the beans, then cut them into small pieces. Bring the lightly salted water to the boil, add the beans to the pan and cook for 3–4 minutes. Drain, reserving the cooking water. Set the beans aside.

COOK'S TIP
Dry fry the coriander seeds for about 2 minutes until the aroma is released.

3 Heat the oil in a wok, and fry the onion until transparent. Remove with a slotted spoon. Add the nut paste to the wok and fry it for 2 minutes without allowing it to brown.

4 Pour in the reserved vegetable water. Spoon off 45–60ml/3–4 tbsp of the cream from the top of the coconut milk and set it aside. Add the remaining coconut milk to the wok, bring to the boil and add the bay leaves. Cook, uncovered, for 15–20 minutes.

5 Just before serving, reserve a few beans, fried onions and beansprouts to garnish and stir the rest into the soup. Add the lemon wedges, reserved coconut cream, lemon juice and seasoning; stir well. Pour into individual soup bowls and serve, garnished with the reserved beans, onion and beansprouts.

Energy 54Kcal/224kJ; Protein 2.1g; Carbohydrate 5.2g, of which sugars 4.2g; Fat 2.8g, of which saturates 0.4g; Cholesterol 0mg; Calcium 38mg; Fibre 1.3g; Sodium 57mg.

SHIITAKE MUSHROOM LAKSA

"NOODLES" OF FINELY SLICED RED ONIONS ENHANCE THE TRADITIONAL FLOUR NOODLES IN THIS SOUP, WHICH IS BASED ON THE CLASSIC MALAYSIAN SOUP KNOWN AS PENANG LAKSA.

SERVES 6

INGREDIENTS

150g/5oz/2½ cups dried shiitake
  mushrooms
1.2 litres/2 pints/5 cups boiling
  vegetable stock
30ml/2 tbsp tamarind paste
250ml/8fl oz/1 cup hot water
6 large dried red chillies, stems
  removed and seeded
2 lemon grass stalks, finely sliced
5ml/1 tsp ground turmeric
15ml/1 tbsp grated fresh galangal
1 onion, chopped
5ml/1 tsp dried shrimp paste
30ml/2 tbsp oil
10ml/2 tsp palm sugar
175g/6oz rice vermicelli
1 red onion, peeled and very
  finely sliced
1 small cucumber, seeded and
  cut into strips
handful of fresh mint leaves,
  to garnish

4 Process the lemon grass, turmeric, galangal, onion, soaked chillies and shrimp paste in a food processor or blender, adding a little soaking water from the chillies to form a paste.

5 Heat the oil in a large, heavy-based pan and cook the paste over a low heat for 4–5 minutes until fragrant. Add the tamarind liquid and bring to the boil, then simmer for 5 minutes. Remove from the heat.

6 Drain the mushrooms and reserve the stock. Discard the stems, then halve or quarter the mushrooms, if large. Add the mushrooms to the pan with their soaking liquid, the remaining stock and the palm sugar. Simmer for 25–30 minutes or until tender.

7 Put the rice vermicelli into a large bowl and cover with boiling water, then leave to soak for 4 minutes or according to the packet instructions. Drain well, then divide among six bowls. Top with onion and cucumber, then ladle in the boiling shiitake soup. Add a small bunch of mint leaves to each bowl and serve immediately.

1 Place the mushrooms in a bowl and pour in enough boiling stock to cover them. Set aside and leave to soak for 30 minutes.

2 Put the tamarind paste into a small bowl and pour in the hot water. Mash the paste against the side of the bowl with a fork to extract as much flavour as possible, then strain and reserve the liquid, discarding the pulp.

3 Soak the chillies in enough hot water to cover for 5 minutes, then drain, reserving the liquid.

Energy 152Kcal/635kJ; Protein 3.2g; Carbohydrate 25.9g, of which sugars 2.6g; Fat 4g, of which saturates 0.5g; Cholesterol 0mg; Calcium 14mg; Fibre 0.6g; Sodium 4mg.

Pasta and Noodle Soups

In Italy hearty pasta soups are often served with bread as a light supper. There are hundreds of little pasta shapes, called pastina, to choose from — which means an endless variety of dishes is possible. In this section you will find Meatballs in Pasta Soup with Basil, as well as Old-Fashioned Chicken and Noodle Soup. Noodles are a key ingredient in many Asian soups including Chiang Mai Noodle Soup, or Tokyo-Style Ramen Noodles in Soup.

AVGOLEMONO WITH PASTA

THIS IS THE MOST POPULAR OF GREEK SOUPS. THE NAME MEANS EGG AND LEMON, THE TWO MOST IMPORTANT INGREDIENTS, WHICH PRODUCE A LIGHT, NOURISHING SOUP. ORZO IS A GREEK RICE-SHAPED PASTA, BUT YOU CAN USE ANY SMALL SOUP PASTA.

SERVES 4–6

INGREDIENTS
1.75 litres/3 pints/7½ cups
  chicken stock
115g/4oz/½ cup orzo pasta
3 eggs
juice of 1 large lemon
salt and ground black pepper
lemon slices, to garnish

COOK'S TIP
This egg and lemon combination is also widely used in Greece as a sauce for pasta or with meatballs.

1 Pour the stock into a large pan, and bring it to a rolling boil. Add the pasta and cook for 5 minutes.

2 Beat the eggs until frothy, then add the lemon juice and 15ml/ 1 tbsp of cold water. Slowly stir in a ladleful of the hot chicken stock, then add one or two more.

3 Return this mixture to the pan, remove from the heat and stir well. (Do not let the soup boil once the eggs have been added or it will curdle.)

4 Season the soup to taste with salt and freshly ground black pepper and serve immediately, garnished with a few lemon slices.

Energy 154Kcal/648kJ; Protein 8.1g; Carbohydrate 21.3g, of which sugars 1g; Fat 4.7g, of which saturates 1.2g; Cholesterol 143mg; Calcium 29mg; Fibre 0.8g; Sodium 53mg.

MEATBALLS IN PASTA SOUP WITH BASIL

THESE CLASSIC HOME-MADE MEATBALLS ARE DELICIOUS — SCENTED WITH ORANGE AND GARLIC, THEY ARE SERVED IN A RUSTIC PASTA SOUP, WHICH IS THICKENED WITH PURÉED CANNELLINI BEANS. THE DISH IS A FILLING AND MAKES A FLAVOURSOME AND AUTHENTIC ITALIAN MEAL.

SERVES 4

INGREDIENTS
   400g/14oz can cannellini beans,
      drained and rinsed
   1 litre/1¾ pints/4 cups
      vegetable stock
   45ml/3 tbsp olive oil
   1 onion, finely chopped
   2 garlic cloves, chopped
   1 small red chilli, seeded and chopped
   2 celery sticks, finely chopped
   1 carrot, finely chopped
   15ml/1 tbsp tomato purée (paste)
   300g/11oz small pasta shapes
   large handful of fresh basil, torn
   salt and ground black pepper
   basil leaves, to garnish
   freshly grated Parmesan cheese,
      to serve
For the meatballs
   1 thick slice white bread,
      crusts removed
   60ml/4 tbsp milk
   350g/12oz lean minced (ground)
      beef or veal
   30ml/2 tbsp chopped fresh parsley
   grated rind of 1 orange
   2 garlic cloves, crushed
   1 egg, beaten
   30ml/2 tbsp olive oil

1 First prepare the meatballs. Break the bread into small pieces and place them in a bowl. Add the milk and leave to soak for about 10 minutes. Add the minced beef or veal, parsley, orange rind and garlic, and season well. Mix well with your hands.

2 When the bread is thoroughly incorporated with the meat, add enough beaten egg to bind the mixture. Shape small spoonfuls of the mixture into balls about the size of a large olive.

COOK'S TIP
Choose hollow pasta shapes for this soup, which will scoop up the soup as you eat. Look for small and medium-size shapes that are made especially for soup.

3 Heat the oil in a frying pan and fry the meatballs in batches for 6–8 minutes until browned all over. Use tongs or a draining spoon to remove them from the pan, and set them aside.

4 Purée the cannellini beans with a little of the stock in a food processor or blender until smooth. Set aside.

5 Heat the olive oil in a large pan. Add the chopped onion and garlic, chilli, celery and carrot, and cook for 4–5 minutes. Cover and cook gently for a further 5 minutes.

6 Stir in the tomato purée, the bean purée and the remaining vegetable stock. Bring the soup to the boil and cook for about 10 minutes.

7 Stir in the pasta shapes and simmer for 8–10 minutes, until the pasta is tender, but not soft. Add the meatballs and basil and cook for a further 5 minutes. Season the soup well before ladling it into warmed bowls. Garnish each bowl of soup with a basil leaf, and serve freshly grated Parmesan cheese with the soup.

Energy 718Kcal/3014kJ; Protein 35g; Carbohydrate 80.9g, of which sugars 10g; Fat 30.5g, of which saturates 8.5g; Cholesterol 53mg; Calcium 152mg; Fibre 9.7g; Sodium 529mg.

OLD-FASHIONED CHICKEN NOODLE SOUP

THIS IS A REALLY TRADITIONAL CHICKEN NOODLE SOUP. IT IS GUARANTEED TO MAKE YOU FEEL BETTER WHENEVER YOU HAVE A COLD. THE SECRET LIES IN BEGINNING WITH A GOOD-QUALITY STOCK.

SERVES 4–6

INGREDIENTS

2kg/4½lb boiling fowl (stewing chicken) with the giblets (except the liver)
1 large onion, peeled and halved
2 large carrots, halved lengthways
6 celery sticks, roughly chopped
1 bay leaf
175g/6oz vermicelli pasta
45ml/3 tbsp chopped fresh parsley or whole parsley leaves
salt and ground black pepper

1 Put the chicken into a large pan with all the vegetables and the bay leaf. Cover with 2.4 litres/4 pints/10 cups cold water.

2 Bring slowly to the boil, carefully skimming off any scum that rises to the top. Add 5ml/1 tsp salt and some ground black pepper.

3 Turn down the heat and simmer the soup slowly for at least 2 hours, or until the fowl is tender. When simmering, the surface of the liquid should just tremble. If it is allowed to boil, the soup will become cloudy.

4 When tender, remove the bird from the broth and strip the flesh off the carcass. (Use the meat in sandwiches or a risotto.) Return the bones to the soup and simmer for another hour.

5 Strain the soup into a bowl, cool, then chill overnight. The next day the soup should have set to a solid jelly and will be covered with a thin layer of solidified chicken fat. Carefully remove the fat.

6 To serve the soup, reheat in a large pan. Add the vermicelli and chopped parsley, and simmer for 6–8 minutes until the pasta is cooked. Taste and season well. Serve piping hot.

VARIATION
For a change you can use the same weight of guinea fowl and chicken wings and thighs, mixed.

Energy 176Kcal/748kJ; Protein 6.3g; Carbohydrate 37.5g, of which sugars 5.7g; Fat 1.2g, of which saturates 0.1g; Cholesterol 0mg; Calcium 66mg; Fibre 3.4g; Sodium 39mg.

THAI CHICKEN NOODLE SOUP

THIS SOUP IS A MEAL IN ITSELF. LOOK FOR STORES THAT SELL BUNCHES OF CORIANDER WITH THE ROOTS STILL ATTACHED, AS THEY ADD EXCELLENT FLAVOUR TO THE STOCK.

SERVES 6

INGREDIENTS

    8 garlic cloves
    small bunch of coriander (cilantro),
      with roots on
    1.2–1.4kg/2½–3lb chicken
    2 star anise
    2 carrots, chopped
    2 celery sticks, chopped
    1 onion, chopped
    30ml/2 tbsp soy sauce
    150g/5oz egg noodles
    30ml/2 tbsp vegetable oil
    60ml/4 tbsp Thai fish sauce
      (nam pla)
    1.5ml/¼ tsp chilli powder
    150g/5oz/1½ cups beansprouts
    2 spring onions (scallions), sliced
    herb sprigs, to garnish
    salt and ground black pepper
For the crab cakes
    5ml/1 tsp Thai red curry paste
    5ml/1 tsp cornflour (cornstarch)
    5ml/1 tsp Thai fish sauce
      (nam pla)
    1 small egg yolk
    15ml/1 tbsp chopped fresh
      coriander
    175g/6oz white crab meat
    50g/2oz/1 cup fresh white
      breadcrumbs
    30ml/2 tbsp vegetable oil

1 Chop four of the garlic cloves, thinly slice the remainder and set aside. Cut the roots off the coriander stems and place in a large pan with the garlic. Pick the coriander leaves off their stems and set aside; discard the stems. Place the chicken in the pan and add the star anise, carrots, celery and onion and soy sauce. Pour in enough water to cover the chicken. Bring to the boil, reduce the heat, cover and simmer for 1 hour.

2 For the crab cakes, mix the curry paste, cornflour, fish sauce and egg yolk in a bowl. Add the coriander, crab meat, breadcrumbs and seasoning, then mix well. Divide the mixture into 12 portions and form each into a small cake.

3 Cook the egg noodles according to the packet instructions. Drain and set aside. Heat the oil in a small pan and fry the sliced garlic until golden brown. Drain and set aside.

4 Remove the chicken from its stock and leave until cool enough to handle. (Reserve the stock.) Discard the chicken skin, take the meat off the bones and tear it into large strips. Set aside. Strain the stock and pour 1.2 litres/2 pints/5 cups into a pan. Stir in the fish sauce, chilli powder and seasoning, then bring to the boil. Reduce the heat and keep hot.

5 To cook the crab cakes, heat the vegetable oil in a large frying pan and fry the crab cakes for 2–3 minutes on each side until golden.

6 Divide the cooked noodles, fried garlic slices, beansprouts, sliced spring onions and chicken strips among six shallow soup bowls.

7 Arrange two of the crab cakes on top of the noodles, then ladle the hot chicken broth into the bowls. Scatter a few fresh coriander leaves over the soups, then garnish with the herb sprigs and serve immediately.

Energy 250Kcal/1049kJ; Protein 10.9g; Carbohydrate 28.8g, of which sugars 3.5g; Fat 10.9g, of which saturates 1.8g; Cholesterol 62mg; Calcium 74mg; Fibre 1.9g; Sodium 638mg.

CHICKEN AND CRAB NOODLE SOUP

THE CHICKEN MAKES A DELICIOUS STOCK FOR THIS LIGHT NOODLE SOUP. HERE IT IS ACCOMPANIED BY A CORIANDER OMELETTE THAT GIVES IT AN ENTICING CHINESE FLAVOUR.

SERVES 6

INGREDIENTS

2 chicken legs, skinned
1.75 litres/3 pints/7½ cups water
bunch of spring onions (scallions)
2.5cm/1in piece fresh root
  ginger, sliced
5ml/1 tsp black peppercorns
2 garlic cloves, halved
75g/3oz rice noodles
115g/4oz fresh white crab meat
30ml/2 tbsp light soy sauce
salt and ground black pepper
coriander (cilantro) leaves, to garnish
For the omelettes
4 eggs
30ml/2 tbsp chopped fresh
  coriander leaves
15ml/1 tbsp extra virgin olive oil

1 Put the chicken and water in a pan. Bring to the boil, reduce the heat and cook gently for 20 minutes; skim the surface occasionally.

2 Slice half the spring onions and add to the pan with the ginger, peppercorns, garlic and salt to taste. Cover and simmer for 1½ hours.

3 Meanwhile, soak the noodles in boiling water for 4 minutes, or according to the packet instructions. Drain and refresh under cold water. Shred the remaining spring onions and set aside.

4 rain and refresh the noodles under cold running water. Shred the remaining spring onions and set aside.

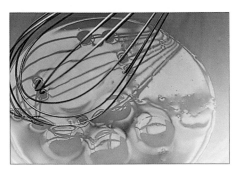

5 To make the omelettes, beat the eggs with the coriander and seasoning.

6 Heat a little of the olive oil in a small frying pan. Add a third of the egg and swirl the pan to coat the base evenly. Cook for 1 minute. Flip over and cook for 30 seconds. Turn the omelette out on to a plate and leave to cool. Repeat twice more to make three omelettes.

7 Roll up the omelettes tightly one at a time and slice thinly.

8 Remove the chicken from the stock and leave to cool. Strain the stock through a sieve (strainer) lined with muslin (cheesecloth) into a clean pan. When the chicken is cool enough to handle, remove and finely shred the meat, discarding the bones.

9 Bring the stock to the boil. Add the noodles, chicken, spring onions and crab meat, then simmer for 1–2 minutes. Stir in the soy sauce and season. Ladle the soup into bowls and top each with sliced omelette and coriander leaves.

Energy 159Kcal/664kJ; Protein 13.5g; Carbohydrate 10.6g, of which sugars 0.4g; Fat 6.9g, of which saturates 1.7g; Cholesterol 157mg; Calcium 46mg; Fibre 0g; Sodium 526mg.

CRAB SOUP WITH CORIANDER RELISH

PREPARED FRESH CRAB IS READILY AVAILABLE, HIGH QUALITY AND CONVENIENT — PERFECT FOR CREATING AN EXOTIC SEAFOOD AND NOODLE SOUP IN MINUTES.

SERVES 4

INGREDIENTS
  45ml/3 tbsp olive oil
  1 red onion, finely chopped
  2 red chillies, seeded and
    finely chopped
  1 garlic clove, finely chopped
  450g/1lb fresh white crab meat
  30ml/2 tbsp chopped fresh parsley
  30ml/2 tbsp chopped fresh
    coriander (cilantro)
  juice of 2 lemons
  1 lemon grass stalk
  1 litre/1¾ pints/4 cups good fish
    or chicken stock
  15ml/1 tbsp Thai fish sauce
    (nam pla)
  150g/5oz vermicelli or angel hair
    pasta, broken into 5 7.5cm/
    2–3in lengths
  salt and ground black pepper
For the relish
  50g/2oz/1 cup fresh coriander
    leaves
  1 green chilli, seeded and chopped
  15ml/1 tbsp sunflower oil
  25ml/1½ tbsp lemon juice
  2.5ml/½ tsp ground roasted
    cumin seeds

1 Heat the oil in a pan and add the onion, chillies and garlic. Cook over a gentle heat for 10 minutes until the onion is very soft.

2 Transfer the cooked onion and chillies to a bowl and stir in the crab meat, parsley, coriander and lemon juice, then set aside.

3 Lay the lemon grass on a chopping board and bruise it with a rolling pin or pestle. Pour the stock and fish sauce into a pan. Add the lemon grass and bring to the boil, then add the pasta. Simmer, uncovered, for 3–4 minutes or until the pasta is just tender.

4 Meanwhile, make the relish. Using a mortar and pestle, make a coarse paste with the fresh coriander, chilli, oil, lemon juice and cumin.

5 Remove and discard the lemon grass from the soup. Stir the chilli and crab mixture into the soup and season it well. Bring to the boil, then reduce the heat and simmer for 2 minutes.

6 Ladle the soup into four deep, warmed bowls and put a spoonful of the coriander relish in the centre of each. Serve at once.

Energy 425Kcal/1773kJ; Protein 26.7g; Carbohydrate 50.7g, of which sugars 1.4g; Fat 12.6g, of which saturates 1.6g; Cholesterol 81mg; Calcium 198mg; Fibre 1.3g; Sodium 632mg.

MALAYSIAN PRAWN LAKSA

THIS SPICY PRAWN AND NOODLE SOUP TASTES JUST AS GOOD WHEN MADE WITH FRESH CRAB MEAT OR ANY FLAKED COOKED FISH INSTEAD OF THE PRAWNS. IF YOU ARE SHORT OF TIME, BUY READY-MADE LAKSA PASTE, WHICH YOU WILL FIND IN ORIENTAL STORES.

SERVES 2–3

INGREDIENTS

115g/4oz rice vermicelli or stir-fry
  rice noodles
15ml/1 tbsp vegetable or groundnut
  (peanut) oil
600ml/1 pint/2½ cups fish stock
400ml/14fl oz/1⅔ cups thin
  coconut milk
30ml/2 tbsp Thai fish sauce
  (nam pla)
½ lime
16–24 cooked peeled prawns
  (shrimp)
salt
cayenne pepper
60ml/4 tbsp fresh coriander (cilantro)
  sprigs and leaves, chopped,
  to garnish

For the spicy paste
2 lemon grass stalks,
  finely chopped
2 fresh red chillies, seeded
  and chopped
2.5cm/1in piece fresh root ginger,
  peeled and sliced
2.5ml/½ tsp shrimp paste
2 garlic cloves, chopped
2.5ml/½ tsp ground turmeric
30ml/2 tbsp tamarind paste

1 Cook the rice vermicelli or noodles in a large pan of boiling salted water for 3–4 minutes, or according to the instructions on the packet.

2 Tip the noodles into a large sieve (strainer) or colander, then rinse under cold water and drain. Set aside.

3 To make the spicy paste, place all the prepared ingredients in a mortar and pound with a pestle. Alternatively, put the ingredients in a food processor until a smooth paste is formed.

4 Heat the vegetable or groundnut oil in a large saucepan, add the spicy paste and fry, stirring constantly, for a few moments to release all the flavours. Be careful not to let it burn.

5 Add the fish stock and coconut milk and bring to the boil. Stir in the fish sauce, then simmer for 5 minutes. Season with salt and cayenne to taste, adding a squeeze of lime. Add the prawns and heat through for a few seconds.

6 Divide the noodles among two or three soup plates. Pour over the soup. Garnish with fresh coriander and serve piping hot.

Energy 436Kcal/1830kJ; Protein 36.9g; Carbohydrate 55.3g, of which sugars 10.2g; Fat 7.6g, of which saturates 1.2g; Cholesterol 341mg; Calcium 239mg; Fibre 0.8g; Sodium 562mg.

CHIANG MAI NOODLE SOUP

NOWADAYS A SIGNATURE DISH OF THE CITY OF CHIANG MAI, THIS DELICIOUS NOODLE SOUP ORIGINATED IN BURMA, NOW CALLED MYANMAR, WHICH LIES ONLY A LITTLE TO THE NORTH OF THE CITY. IT IS ALSO THE THAI EQUIVALENT OF THE FAMOUS MALAYSIAN "LAKSA".

SERVES 4–6

INGREDIENTS

600ml/1 pint/2½ cups coconut milk
30ml/2 tbsp Thai red curry paste
5ml/1 tsp ground turmeric
450g/1lb chicken thighs, boned and
   cut into bitesize chunks
600ml/1 pint/2½ cups
   chicken stock
60ml/4 tbsp Thai fish sauce (nam pla)
15ml/1 tbsp dark soy sauce
juice of ½–1 lime
450g/1lb fresh egg noodles, blanched
   briefly in boiling water
salt and ground black pepper
To garnish
   3 spring onions (scallions), chopped
   4 fresh red chillies, chopped
   4 shallots, chopped
   60ml/4 tbsp sliced pickled mustard
      leaves, rinsed
   30ml/2 tbsp fried sliced garlic
   coriander (cilantro) leaves
   4–6 fried noodle nests (optional)

1 Pour about one third of the coconut milk into a large, heavy pan or wok. Bring to the boil over a medium heat, stirring frequently with a wooden spoon until the milk separates.

2 Add the curry paste and ground turmeric, stir to mix completely and cook until the mixture is fragrant.

3 Add the chunks of chicken and toss over the heat for about 2 minutes, making sure that all the chunks are thoroughly coated with the paste.

4 Add the remaining coconut milk, the chicken stock, fish sauce and soy sauce. Season with salt and pepper to taste. Bring to simmering point, stirring frequently, then lower the heat and cook gently for 7–10 minutes. Remove from the heat and stir in lime juice to taste.

5 Reheat the fresh egg noodles in boiling water, drain and divide among four to six warmed bowls. Divide the chunks of chicken among the bowls and ladle in the hot soup. Top each serving with spring onions, chillies, shallots, pickled mustard leaves, fried garlic, coriander leaves and a fried noodle nest, if using. Serve immediately.

Energy 679Kcal/2873kJ; Protein 43.2g; Carbohydrate 88.7g, of which sugars 10.1g; Fat 19.4g, of which saturates 5.6g; Cholesterol 180mg; Calcium 95mg; Fibre 3.4g; Sodium 769mg.

TOKYO-STYLE RAMEN NOODLES IN SOUP

RAMEN IS A HYBRID CHINESE NOODLE DISH PRESENTED IN A JAPANESE WAY, AND THERE ARE MANY REGIONAL VARIATIONS FEATURING LOCAL SPECIALITIES. THIS IS A LEGENDARY TOKYO VERSION.

SERVES 4

INGREDIENTS
  250g/9oz dried ramen noodles
For the soup stock
  4 spring onions (scallions)
  7.5cm/3in fresh root ginger, quartered
  raw bones from 2 chickens, washed
  1 large onion, quartered
  4 garlic cloves, peeled
  1 large carrot, roughly chopped
  1 egg shell
  120ml/4fl oz/½ cup sake
  about 60ml/4 tbsp Japanese soy
    sauce (shoyu)
  2.5ml/½ tsp salt
For the *cha-shu* (pot-roast pork)
  500g/1¼lb pork shoulder, boned
  30ml/2 tbsp vegetable oil
  2 spring onions, chopped
  2.5cm/1in fresh root ginger, peeled
    and sliced
  15ml/1 tbsp sake
  45ml/3 tbsp Japanese soy sauce
  15ml/1 tbsp caster (superfine) sugar
For the toppings
  2 hard-boiled (hard-cooked) eggs
  150g/5oz menma, soaked for
    30 minutes and drained
  ½ nori sheet, broken into pieces
  2 spring onions, chopped
  ground white pepper
  sesame oil or chilli oil

1 To make the soup stock, bruise the spring onions and ginger by hitting with the side of a large knife. Pour 1.5 litres/ 2½ pints/6¼ cups water into a wok and bring to the boil. Add the chicken bones and boil until meat changes colour. Discard the water and wash the bones.

2 Wash the wok, bring 2 litres/ 3½ pints/ 9 cups water to the boil and add the bones and other stock ingredients, except the soy sauce and salt. Reduce the heat to low, and simmer until the water has reduced by half, skimming off any scum. Strain into a bowl through a sieve (strainer) lined with muslin (cheesecloth). This will take 1–2 hours.

3 Make the *cha-shu*. Roll the meat up tightly, 8cm/3½in in diameter, and tie it with kitchen string.

4 Wash the wok and dry over a high heat. Heat the oil to smoking point in the wok and add the chopped spring onions and ginger. Cook briefly, then add the meat. Turn often to brown the outside evenly.

5 Sprinkle with sake and add 400ml/ 14fl oz/1⅔ cups water, the soy sauce and sugar. Boil, then reduce the heat to low and cover. Cook for 25–30 minutes, turning every 5 minutes. Remove from the heat.

6 Slice the pork into 12 fine slices. Use any leftover pork for another recipe.

7 Shell and halve the boiled eggs, and sprinkle some salt on to the yolks.

8 Pour 1 litre/1¾ pints/4 cups soup stock from the bowl into a large pan. Boil and add the soy sauce and salt. Check the seasoning; add more sauce if required.

9 Wash the wok again and bring 2 litres/ 3½ pints/9 cups water to the boil. Cook the ramen noodles according to the packet instructions until just soft. Stir constantly to prevent sticking. If the water bubbles up, pour in 50ml/2fl oz/ ¼ cup cold water. Drain well and divide among four bowls.

10 Pour the soup over the noodles to cover. Arrange half a boiled egg, pork slices, menma and nori on top, and sprinkle with spring onions. Serve with pepper and sesame or chilli oil. Season to taste with a little salt, if you like.

COOK'S TIPS
• Sake, made from fermented rice, can be stored in the refrigerator for at least 3 weeks in a sealed container.
• Menma are pickled bamboo shoots, and need soaking before use.

Energy 466Kcal/1947kJ; Protein 35.1g; Carbohydrate 49.9g, of which sugars 0.9g; Fat 13.9g, of which saturates 3.2g; Cholesterol 175mg; Calcium 43mg; Fibre 0.3g; Sodium 489mg.

Soba Noodles in Hot Soup with Tempura

When you cook Japanese noodle dishes, everyone should be ready at the dinner table, because cooked noodles start to soften and lose their taste and texture quite quickly.

3 To make the batter, pour the ice-cold water into a bowl and mix in the beaten egg. Sift in the flour and stir briefly; it should remain fairly lumpy.

4 Heat the oil in a wok or deep-fryer to 180°C/350°F. Hold the tail of a prawn, dunk it in the batter, then plunge it into the hot oil. Deep-fry two prawns at a time until crisp and golden. Drain on kitchen paper and keep warm.

5 Put the noodles in a large pan with at least 2 litres/3½ pints/9 cups rapidly boiling water, and stir frequently to stop them sticking.

6 When the water foams, pour in about 50ml/2fl oz/¼ cup cold water to lower the temperature. Repeat when the water foams once again. The noodles should be slightly softer than *al dente* pasta.

7 Tip the noodles into a sieve (strainer) and wash under cold water with your hands to rinse off any oil.

8 Heat the soup. Warm the noodles with hot water, and divide among individual serving bowls.

9 Place the prawns attractively on the noodles and add the soup. Sprinkle with sliced spring onion and some shichimi togarashi, if you like. Serve immediately.

COOK'S TIPS
• Shichimi togarashi is a peppery condiment made of seven seasonings.
• Kezuri-bushi is ready-shaved dried fish, one of the main ingredients used in dashi stock.
• Dashi is a fish stock that is frequently used in Japanese cooking. Freeze-dried granules are called dashi-no-moto, and these can be used to make a quick dashi.

SERVES 4

INGREDIENTS
  400g/14oz dried soba noodles
  1 spring onion (scallion), sliced
  shichimi togarashi (optional)
For the tempura
  16 medium raw tiger or king prawns
    (jumbo shrimp), heads and shell
    removed, tails intact
  400ml/14fl oz/1⅔ cups ice-cold water
  1 large (US extra large) egg, beaten
  200g/7oz/scant 2 cups plain
    (all-purpose) flour
  vegetable oil, for deep-frying
For the soup
  150ml/¼ pint/⅔ cup mirin
  150ml/¼ pint/⅔ cup shoyu
  900ml/1½ pints/3¾ cups water
  25g/1oz kezuri-bushi or 2 × 15g/
    ½oz packets
  15ml/1 tbsp caster (superfine) sugar
  5ml/1 tsp salt
  900ml/1½ pints/3¾ cups first dashi
    stock or the same amount of water
    and 12.5ml/2½ tsp dashi-no-moto

1 To make the soup, put the mirin in a large pan. Bring to the boil, then add the rest of the soup ingredients apart from the dashi stock. Bring back to the boil, then reduce the heat to low. Skim off the scum and cook for 2 minutes. Strain the soup and put back into a clean pan with the dashi stock.

2 Remove the vein from the prawns, then make five shallow cuts into each prawn's belly. Clip the tip of the tail with scissors and squeeze out any moisture from the tail.

Energy 728Kcal/3053kJ; Protein 30.7g; Carbohydrate 121.8g, of which sugars 5.3g; Fat 14g, of which saturates 1.9g; Cholesterol 218mg; Calcium 173mg; Fibre 1.6g; Sodium 728mg.

SAPPORO-STYLE RAMEN NOODLES IN SOUP

THIS IS A RICH AND TANGY SOUP FROM SAPPORO, THE CAPITAL OF HOKKAIDO, WHICH IS JAPAN'S MOST NORTHERLY ISLAND. RAW GRATED GARLIC AND CHILLI OIL ARE ADDED TO WARM THE BODY.

SERVES 4

INGREDIENTS
  250g/9oz dried ramen noodles
For the soup stock
  4 spring onions (scallions)
  6cm/2½in fresh root ginger, quartered
  raw bones from 2 chickens, washed
  1 large onion, quartered
  4 garlic cloves
  1 large carrot, roughly chopped
  1 egg shell
  120ml/4fl oz/½ cup sake
  90ml/6 tbsp miso (any colour)
  30ml/2 tbsp Japanese soy sauce
    (shoyu)
For the toppings
  115g/4oz pork belly
  5cm/2in carrot
  12 mangetouts (snow peas)
  8 baby corn
  15ml/1 tbsp sesame oil
  1 dried red chilli, seeded and crushed
  225g/8oz/1 cup beansprouts
  2 spring onions, chopped
  2 garlic cloves, finely grated
  chilli oil
  salt

1 To make the soup stock, bruise the spring onions and ginger by hitting with a rolling pin. Boil 1.5 litres/2½ pints/6¼ cups water in a heavy pan, add the bones, and cook until the meat changes colour. Discard the water and wash the bones under running water.

2 Wash the pan and boil 2 litres/3½ pints/9 cups water, then add the bones and other stock ingredients except for the miso and soy sauce. Reduce the heat to low, and simmer for 2 hours, skimming any scum off. Strain into a bowl through a sieve (strainer) lined with muslin (cheesecloth); this will take about 1–2 hours. Do not squeeze the muslin.

3 Cut the pork into 5mm/¼in slices. Peel and halve the carrot lengthways then cut into 3mm/⅛in thick, 5cm/2in long slices. Boil the carrot, mangetouts and corn for 3 minutes in water. Drain.

4 Heat the sesame oil in a wok and fry the pork slices and chilli. When the colour of the meat has changed, add the beansprouts. Reduce the heat to medium and add 1 litre/1¾ pints/4 cups soup stock. Cook for 5 minutes.

5 Scoop 60ml/4 tbsp soup stock from the wok and mix well with the miso and soy sauce in a bowl. Stir back into the soup. Reduce the heat to low.

6 Bring 2 litres/3½ pints/9 cups water to the boil. Cook the noodles until just soft, following the instructions on the packet. Stir constantly. If the water bubbles up, pour in 50ml/2fl oz/¼ cup cold water. Drain well and divide among four bowls.

7 Pour the hot soup on to the noodles and heap the beansprouts and pork on top. Add the carrot, mangetouts and corn. Sprinkle with the spring onions and serve with garlic and chilli oil.

Energy 365Kcal/1522kJ; Protein 12.5g; Carbohydrate 54.1g, of which sugars 3.9g; Fat 10.9g, of which saturates 3.9g; Cholesterol 21mg; Calcium 43mg; Fibre 1.7g; Sodium 569mg.

POT-COOKED UDON IN MISO SOUP

UDON IS A WHITE WHEAT NOODLE EATEN WITH VARIOUS HOT AND COLD SOUPS. IN THIS DISH, KNOWN AS MISO NIKOMI UDON, THE NOODLES ARE COOKED IN A CLAY POT WITH A RICH MISO SOUP.

SERVES 4

INGREDIENTS
  200g/7oz chicken breast portion,
    boned and skinned
  10ml/2 tsp sake
  2 abura-age
  900ml/1½ pints/3¾ cups second
    dashi stock, or the same amount
    of water and 7.5ml/1½ tsp
    dashi-no-moto
  6 large fresh shiitake mushrooms,
    stalks removed, quartered
  4 spring onions (scallions), trimmed
    and chopped into 3mm/⅛in lengths
  30ml/2 tbsp mirin
  about 90g/3½oz aka miso or
    hatcho miso
  300g/11oz dried udon noodles
  4 eggs
  shichimi togarashi (optional)

1 Cut the chicken into bitesize pieces. Sprinkle with sake and leave to marinate for 15 minutes.

2 Put the abura-age in a sieve (strainer) and thoroughly rinse with hot water from the kettle to wash off the oil. Drain on kitchen paper and cut each abura-age into 4 squares.

3 To make the soup, heat the second dashi stock in a large pan. When it has come to the boil, add the chicken pieces, shiitake mushrooms and abura-age and cook for 5 minutes. Remove the pan from the heat and add the spring onions.

4 Put the mirin and miso paste into a small bowl. Scoop 30ml/2 tbsp soup from the pan and mix this in well.

5 To cook the udon, boil at least 2 litres/ 3½ pints/9 cups water in a large pan. The water should not come higher than two-thirds the depth of the pan. Cook the udon for 6 minutes and drain.

6 Put the udon in one large flameproof clay pot or casserole (or divide among four small pots). Mix the miso paste into the soup and check the taste. Add more miso if required. Ladle in enough soup to cover the udon, and arrange the soup ingredients on top of the udon.

7 Put the soup on a medium heat and break an egg on top. When the soup bubbles, wait for 1 minute, then cover and remove from the heat. Leave to stand for 2 minutes. Serve with shichimi togarashi, if you like.

COOK'S TIPS
Look for the traditional ingredients in Japanese food stores:
• Abura-age is a thin deep-fried tofu, used in traditional Japanese soups.
• Dashi-no-moto are freeze-dried granules of dashi fish stock.
• Hatcho miso is a paste made from soybeans using traditional methods.
• Shichimi togarashi is a peppery condiment made of seven seasonings.

Energy 431Kcal/1819kJ; Protein 28.6g; Carbohydrate 54.7g, of which sugars 2.2g; Fat 12.6g, of which saturates 3.5g; Cholesterol 248mg; Calcium 60mg; Fibre 2.9g; Sodium 594mg.

NOODLE, PAK CHOI AND SALMON RAMEN

THIS LIGHTLY SPICED JAPANESE NOODLE SOUP IS ENHANCED BY SLICES OF SEARED FRESH SALMON AND CRISP VEGETABLES. THE CONTRASTS IN TEXTURE ARE AS APPEALING AS THE DELICIOUS TASTE.

SERVES 4

INGREDIENTS

1.5 litres/2½ pints/6 cups good vegetable stock
2.5cm/1in piece fresh root ginger, finely sliced
2 garlic cloves, crushed
6 spring onions (scallions), sliced
45ml/3 tbsp soy sauce
45ml/3 tbsp sake
450g/1lb salmon fillet, skinned
5ml/1 tsp groundnut (peanut) oil
350g/12oz ramen or udon noodles
4 small heads pak choi (bok choy), broken into leaves
1 fresh red chilli, seeded and sliced
50g/2oz/1 cup beansprouts
salt and ground black pepper

1 Pour the stock into a large pan and add the ginger, garlic, and a third of the spring onions.

2 Add the soy sauce and sake. Bring to the boil, then reduce the heat and simmer for 30 minutes.

3 Meanwhile, remove any pin bones from the salmon using tweezers, then cut the salmon on the slant into 12 slices, using a very sharp knife.

4 Brush a ridged griddle or frying pan with the oil and heat until very hot. Sear the salmon slices for 1–2 minutes on each side until tender and marked by the ridges of the pan. Set aside.

5 Cook the ramen or udon noodles in a large pan of boiling water for 4–5 minutes or according to the instructions on the packet. Tip into a colander, drain well and refresh under cold running water. Drain again and set aside.

6 Strain the broth into a clean pan and season, then bring to the boil. Add the pak choi. Using a fork, twist the noodles into four nests and put these into deep bowls. Divide the salmon slices, spring onions, chilli and beansprouts among the bowls. Ladle in the broth.

Energy 569Kcal/2394kJ; Protein 34.6g; Carbohydrate 65.6g, of which sugars 4.1g; Fat 20.5g, of which saturates 4.3g; Cholesterol 83mg; Calcium 70mg; Fibre 3.5g; Sodium 746mg.

FISH SOUPS

Fish soups are always delicious and can be eaten either as a first course or as an entire meal. Chunky soups such as Matelote, Bouillabaisse and Fish Soup with Tomatoes and Mushrooms are perfect for winter and so hearty that they can be eaten as a meal in themselves. Sophisticated soups such as Pad Thai Red Monkfish Soup, Bourride of Red Mullet and Fennel and Soup Niçoise with Seared Tuna are great for entertaining and sure to impress guests.

FISH SOUP WITH TOMATOES AND MUSHROOMS

WITH SOME FRESH CRUSTY HOME-MADE BROWN BREAD OR GARLIC BREAD, THIS QUICK-AND-EASY SOUP CAN BE SERVED LIKE A STEW AND WILL MAKE A DELICIOUS FIRST COURSE OR SUPPER.

SERVES 6

INGREDIENTS
25g/1oz/2 tbsp butter
1 onion, finely chopped
1 garlic clove, crushed
1 small red (bell) pepper, chopped
salt and ground black pepper
2.5ml/½ tsp sugar
a dash of Tabasco sauce
25g/1oz/¼ cup plain
  (all-purpose) flour
600ml/1 pint/2½ cups fish stock
400g/14oz can chopped tomatoes
115g/4oz/1½ cups mushrooms,
  chopped
about 300ml/½ pint/1¼ cups milk
225g/8oz white fish, cut into cubes
115g/4oz smoked haddock or cod,
  skinned, and cut into bitesize cubes
12–18 mussels, cleaned (optional)
chopped fresh parsley, to garnish

1 Melt the butter in a large heavy pan and cook the chopped onion and crushed garlic gently in it until softened but not browned.

2 Add the chopped red pepper. Season with salt and pepper, the sugar and Tabasco sauce.

3 Sprinkle the flour over and cook gently for 2 minutes, stirring.

4 Gradually stir in the stock and add the canned tomatoes, with their juices and the mushrooms.

5 Bring to the boil over medium heat, stir well, then reduce the heat and simmer gently until the vegetables are soft. Add the milk and bring back to the boil. Add the fish to the pan and simmer for 3 minutes.

6 Add the mussels, if using, and cook for another 3–4 minutes, or until the fish is just tender but not breaking up. Discard any mussels that remain closed. Adjust the consistency with a little extra fish stock or milk, if necessary. Check the seasoning.

7 Ladle the soup into six warmed bowls and serve piping hot, garnished with chopped parsley.

Energy 132Kcal/556kJ; Protein 15.6g; Carbohydrate 8g, of which sugars 4.5g; Fat 4.4g, of which saturates 2.4g; Cholesterol 40mg; Calcium 29mg; Fibre 1.6g; Sodium 341mg.

FISH SOUP WITH ROUILLE

MAKING THIS SOUP IS SIMPLICITY ITSELF, YET THE FLAVOUR SUGGESTS IT IS THE PRODUCT OF PAINSTAKING PREPARATION AND COOKING. SERVE WITH CHEESE-TOPPED CRUSTY BREAD ON THE SIDE.

SERVES 6

INGREDIENTS
  1kg/2¼lb mixed fish
  30ml/2 tbsp olive oil
  1 onion, chopped
  1 carrot, chopped
  1 leek, chopped
  2 large ripe tomatoes, chopped
  1 red (bell) pepper, seeded
    and chopped
  2 garlic cloves, peeled
  150g/5oz/⅔ cup tomato
    purée (paste)
  1 large fresh bouquet garni
  300ml/½ pint/1¼ cups dry
    white wine
  salt and ground black pepper
For the rouille
  2 garlic cloves, roughly chopped
  5ml/1 tsp coarse salt
  1 thick slice of white bread, crust
    removed, soaked in water and
    squeezed dry
  1 fresh red chilli, seeded and
    roughly chopped
  45ml/3 tbsp olive oil
  salt and cayenne pepper
For the garnish
  12 slices of baguette, toasted in
    the oven
  50g/2oz Gruyère cheese,
    finely grated

1 Cut the fish into 7.5cm/3in chunks, removing any obvious bones. Heat the oil in a large pan, then add the fish and chopped vegetables. Stir until these begin to colour.

2 Add all the other soup ingredients, then pour in just enough cold water to cover the mixture. Season well and bring to just below boiling point, then lower the heat to a bare simmer, cover and cook for 1 hour.

3 Meanwhile, make the rouille. Put the garlic and coarse salt in a mortar and crush to a paste with a pestle. Add the soaked bread and chilli and pound until smooth, or purée in a food processor. Whisk in the olive oil, a drop at a time, to make a smooth, shiny sauce that resembles mayonnaise. Season with salt and add a pinch of cayenne if you like a fiery taste. Set the rouille aside.

4 Lift out and discard the bouquet garni from the soup. Purée the soup in batches in a food processor, then strain through a fine sieve (strainer) placed over a clean pan, pushing the solids through with the back of a ladle.

5 Reheat the soup without letting it boil. Check the seasoning and ladle into individual bowls. Top each serving with two slices of toasted baguette, a spoonful of rouille and some grated Gruyère.

COOK'S TIP
Any firm fish can be used for this recipe. If you use whole fish, include the heads, which enhance the flavour of the soup.

Energy 518Kcal/2179kJ; Protein 41.5g; Carbohydrate 49g, of which sugars 10.8g; Fat 14.9g, of which saturates 3.6g; Cholesterol 85mg; Calcium 193mg; Fibre 4.3g; Sodium 665mg.

SPANISH FISH SOUP WITH ORANGE

THE SPANISH NAME FOR THIS SOUP IS SOPA CACHORREÑA — *SEVILLE ORANGE SOUP* — *AND IT IS GOOD SERVED POST-CHRISTMAS, WHEN BITTER SEVILLE ORANGES ARE IN SEASON.*

2 Heat the oil in a large flameproof casserole over a high heat. Smash the garlic cloves with the flat of a knife and fry until they are well-coloured. Discard them and turn down the heat. Fry the onion gently until it is softened, adding the tomato halfway through.

3 Strain in the hot fish stock (adding the orange spiral if you wish) and bring back to the boil. Add the potatoes to the pan and cook them for about 5 minutes.

4 Add the fish pieces to the soup, a few at a time, without letting it go off the boil. Cook for about 15 minutes. Add the squeezed orange juice and lemon juice, if using, and the paprika, with salt and pepper to taste. Serve in bowls, garnished with a little parsley.

SERVES 6

INGREDIENTS
   1kg/2¼lb small hake or whiting,
     whole but cleaned
   1.2 litres/2 pints/5 cups water
   4 bitter oranges or 4 sweet oranges
     and 2 lemons
   30ml/2 tbsp olive oil
   5 garlic cloves, unpeeled
   1 large onion, finely chopped
   1 tomato, peeled, seeded
     and chopped
   4 small potatoes, cut into rounds
   5ml/1 tsp paprika
   salt and ground black pepper
   15–30ml/1–2 tbsp finely chopped
     fresh parsley, to garnish

1 Fillet the fish and cut each fillet into three, reserving all the trimmings. Put the fillets on a plate, salt lightly and chill. Put the trimmings in a pan, add the water and a spiral of orange rind. Bring to a simmer, skim, then cover and cook gently for 30 minutes.

Energy 175Kcal/738kJ; Protein 20.2g; Carbohydrate 18.8g, of which sugars 8.7g; Fat 2.6g, of which saturates 0.4g; Cholesterol 23mg; Calcium 59mg; Fibre 2.3g; Sodium 113mg.

MEDITERRANEAN LEEK <u>AND</u> FISH SOUP

THIS CHUNKY SOUP, WHICH IS ALMOST A STEW, MAKES A ROBUST AND WONDERFULLY AROMATIC MEAL IN A BOWL. SERVE IT WITH CRISP-BAKED CROÛTES SPREAD WITH A TASTY GARLIC MAYONNAISE.

SERVES 4

INGREDIENTS
    2 large thick leeks
    30ml/2 tbsp olive oil
    5ml/1 tsp crushed coriander seeds
    a good pinch of dried red chilli flakes
    300g/11oz small salad potatoes,
      peeled and thickly sliced
    400g/14oz can chopped tomatoes
    600ml/1 pint/2½ cups fish stock
    150ml/¼ pint/⅔ cup white wine
    1 fresh bay leaf
    1 star anise
    strip of pared orange rind
    good pinch of saffron threads
    450g/1lb white fish fillets, such
      as monkfish, sea bass, cod or
      haddock
    450g/1lb small squid, cleaned
    250g/9oz raw peeled prawns (shrimp)
    30–45ml/2–3 tbsp chopped flat
      leaf parsley
    salt and ground black pepper
To serve
    1 short French loaf, sliced and toasted
    garlic mayonnaise

3 Add the potatoes and tomatoes, and pour in the stock and wine. Add the bay leaf, star anise, orange rind and saffron. Bring to the boil, lower the heat and partially cover the pan. Simmer for 20 minutes or until the potatoes are tender. Taste and adjust the seasoning.

4 Cut the white fish fillets into chunks. Cut the squid sacs into rectangles and score a criss-cross pattern into them without cutting right through.

5 Add the fish to the soup and cook gently for 4 minutes. Add the prawns and cook for 1 minute. Add the squid and the sliced white part of the leek and cook, stirring occasionally, for a further 2 minutes.

6 Finally, stir in the chopped parsley and serve immediately, ladling the soup into warmed bowls. Offer the toasted French bread and garlic mayonnaise with the soup.

1 Slice the leeks, keeping the green tops separate from the white bottom pieces. Wash the leek slices thoroughly in a colander and drain them well. Set the white slices aside for later.

2 Heat the oil in a heavy pan over a low heat, then add the green leek slices, the crushed coriander seeds and the dried red chilli flakes. Cook, stirring occasionally, for 5 minutes.

Energy 340Kcal/1437kJ; Protein 51.8g; Carbohydrate 7.2g, of which sugars 5.3g; Fat 9.2g, of which saturates 1.6g; Cholesterol 416mg; Calcium 111mg; Fibre 2.9g; Sodium 330mg.

MATELOTE

THIS FISHERMEN'S CHUNKY SOUP IS TRADITIONALLY MADE FROM FRESHWATER FISH, INCLUDING EEL, BUT ANY FIRM FISH WORKS WELL IN THIS DISH. DO TRY TO INCLUDE AT LEAST SOME EEL, AND USE A ROBUST DRY WHITE OR RED WINE FOR A STRONGER FLAVOUR.

SERVES 6

INGREDIENTS

1kg/2¼ lb mixed fish, including
   450g/1lb conger eel if possible
50g/2oz/¼ cup butter
1 onion, thickly sliced
2 celery sticks, thickly sliced
2 carrots, thickly sliced
1 bottle dry white or red wine
1 fresh bouquet garni containing
   parsley, bay leaf and chervil
2 cloves
6 black peppercorns
beurre manié for thickening, see
   Cook's Tip
salt and cayenne pepper
For the garnish
   25g/1oz/2 tbsp butter
   12 baby onions, peeled
   12 button (white) mushrooms
   chopped flat leaf parsley

1 Cut all the fish into thick slices, removing any obvious bones. Melt the butter in a large pan, put in the fish and sliced vegetables and stir over a medium heat until lightly browned. Pour in the wine and enough cold water to cover. Add the bouquet garni and spices and season. Bring to the boil, lower the heat and simmer gently for 20–30 minutes, until the fish is tender, skimming the surface occasionally.

2 Meanwhile, prepare the garnish. Heat the butter in a deep frying pan and sauté the baby onions until golden and tender. Add the mushrooms and fry until golden. Season and keep hot.

3 Strain the soup through a large sieve (strainer) into a clean pan. Discard the herbs and spices in the sieve, then divide the fish among deep soup plates (you can skin the fish if you wish, but this is not essential) and keep hot.

4 Reheat the soup until it boils. Lower the heat and whisk in the *beurre manié* little by little until the soup thickens. Season it and pour over the fish. Garnish each portion with the fried baby onions and mushrooms and sprinkle with chopped parsley.

COOK'S TIP
To make the *beurre manié* for thickening, mix 15g/½ oz/1 tbsp softened butter with 15ml/1 tbsp plain (all-purpose) flour. Add to the boiling soup a pinch at a time, whisking all the time.

Energy 323Kcal/1346kJ; Protein 31.4g; Carbohydrate 2.3g, of which sugars 1.9g; Fat 11.6g, of which saturates 6.7g; Cholesterol 103mg; Calcium 35mg; Fibre 0.8g; Sodium 192mg.

BOUILLABAISSE

AUTHENTIC BOUILLABAISSE COMES FROM THE SOUTH OF FRANCE AND INCLUDES RASCASSE (SCORPION FISH) AS A CHARACTERISTIC INGREDIENT. IT IS, HOWEVER, PERFECTLY POSSIBLE TO MAKE THIS WONDERFUL MAIN-COURSE SOUP WITHOUT IT. USE AS LARGE A VARIETY OF FISH AS YOU CAN.

SERVES 4

INGREDIENTS
    45ml/3 tbsp olive oil
    2 onions, chopped
    2 leeks, white parts only, cleaned
        and chopped
    4 garlic cloves, chopped
    450g/1lb ripe tomatoes, peeled
        and chopped
    3 litres/5 pints/12 cups boiling fish
        stock or water
    15ml/1 tbsp tomato purée (paste)
    large pinch of saffron threads
    1 fresh bouquet garni, containing
        2 thyme sprigs, 2 bay leaves and
        2 fennel sprigs
    3kg/6½lb mixed fish, cleaned and
        cut into large chunks
    4 potatoes, peeled and thickly sliced
    salt, pepper and cayenne pepper
    rouille and aioli (see Cook's Tip),
        to serve
For the garnish
    16 slices of French bread, toasted
        and rubbed with garlic
    30ml/2 tbsp chopped parsley

1 Heat the oil in a large pan. Add the onions, leeks, garlic and tomatoes. Cook until slightly softened. Stir in the stock or water, tomato purée and saffron. Add the bouquet garni and boil until the oil is amalgamated. Lower the heat; add the fish and potatoes.

COOK'S TIP
For aioli, mix together 600ml/1 pint/2½ cups mayonnaise with 2 crushed garlic cloves and cayenne pepper.

2 Simmer the soup for 5–8 minutes, removing each type of fish as it becomes cooked. Continue to cook until the potatoes are very tender. Season well with salt, pepper and cayenne.

3 Divide the fish and potatoes among individual soup plates. Strain the soup and ladle it over the fish. Garnish with toasted French bread and parsley, and serve with rouille and aioli.

Energy 888Kcal/3748kJ; Protein 105.5g; Carbohydrate 88g, of which sugars 14g; Fat 14.8g, of which saturates 2.3g; Cholesterol 230mg; Calcium 217mg; Fibre 7.3g; Sodium 953mg.

THAI FISH BROTH

LEMON GRASS, CHILLIES AND GALANGAL ARE AMONG THE FLAVOURINGS USED IN THIS FRAGRANT SOUP.

SERVES 2–3

INGREDIENTS

1 litre/1¾ pints/4 cups fish or
  light chicken stock
4 lemon grass stalks
3 limes
2 small fresh hot red chillies,
  seeded and thinly sliced
2cm/¾ in piece fresh galangal,
  peeled and thinly sliced
6 coriander (cilantro) stalks and leaves
2 kaffir lime leaves, coarsely
  chopped (optional)
350g/12oz monkfish fillet, skinned
  and cut into 2.5cm/1in pieces
15ml/1 tbsp rice vinegar
45ml/3 tbsp Thai fish sauce
30ml/2 tbsp chopped coriander
  leaves, to garnish

1 Pour the stock into a pan and bring it to the boil. Meanwhile, slice the bulb end of each lemon grass stalk diagonally into pieces about 3mm/⅛in thick. Peel off four wide strips of lime rind with a potato peeler, taking care to avoid the white pith underneath which would make the soup bitter. Squeeze the limes and reserve the juice.

2 Add the sliced lemon grass, lime rind, chillies, galangal and coriander stalks to the stock, with the kaffir lime leaves, if using. Simmer for 1–2 minutes.

VARIATIONS
Prawns (shrimp), scallops, squid or sole can be substituted for the monkfish. If you use kaffir lime leaves, you will need the juice of only 2 limes.

3 Add the monkfish, rice vinegar and fish sauce, with half the reserved lime juice. Simmer for about 3 minutes, until the fish is just cooked. Lift out and discard the coriander stalks, taste the broth and add more lime juice if necessary; the soup should taste quite sour. Sprinkle with the coriander leaves and serve very hot.

Energy 124Kcal/529kJ; Protein 28.3g; Carbohydrate 0.7g, of which sugars 0.6g; Fat 1g, of which saturates 0.2g; Cholesterol 25mg; Calcium 64mg; Fibre 1.3g; Sodium 40mg.

PAD THAI RED MONKFISH SOUP

THIS LIGHT COCONUT SOUP IS BASED ON THAILAND'S CLASSIC STIR-FRIED NOODLE DISH.

SERVES 4

INGREDIENTS
175g/6oz flat rice noodles
30ml/2 tbsp vegetable oil
2 garlic cloves, chopped
15ml/1 tbsp red curry paste
450g/1lb monkfish tail, cut into
    bitesize pieces
300ml/½ pint/1¼ cups
    coconut cream
750ml/1¼ pints/3 cups hot
    chicken stock
45ml/3 tbsp Thai fish sauce
15ml/1 tbsp palm sugar
60ml/4 tbsp roughly chopped
    roasted peanuts
4 spring onions (scallions),
    shredded lengthways
50g/2oz beansprouts
large handful of fresh Thai
    basil leaves
salt and ground black pepper
1 red chilli, seeded and cut
    lengthways into slivers,
    to garnish

1 Soak the noodles in boiling water for 10 minutes, or according to the packet instructions. Drain.

2 Heat the oil in a wok or saucepan over a high heat. Add the garlic and cook for 2 minutes. Stir in the curry paste and cook for 1 minute.

COOK'S TIP
Thai fish sauce (nam pla) is made from salted, fermented fish. The colour of the sauce can vary considerably. Look for a light-coloured sauce, as it is considered better than the darker version.

3 Add the monkfish and stir-fry over a high heat for 4–5 minutes, until just tender. Pour in the coconut cream and stock. Stir in the fish sauce and sugar, and bring just to the boil. Add the drained noodles and cook for 1–2 minutes, until tender.

4 Stir in half the peanuts, half the spring onions, half the beansprouts, the basil and seasoning. Ladle the soup into deep bowls and scatter over the remaining peanuts. Garnish with the rest of the spring onions and beansprouts, and the red chilli.

Energy 379Kcal/1589kJ; Protein 25.5g; Carbohydrate 11.2g, of which sugars 4.7g; Fat 12g, of which saturates 2g; Cholesterol 18mg; Calcium 49mg; Fibre 0.9g; Sodium 111mg.

BOURRIDE OF RED MULLET AND FENNEL

THIS AROMATIC FISH SOUP FROM PROVENCE IN FRANCE IS MADE WITH FRESH MAYONNAISE. THE SECRET OF SUCCESS IS TO COOK THE SOUP GENTLY OVER A LOW HEAT.

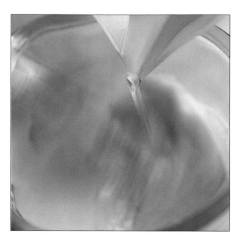

SERVES 4

INGREDIENTS
  25ml/1½ tbsp olive oil
  1 onion, chopped
  3 garlic cloves, chopped
  2 fennel bulbs, halved, cored and
    thinly sliced
  4 tomatoes, chopped
  1 bay leaf
  1 fresh thyme sprig
  1.2 litres/2 pints/5 cups fish stock
  675g/1½lb red mullet or snapper
  8 slices baguette
  1 garlic clove
  30ml/2 tbsp sun-dried tomato paste
  12 black olives, stoned and quartered
  salt and ground black pepper
  fresh fennel fronds, to garnish

For the mayonnaise
  2 egg yolks
  10ml/2 tsp white wine vinegar
  300ml/½ pint/1¼ cups extra
    virgin olive oil

1 Heat the olive oil in a large, heavy-based pan. Add the onion and garlic and cook for 5 minutes, until softened.

2 Add the fennel and cook for a further 2–3 minutes. Stir in the tomatoes, bay leaf, thyme and fish stock. Bring the mixture to the boil, then reduce the heat and simmer for 30 minutes.

COOK'S TIP
Use any firm fish for this recipe if red mullet or snapper isn't available.

3 Meanwhile, make the mayonnaise. Put the egg yolks and vinegar in a bowl. Season and whisk well. Whisk in the oil, a little at a time, increasing the speed from a few drops at a time to a slow trickle. Transfer to a bowl and set aside.

4 Scale and fillet the mullet. Cut each fillet into two or three pieces, then add them to the soup and cook gently for 5 minutes. Use a slotted spoon to remove the mullet, and set aside.

5 Strain the cooking liquid through a fine sieve (strainer), pressing the vegetables with a ladle to extract as much of the flavour as possible.

6 Whisk about a ladleful of the soup into the mayonnaise, then whisk in the remaining soup in one go.

7 Return the soup to a clean pan and cook very gently, whisking continuously, until the mixture is slightly thickened. Add the fish to the soup and set aside.

8 Toast the baguette slices on both sides. Rub each slice with the clove of garlic and spread with sun-dried tomato paste. Divide the olives among the toasted bread slices.

9 Reheat the soup, but do not allow it to boil. Ladle it into bowls and top each with two toasts. Garnish with fennel.

Energy 322Kcal/1354kJ; Protein 35.3g; Carbohydrate 17.5g, of which sugars 6.4g; Fat 12.9g, of which saturates 1g; Cholesterol 0mg; Calcium 173mg; Fibre 4.4g; Sodium 299mg.

SOUP NIÇOISE ^{WITH} SEARED TUNA

INGREDIENTS FOR THE FAMOUS SALAD FROM NICE IN THE SOUTH OF FRANCE ARE TRANSFORMED INTO A SIMPLE, YET ELEGANT, SOUP BY ADDING A HOT GARLIC-INFUSED STOCK.

SERVES 4

INGREDIENTS
  12 bottled anchovy fillets, drained
  30ml/2 tbsp milk
  115g/4oz green beans, halved
  4 plum tomatoes
  16 black olives, stoned
  1 litre/1¾ pints/4 cups good
    vegetable stock
  3 garlic cloves, crushed
  30ml/2 tbsp lemon juice
  15ml/1 tbsp olive oil
  4 tuna steaks, about 75g/3oz each
  small bunch of spring onions
    (scallions), shredded lengthways
  handful of fresh basil leaves,
    finely shredded
  salt and ground black pepper
  fresh crusty bread, to serve

1 Soak the anchovies in the milk for 10 minutes. Drain well and dry on kitchen paper.

2 Cook the green beans in boiling salted water for 2–3 minutes. Drain, refresh under cold running water and drain. Split any thick beans diagonally lengthways. Wash the olives to remove any oil, then cut into quarters.

3 Peel, halve and seed the tomatoes, then cut into wedges. Set all the prepared ingredients aside.

4 Bring the stock to the boil in a large, heavy-based pan. Add the garlic, reduce the heat and simmer for 10 minutes. Season the stock well and add the lemon juice.

5 Meanwhile, brush a griddle pan or frying pan with the oil and heat until very hot. Season the tuna and cook for about 2 minutes on each side. Do not overcook the tuna or it will become dry.

6 Gently toss together the green beans, tomatoes, spring onions, anchovies, black olives and shredded basil leaves.

7 Put the seared tuna steaks into four bowls and pile the vegetable mixture on top. Carefully ladle the hot garlic stock around the ingredients. Serve at once, with crusty bread.

COOK'S TIP
Buy anchovy fillets that have been bottled in extra virgin olive oil if you can, as they have a far superior flavour to the smaller anchovy fillets.

Energy 217Kcal/909kJ; Protein 27.4g; Carbohydrate 3g, of which sugars 2.7g; Fat 10.7g, of which saturates 2.2g; Cholesterol 34mg, Calcium 76mg; Fibre 2g; Sodium 829mg.

SALMON SOUP *WITH* SALSA *AND* ROUILLE

THIS SMART FISH SOUP IS THE PERFECT CHOICE FOR SUMMER ENTERTAINING. SORREL IS A GOOD PARTNER FOR SALMON, BUT DILL OR FENNEL ARE EQUALLY DELICIOUS ALTERNATIVES.

SERVES 4

INGREDIENTS
90ml/6 tbsp olive oil
1 onion, chopped
1 leek, chopped
1 celery stick, chopped
1 fennel bulb, roughly chopped
1 red (bell) pepper, seeded
  and sliced
3 garlic cloves, chopped
grated rind and juice of 2 oranges
1 bay leaf
400g/14oz can chopped tomatoes
1.2 litres/2 pints/5 cups fish stock
pinch of cayenne pepper
800g/1¾lb salmon fillet, skinned
300ml/½ pint/1¼ cups double
  (heavy) cream
salt and ground black pepper
4 thin slices baguette, to serve

For the ruby salsa
2 tomatoes, peeled, seeded
  and diced
½ small red onion, very
  finely chopped
15ml/1 tbsp cod's roe
15ml/1 tbsp chopped fresh sorrel

For the rouille
120ml/4fl oz/½ cup mayonnaise
1 garlic clove, crushed
5ml/1 tsp sun-dried tomato paste

1 Heat the oil in a large pan and add the chopped onion, leek, celery, fennel, pepper and garlic. Cover the pan and cook gently for 20 minutes or until all the vegetables have softened. Do not allow the onion and garlic to brown.

2 Add the orange rind and juice, bay leaf and tomatoes. Cover and cook for 4–5 minutes, stirring occasionally. Add the stock and cayenne, cover the pan and simmer for 30 minutes.

3 Add the salmon and cook gently for 8–10 minutes, until just cooked. Using a slotted spoon, remove the salmon and place it on a large plate.

4 Flake the salmon into large pieces, and remove any bones that were missed when the fish was originally filleted. Put the flaked salmon in a dish and set it aside.

COOK'S TIP
For a smart presentation, choose wide, shallow soup plates, so that there is plenty of room for the rouille-topped toast on top of the flaked salmon. The ruby salsa adds the finishing touch.

5 Meanwhile, make the salsa. Put the tomatoes in a bowl and add the finely chopped red onion. Stir in the cod's roe and the chopped fresh sorrel. Transfer the mixture to a serving dish and set it aside.

6 To make the rouille to top the toast, mix the mayonnaise with the crushed garlic and the sun-dried tomato paste in a bowl.

7 Leave the soup to cool slightly, then remove and discard the bay leaf. Purée the soup in a food processor or blender until smooth, then press it through a fine sieve (strainer) into the rinsed pan.

8 Stir in the cream and season well, then add the flaked salmon. Toast the baguette slices under a hot grill (broiler) on both sides and set aside.

9 Reheat the soup gently without letting it boil. Ladle it into bowls and float the toasted baguette slices on top. Add a spoonful of rouille to each slice of baguette and spoon some ruby salsa on top. Serve immediately.

Energy 1153Kcal/4772kJ; Protein 44.9g; Carbohydrate 13.7g, of which sugars 12.5g; Fat 102.5g, of which saturates 34.9g; Cholesterol 225mg; Calcium 127mg; Fibre 4.7g; Sodium 268mg.

SALMON CHOWDER

DILL IS THE PERFECT PARTNER FOR SALMON IN THIS CREAMY SOUP FROM THE USA. IT IS BEST SERVED IMMEDIATELY AFTER COOKING, WHEN THE SALMON IS JUST TENDER.

3 Add the fish stock and potatoes to the mixture in the pan. Season with a little salt and ground black pepper. Bring to the boil, then reduce the heat, cover and simmer gently for about 20 minutes or until the potatoes are tender when tested with a fork.

4 Add the cubed salmon fillet and simmer gently for 3–5 minutes until it is just cooked.

SERVES 4

INGREDIENTS
  20g/¾oz/1½ tbsp butter
  1 onion, finely chopped
  1 leek, finely chopped
  1 small fennel bulb, finely chopped
  25g/1oz/¼ cup plain
   (all-purpose) flour
  1.75 litres/3 pints/7 cups fish stock
  2 medium potatoes, cut into
   1cm/½in cubes
  450g/1lb salmon fillet, skinned and
   cut into 2cm/¾in cubes
  175ml/6fl oz/¾ cup milk
  120ml/4fl oz/½ cup whipping cream
  30ml/2 tbsp chopped fresh dill
  salt and ground black pepper

1 Melt the butter in a large pan. Add the onion, leek and chopped fennel and cook for 6 minutes until softened.

2 Stir in the flour. Reduce the heat to low and cook for 3 minutes, stirring occasionally with a wooden spoon.

5 Stir the milk, cream and chopped dill into the contents of the pan. Cook until just warmed through, stirring occasionally, but do not allow to boil. Adjust the seasoning to taste, then ladle into warmed soup bowls to serve.

Energy 464Kcal/1934kJ; Protein 27.9g; Carbohydrate 22.1g, of which sugars 6.5g; Fat 30g, of which saturates 12.9g; Cholesterol 101mg; Calcium 131mg; Fibre 3.1g; Sodium 122mg.

SMOKED HADDOCK CHOWDER

BASED ON A TRADITIONAL SCOTTISH RECIPE, THIS SOUP HAS AMERICAN-STYLE SWEETNESS FROM THE SWEET POTATOES AND BUTTERNUT SQUASH, AND IS FLAVOURED WITH A HINT OF THAI BASIL.

SERVES 6

INGREDIENTS
  400g/14oz sweet potatoes
    (pink-fleshed variety)
  225g/8oz butternut squash
  50g/2oz/¼ cup butter
  1 onion, chopped
  450g/1lb smoked haddock fillets
  300ml/½ pint/1¼ cups water
  600ml/1 pint/2½ cups milk
  small handful of Thai basil leaves
  60ml/4 tbsp double (heavy) cream
  salt and ground black pepper

3 Use a sharp knife to skin the smoked haddock fillets.

4 Add the fillets and water to the pan. Bring to the boil, reduce the heat and simmer for 10 minutes, until the fish is cooked. Use a slotted spoon to lift the fish out of the pan, and leave to cool. Set the cooking liquid aside.

5 When cool enough to handle, carefully break the flesh into large flakes, discarding the skin and bones. Set the fish aside.

6 Press the sweet potatoes through a sieve (strainer) and beat in the remaining butter with seasoning to taste. Strain the reserved fish cooking liquid and return it to the rinsed pan, then whisk in the sweet potato. Stir in the milk and bring to the boil. Simmer for about 2–3 minutes.

7 Stir in the butternut squash, fish, Thai basil leaves and cream. Season the soup to taste and heat through without boiling. Ladle the soup into six warmed soup bowls and serve immediately.

1 Peel the sweet potatoes and butternut squash and cut into small, bitesize pieces. Cook them separately in boiling salted water for 15 minutes or until just tender. Drain both well.

2 Melt half the butter in a large, heavy-based pan. Add the onion and cook for 4–5 minutes, until soft.

COOK'S TIP
The best type of smoked fish to use in this recipe is Finnan haddock, but other types of smoked haddock can be used with equal success.

Energy 285Kcal/1196kJ; Protein 19.1g; Carbohydrate 20.7g, of which sugars 9.9g; Fat 14.7g, of which saturates 8.9g; Cholesterol 64mg; Calcium 166mg; Fibre 2.1g; Sodium 173mg

SMOKED MACKEREL AND TOMATO SOUP

ALL THE INGREDIENTS FOR THIS UNUSUAL SOUP ARE COOKED IN A SINGLE PAN, SO IT IS NOT ONLY QUICK AND EASY TO PREPARE, BUT REDUCES THE CLEARING UP. SMOKED MACKEREL GIVES THE SOUP A ROBUST FLAVOUR, BUT THIS IS TEMPERED BY THE CITRUS TONES IN THE LEMON GRASS AND TAMARIND.

SERVES 4

INGREDIENTS

   200g/7oz smoked mackerel fillets
   4 tomatoes
   1 litre/1¾ pints/4 cups
     vegetable stock
   1 lemon grass stalk, finely chopped
   5cm/2in piece fresh galangal,
     finely diced
   4 shallots, finely chopped
   2 garlic cloves, finely chopped
   2.5ml/½ tsp dried chilli flakes
   15ml/1 tbsp Thai fish sauce
   5ml/1 tsp palm sugar or light
     muscovado (brown) sugar
   45ml/3 tbsp thick tamarind juice,
     made by mixing tamarind paste
     with warm water
   small bunch of fresh chives or spring
     onions (scallions), to garnish

1 Prepare the smoked mackerel fillets. Remove and discard the skin, if necessary, then chop the flesh into large pieces. Remove any stray bones with your fingers or a pair of tweezers.

2 Cut the tomatoes in half, squeeze out most of the seeds with your fingers, then finely dice the flesh with a sharp knife. Set aside.

3 Pour the stock into a large pan and add the lemon grass, galangal, shallots and garlic. Bring to the boil, reduce the heat and simmer for 15 minutes.

4 Add the fish, tomatoes, chilli flakes, fish sauce, sugar and tamarind juice. Simmer for 4–5 minutes, until the fish and tomatoes are heated through. Serve garnished with chives or spring onions.

Energy 203Kcal/845kJ; Protein 10.3g; Carbohydrate 5.3g, of which sugars 5g; Fat 15.8g, of which saturates 3.3g; Cholesterol 53mg; Calcium 21mg; Fibre 1.2g; Sodium 385mg.

COD, BROAD BEAN <u>AND</u> SPINACH CHOWDER

FRESH COD AND VEGETABLES ARE ABUNDANT IN THIS THICK AND CREAMY SOUP, WHICH IS FINISHED WITH CRISP GRANARY CROÛTONS TO SOAK UP THE DELICIOUS LIQUID. MAKE IT EARLY IN THE SUMMER TO TAKE ADVANTAGE OF THE YOUNGEST, SWEETEST FRESH BEANS.

SERVES 6

INGREDIENTS
1 litre/1¾ pints/4 cups milk
150ml/¼ pint/⅔ cup double (heavy) cream
675g/1½lb cod fillet, skinned and boned
45ml/3 tbsp olive oil
1 onion, sliced
2 garlic cloves, finely chopped
450g/1lb potatoes, thickly sliced
450g/1lb fresh broad (fava) beans, podded
225g/8oz baby spinach leaves
pinch of grated nutmeg
30ml/2 tbsp chopped fresh chives
salt and ground black pepper
fresh chives, to garnish

For the croûtons
60ml/4 tbsp olive oil
6 slices Granary (whole-wheat) bread, crusts removed, cut into large cubes

1 Pour the milk and cream into a large pan and bring to the boil. Add the cod and bring back to the boil. Reduce the heat and simmer for 2–3 minutes, then remove from the heat and leave to stand for about 6 minutes, until the fish is just cooked. Use a slotted spoon to remove the fish from the cooking liquid.

2 Using a fork, flake the cooked cod into chunky pieces, removing any bones or skin, then cover and set aside.

3 Heat the olive oil in a large pan and add the onion and garlic. Cook for about 5 minutes, until softened, stirring occasionally. Add the potatoes, stir in the milk mixture and bring to the boil. Reduce the heat and cover the pan. Cook for 10 minutes. Add the broad beans; cook for 10 minutes more or until the beans are tender and the potatoes just begin to break up.

4 Meanwhile, to make the croûtons, heat the oil in a frying pan and add the bread cubes. Cook over a medium heat, stirring often, until golden all over. Remove using a slotted spoon and leave to drain on kitchen paper.

5 Add the cod to the soup and heat through gently. Just before serving, add the spinach and stir for 1–2 minutes, until wilted. Season the soup well and stir in the nutmeg and chives.

6 Ladle the soup into six warmed soup bowls and pile the croûtons on top. Garnish with fresh chives and serve immediately.

COOK'S TIP
When fresh broad (fava) beans are out of season, frozen beans are acceptable as an alternative. Make sure that you cook them for the time recommended on the packet.

Energy 603Kcal/2525kJ; Protein 37.9g; Carbohydrate 44.7g, of which sugars 12.2g; Fat 31.6g, of which saturates 12.4g; Cholesterol 96mg; Calcium 398mg; Fibre 7.6g; Sodium 375mg.

SHELLFISH SOUPS

If you like shellfish, you will find a wealth of delicious and luxurious soups in this section. Provençal Fish Soup, or Lobster Bisque is a marvellous party dish. Or you could try Spanish Seafood Soup, a hearty dish that has all the colours and flavours of the Mediterranean. From Japan there is a delicate Clear Soup with Seafood Sticks, often eaten with sushi, and from China there is Wonton and Prawn Tail Soup.

CLEAR SOUP WITH SEAFOOD STICKS

THIS DELICATE JAPANESE SOUP, WHICH IS OFTEN EATEN WITH SUSHI, IS VERY QUICK TO MAKE IF YOU PREPARE THE FIRST DASHI BEFOREHAND OR IF YOU USE FREEZE-DRIED DASHI-NO-MOTO.

SERVES 4

INGREDIENTS

    4 mitsuba sprigs or 4 chives
      and a few sprigs of mustard and
      cress
    4 seafood sticks
    400ml/14fl oz/1⅔ cups first dashi
      stock, or the same amount of water
      and 5ml/1 tsp dashi-no-moto
    15ml/1 tbsp Japanese soy
      sauce (shoyu)
    7.5ml/1½ tsp salt
    grated rind of yuzu (optional),
      to garnish

1 Mitsuba leaves are normally sold with the stems and roots on to retain freshness. Cut off the root, then cut 5cm/2in from the top, retaining both the long straw-like stem and the leaf.

2 Blanch the stems in hot water from the kettle. If you use chives, choose them at least 10cm/4in in length and blanch them, too.

3 Take a seafood stick and carefully tie around the middle with a mitsuba stem or chive, holding it in place with a knot. Do not pull too tightly, as the bow will easily break. Repeat the process to make four tied seafood sticks.

4 Hold one seafood stick in your hand. With your finger, carefully loosen both ends to make it look like a tassel.

5 Place one seafood stick in each soup bowl, then put the four mitsuba leaves or mustard and cress on top.

6 Heat the stock in a pan and bring to the boil. Add shoyu and salt to taste. Pour the stock gently over the mitsuba and seafood stick. Sprinkle with grated yuzu rind, if using.

COOK'S TIPS
• Mitsuba is a member of the parsley family and is available from Asian stores.
• Dashi stock can be bought as instant dashi-no-moto, or you can make your own.
• Yuzu is a popular Japanese citrus fruit, about the same size as a clementine, with a firm, thick, yellow skin.

Energy 9Kcal/36kJ; Protein 1.1g; Carbohydrate 1g, of which sugars 0.3g; Fat 0.1g, of which saturates 0g; Cholesterol 4mg; Calcium 2mg; Fibre 0g; Sodium 1025mg.

COCONUT AND SEAFOOD SOUP

THE LONG LIST OF INGREDIENTS COULD MISLEAD YOU INTO THINKING THAT THIS
COMPLICATED AND VERY TIME-CONSUMING TO PREPARE. IN FACT, IT IS EXTREMEL
TOGETHER AND THE MARRIAGE OF FLAVOURS WORKS BEAUTIFULLY.

SERVES 4

INGREDIENTS
600ml/1 pint/2½ cups fish stock
5 thin slices fresh galangal or fresh
    root ginger
2 lemon grass stalks, chopped
3 kaffir lime leaves, shredded
bunch garlic chives, about 25g/1oz
small bunch fresh coriander
    (cilantro), about 15g/½oz
15ml/1 tbsp vegetable oil
4 shallots, chopped
400ml/14fl oz can coconut milk
30–45ml/2–3 tbsp Thai fish sauce
45–60ml/3–4 tbsp Thai green
    curry paste
450g/1lb raw large prawns (shrimp),
    peeled and deveined
450g/1lb prepared squid
a little fresh lime juice (optional)
salt and ground black pepper
60ml/4 tbsp crisp fried shallot
    slices, to serve

1 Pour the fish stock into a large pan
and add the slices of galangal or ginger,
the lemon grass and half the shredded
kaffir lime leaves.

VARIATIONS
• Instead of squid, you could add 400g/
14oz firm white fish, such as monkfish,
cut into small pieces.
• You could also replace the squid with
mussels. Steam 675g/1½lb live mussels
in a tightly covered pan for 3–4 minutes,
or until they have opened. Discard any
that remain shut, then remove them from
their shells and add to the soup.

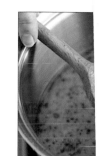

2 Reserve a few garlic chives for the
garnish, then chop the remainder. Add
half the chopped garlic chives to the
pan. Strip the coriander leaves from the
stalks and set the leaves aside. Add
the stalks to the pan. Bring to the boil,
reduce the heat to low and cover the
pan, then simmer gently for 20 minutes.
Strain the stock into a bowl.

3 Rinse and dry the pan. Add the oil
and shallots. Cook over a medium heat
for 5–10 minutes, until the shallots are
just beginning to brown.

4 Stir in the strained stock, coconut
milk, the remaining kaffir lime leaves
and 30ml/2 tbsp of the fish sauce. Heat
gently until simmering and cook over a
low heat for 5–10 minutes.

5 Stir in the cu
then cook for 3
and cook for a
the lime juice,
adding more fl
the remaining
coriander leave
sprinkle each p
and whole garli

PRAWN AND EGG-KNOT SOUP

OMELETTES AND PANCAKES ARE OFTEN USED TO ADD PROTEIN TO LIGHT ORIENTAL SOUPS. IN THIS
RECIPE, THIN OMELETTES ARE TWISTED INTO LITTLE KNOTS AND ADDED AT THE LAST MINUTE.

SERVES 4

INGREDIENTS
1 spring onion (scallion), shredded
800ml/1⅓ pints/3½ cups well-
    flavoured stock or instant dashi
5ml/1 tsp soy sauce
dash of sake or dry white wine
pinch of salt
For the prawn (shrimp) balls
200g/7oz/generous 1 cup raw large
    prawns, shelled, thawed if frozen
65g/2½oz cod fillet, skinned
5ml/1 tsp egg white
5ml/1 tsp sake or dry white wine,
    plus a dash extra
22.5ml/4½ tsp cornflour (cornstarch)
    or potato flour
2–3 drops soy sauce
pinch of salt
For the omelette
1 egg, beaten
dash of mirin
pinch of salt
oil, for cooking

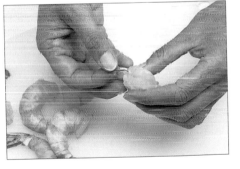

1 To make the prawn balls, use a pin to
remove the black vein running down the
back of each prawn. Place the prawns,
cod, egg white, sake or dry white wine,
cornflour or potato flour, soy sauce and
a pinch of salt in a food processor or
blender and process to a thick, sticky
paste. Shape the mixture into 4 balls,
place in a steaming basket and steam
over a pan of vigorously boiling water
for about 10 minutes.

2 To make the garnish, soak the spring
onion shreds in iced water for about
5 minutes, until they curl, then drain.

3 To make the omelette, mix the egg
with the mirin and salt. Heat a little
oil in a frying pan and pour in the egg
mixture, coating the pan evenly. When
the omelette has set, turn it over and
cook for 30 seconds. Leave to cool.

4 Cut the omelette into strips and tie
each in a knot. Heat the stock or dashi,
then add the soy sauce, sake or wine
and salt. Divide the prawn balls and
egg-knots among 4 bowls and add the
soup. Garnish with the spring onion.

WONTON AND PRAWN TAIL SOUP

A WELL-FLAVOURED CHICKEN STOCK OR BROTH IS A MUST FOR THIS CLASSIC
IS POPULAR ON FAST-FOOD STALLS IN TOWNS AND CITIES THROUGHOUT SOUT
AN APPETIZER OR PART OF A MAIN MEAL WITH A SELECTION OF DIM SUM OR

SERVES 4

INGREDIENTS
200g/7oz minced (ground) pork
200g/7oz cooked, peeled prawns
  (shrimp), thawed if frozen
10ml/2 tsp rice wine or dry sherry
10ml/2 tsp light soy sauce
5ml/1 tsp sesame oil
24 thin wonton wrappers
1.2 litres/2 pints/5 cups
  chicken stock
12 tiger prawns, shelled, with
  tails still on
350g/12oz pak choi (bok choy),
  coarsely shredded
salt and ground black pepper
4 spring onions (scallions),
  sliced, and 1cm/½in piece fresh
  root ginger, finely shredded,
  to garnish

1 Put the pork, prawns, rice wine or sherry, soy sauce and sesame oil in a large bowl. Add plenty of seasoning and mix the ingredients.

2 Put about 10ml/2 tsp of pork mixture in the centre of each wonton wrapper. Bring up the sides of the wrapper and pinch them together to seal the filling in a small bundle.

3 Bring a
boil. Add
3 minutes

4 Pour the
the boil. S
prawns an
just tender
choi and c
with spring

CHICKEN AND LEEK SOUP

THIS RECIPE IS BASED ON THE TRADITIONAL SCOTTISH SOUP, COCK-A-LEEKIE. THE UNUSUAL COMBINATION OF LEEKS AND PRUNES IS SURPRISINGLY DELICIOUS.

SERVES 6

INGREDIENTS

  1 chicken, weighing about 2kg/4¼lb
  900g/2lb leeks
  1 fresh bay leaf
  a few each fresh parsley stalks and
    thyme sprigs
  1 large carrot, thickly sliced
  2.4 litres/4 pints/10 cups chicken
    or beef stock
  115g/4oz/generous ½ cup
    pearl barley
  400g/14oz ready-to-eat prunes
  salt and ground black pepper
  chopped fresh parsley, to garnish

1 Cut the breasts off the chicken and set aside. Place the remaining chicken carcass in a large pan. Cut half the leeks into 5cm/2in lengths and add them to the pan. Tie the bay leaf, parsley and thyme into a bouquet garni and add to the pan with the carrot and the stock. Bring to the boil, then reduce the heat and cover. Simmer gently for 1 hour. Skim off any scum when the water first boils and occasionally during simmering.

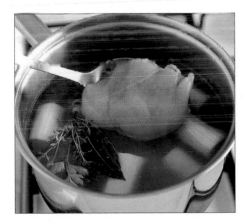

2 Add the chicken breasts and cook for another 30 minutes, until they are just cooked. Leave until cool enough to handle, then strain the stock. Reserve the chicken breasts and meat from the chicken carcass. Discard all the skin, bones, cooked vegetables and herbs. Skim as much fat as you can from the stock, then return it to the pan.

3 Meanwhile, rinse the pearl barley thoroughly in a sieve (strainer) under cold running water, then cook it in a large pan of boiling water for about 10 minutes. Drain, rinse well again and drain thoroughly.

4 Add the pearl barley to the stock. Bring to the boil over a medium heat, then lower the heat and cook very gently for 15–20 minutes, until the barley is just cooked and tender. Season the soup with 5ml/1 tsp salt and black pepper.

5 Add the prunes. Slice the remaining leeks and add them to the pan. Bring to the boil, then simmer for 10 minutes or until the leeks are just cooked.

6 Slice the chicken breasts and add them to the soup with the remaining chicken meat, sliced or cut into neat pieces. Reheat if necessary, then ladle the soup into deep plates and sprinkle with chopped parsley.

Energy 359Kcal/1526kJ; Protein 41.7g; Carbohydrate 44g, of which sugars 26.9g; Fat 3g, of which saturates 0.6g; Cholesterol 105mg; Calcium 73mg; Fibre 7.4g; Sodium 104mg.

CHICKEN, LEEK AND CELERY SOUP

THIS MAKES A SUBSTANTIAL MAIN COURSE SOUP WITH FRESH CRUSTY BREAD. YOU WILL NEED NOTHING MORE THAN A SALAD AND CHEESE, OR JUST FRESH FRUIT TO FOLLOW THIS DISH.

SERVES 4–6

INGREDIENTS
1.4kg/3lb free-range chicken
1 small head of celery, trimmed
1 onion, coarsely chopped
1 fresh bay leaf
a few fresh parsley stalks
a few fresh tarragon sprigs
2.4 litres/4 pints/10 cups cold water
3 large leeks
65g/2½oz/5 tbsp butter
2 potatoes, cut into chunks
150ml/¼ pint/⅔ cup dry white wine
30–45ml/2–3 tbsp single (light)
  cream (optional)
salt and ground black pepper
90g/3½oz pancetta, grilled until
  crisp, to garnish

1 Cut the breasts off the chicken and set aside. Chop the rest of the chicken carcass into 8–10 pieces and place in a large pan.

2 Chop 4–5 of the outer sticks of the celery and add them to the pan with the onion. Tie the bay leaf, parsley and tarragon together and add to the pan. Pour in the cold water to cover the ingredients and bring to the boil. Reduce the heat and cover the pan, then simmer for 1½ hours.

3 Remove the chicken and cut off and reserve the meat. Strain the stock, then return it to the pan and boil rapidly until it has reduced to about 1.5 litres/ 2½ pints/6¼ cups.

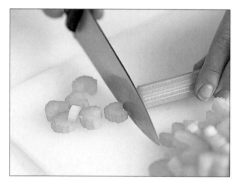

4 Meanwhile, set about 150g/5oz of the leeks aside. Slice the remaining leeks and the remaining celery, reserving any celery leaves. Chop the celery leaves and set aside to garnish the soup.

5 Melt half the butter in a large, heavy-based pan. Add the sliced leeks and celery, cover and cook over a low heat for about 10 minutes, or until softened but not browned. Add the potatoes, wine and 1.2 litres/2 pints/ 5 cups of the stock.

6 Season well with salt and pepper, bring to the boil and reduce the heat. Part-cover the pan and simmer the soup for 15–20 minutes, or until the potatoes are cooked.

7 Meanwhile, skin the reserved chicken breasts and cut the flesh into small pieces. Melt the remaining butter in a frying pan, add the chicken and fry for 5–7 minutes, until cooked.

8 Thickly slice the remaining leeks, add to the pan and cook, stirring occasionally, for a further 3–4 minutes, until just cooked.

9 Process the soup with the cooked chicken from the stock in a blender or food processor. Taste and adjust the seasoning, and add more stock if the soup is very thick.

10 Stir in the cream, if using, and the chicken and leek mixture. Reheat gently and serve in warmed bowls. Crumble the pancetta over the soup and sprinkle with the chopped celery leaves.

Energy 294Kcal/1246kJ; Protein 40.5g; Carbohydrate 22.1g, of which sugars 5.9g; Fat 2.8g, of which saturates 0.7g; Cholesterol 105mg; Calcium 69mg; Fibre 4.9g; Sodium 124mg.

MOROCCAN CHICKEN SOUP
WITH CHARMOULA BUTTER

THIS TASTY SOUP, INSPIRED BY THE INGREDIENTS OF NORTH AFRICA, IS SPICED WITH CHILLI AND SERVED WITH A RICH AND PUNGENT LEMON BUTTER CREAMED WITH CRISP BREADCRUMBS.

1 Melt the butter in a large, heavy-based pan. Add the chicken strips and cook for 5–6 minutes, turning with a wooden spatula, until beginning to brown. Use a slotted spoon to remove the chicken from the pan and set aside.

2 Add the onion and garlic to the pan and cook over a gentle heat for 4–5 minutes, until softened but not brown.

3 Stir in the flour and cook for 3–4 minutes, stirring continuously, until beginning to brown.

4 Stir in the harissa and cook for a further 1 minute. Gradually pour in the stock and cook for 2–3 minutes, until slightly thickened. Stir in the tomatoes.

5 Return the chicken to the soup and add the chickpeas. Cover and cook over a low heat for 20 minutes. Season well with salt and black pepper.

6 Meanwhile, to make the charmoula, put the butter into a bowl and beat in the coriander, garlic, cumin, chilli, saffron strands, lemon rind and paprika. When the mixture is well combined, stir in the coarse breadcrumbs.

7 Ladle the soup into six warmed bowls. Spoon a little of the charmoula into the centre of each and leave for a few seconds to allow the butter to melt into the soup before serving with lemon wedges.

SERVES 6

INGREDIENTS
50g/2oz/¼ cup butter
450g/1lb chicken breasts, cut into strips
1 onion, chopped
2 garlic cloves, crushed
7.5ml/1½ tsp plain (all-purpose) flour
15ml/1 tbsp harissa
1 litre/1¾ pints/4 cups chicken stock
400g/14oz can chopped tomatoes
400g/14oz can chickpeas, drained and rinsed
salt and ground black pepper
lemon wedges, to serve

For the charmoula
50g/2oz/¼ cup slightly salted butter, at room temperature
30ml/2 tbsp chopped fresh coriander (cilantro)
2 garlic cloves, crushed
5ml/1 tsp ground cumin
1 red chilli, seeded and chopped
pinch of saffron strands
finely grated rind of ½ lemon
5ml/1 tsp paprika
25g/1oz/1 cup dried breadcrumbs

Energy 313Kcal/1312kJ; Protein 25g; Carbohydrate 18.3g, of which sugars 3.3g; Fat 16.1g, of which saturates 9g; Cholesterol 88mg; Calcium 53mg; Fibre 3.6g; Sodium 207mg.

SOUTHERN AMERICAN SUCCOTASH SOUP
WITH CHICKEN

BASED ON A VEGETABLE DISH FROM THE SOUTHERN STATES OF AMERICA, THIS SOUP INCLUDES SUCCULENT FRESH CORN KERNELS, WHICH GIVE IT A RICHNESS THAT COMPLEMENTS THE CHICKEN.

SERVES 4

INGREDIENTS

750ml/1¼ pints/3 cups chicken stock
4 boneless, skinless chicken breasts
50g/2oz/¼ cup butter
2 onions, chopped
115g/4oz piece rindless smoked
   streaky (fatty) bacon, chopped
25g/1oz/¼ cup plain
   (all-purpose) flour
4 cobs of corn
300ml/½ pint/1¼ cups milk
400g/14oz can butter (lima)
   beans, drained
45ml/3 tbsp chopped fresh parsley
salt and ground black pepper

1 Bring the chicken stock to the boil in a large pan. Add the chicken breasts and bring back to the boil. Reduce the heat and cook for 12–15 minutes, until cooked through and tender. Use a slotted spoon to remove the chicken from the pan and leave to cool. Reserve the stock.

2 Melt the butter in a pan. Add the onions and cook for 4–5 minutes, until softened but not brown.

3 Add the bacon and cook for 5–6 minutes, until beginning to brown. Sprinkle in the flour and cook for 1 minute, stirring continuously.

4 Gradually stir in the hot stock and bring to the boil, stirring until thickened. Remove from the heat.

5 Using a sharp knife, remove the kernels from the corn cobs. Stir the kernels into the pan with half the milk. Return to the heat and cook, stirring occasionally, for 12–15 minutes, until the corn is tender.

VARIATION
Canned corn can be used instead of fresh corn.

6 Cut the chicken into bitesize pieces and stir into the soup. Stir in the butter beans and the remaining milk. Bring to the boil and cook for 5 minutes, then season well and stir in the parsley.

Energy 539Kcal/2267kJ; Protein 51.8g; Carbohydrate 37.4g, of which sugars 11.5g; Fat 21.4g, of which saturates 10.3g; Cholesterol 155mg; Calcium 155mg; Fibre 6.4g; Sodium 1120mg.

CHICKEN AND COCONUT SOUP

THIS RECIPE COMBINES THE ORIENTAL FLAVOURS OF THAILAND IN A SMOOTH EUROPEAN-STYLE SOUP, AND THE FINISHED DISH IS COMPLEMENTED BY A TOPPING OF CRISP SHALLOTS.

1 Melt the butter in a large, heavy-based pan. Add the onion, garlic and ginger. Cook for 4–5 minutes, until soft. Stir in the curry paste and turmeric, and cook for a further 2–3 minutes, stirring continuously.

2 Pour in two-thirds of the coconut milk; cook for 5 minutes.

3 Add the stock, lime leaves, lemon grass and chicken. Heat until simmering; cook for 15 minutes or until the chicken is tender.

4 Use a slotted spoon to remove the chicken thighs. Set them aside to cool.

5 Add the spinach to the pan and cook for 3–4 minutes. Stir in the remaining coconut milk and seasoning, then process the soup in a food processor or blender until almost smooth. Return the soup to the rinsed-out pan.

6 Cut the chicken thighs into bite-size pieces and stir these into the soup with the fish sauce and lime juice.

7 Reheat the soup gently until hot, but do not let it boil. Meanwhile, heat the oil in a frying pan and cook the shallots for 6–8 minutes, until crisp and golden, stirring occasionally.

8 Drain on kitchen paper. Ladle the soup into bowls, then top with the basil leaves and fried shallots, and serve.

SERVES 6

INGREDIENTS
  40g/1½oz/3 tbsp butter
  1 onion, finely chopped
  2 garlic cloves, chopped
  2.5cm/1in piece fresh root ginger,
    finely chopped
  10ml/2 tsp Thai green curry paste
  2.5ml/½ tsp turmeric
  400ml/14fl oz can coconut milk
  475ml/16fl oz/2 cups chicken stock

  2 lime leaves, shredded
  1 lemon grass stalk, finely chopped
  8 skinless, boneless chicken thighs
  350g/12oz spinach, roughly
    chopped
  10ml/2 tsp Thai fish sauce
  30ml/2 tbsp lime juice
  30ml/2 tbsp vegetable oil
  2 shallots, thinly sliced
  small handful of Thai purple
    basil leaves
salt and ground black pepper

Energy 136Kcal/570kJ; Protein 14.1g; Carbohydrate 5.2g, of which sugars 4.9g; Fat 6.7g, of which saturates 3.8g; Cholesterol 49mg; Calcium 125mg; Fibre 1.4g; Sodium 344mg.

CHINESE CHICKEN AND CHILLI SOUP

GINGER AND LEMON GRASS ADD AN AROMATIC NOTE TO THIS TASTY, REFRESHING SOUP, WHICH CAN BE SERVED AS A LIGHT LUNCH OR APPETIZER. SERVE WITH A SWEET CHILLI SAUCE FOR EXTRA SPICE.

SERVES 4

INGREDIENTS

150g/5oz boneless chicken breast
   portion, cut into thin strips
2.5cm/1in piece fresh root ginger,
   finely chopped
5cm/2in piece lemon grass stalk,
   finely chopped
1 red chilli, seeded and
   thinly sliced
8 baby corn cobs, halved lengthways
1 large carrot, cut into thin sticks
1 litre/1¾ pints/4 cups hot
   chicken stock
4 spring onions (scallions),
   thinly sliced
12 small shiitake mushrooms, sliced
115g/4oz/1 cup vermicelli
   rice noodles
30ml/2 tbsp soy sauce
salt and ground black pepper

2 Place the Chinese sand pot in an unheated oven. Set the temperature to 200°C/400°F/Gas 6 and cook the soup for 30–40 minutes, or until the stock is simmering and the chicken and vegetables are tender.

3 Add the spring onions and the mushrooms, cover and return the pot to the oven for 10 minutes.

4 Meanwhile place the noodles in a large bowl and cover with boiling water. Soak for the required time, following the packet instructions.

5 Stir the soy sauce into the soup, taste for seasoning and add salt and pepper as required.

6 Drain the noodles and divide them among four warmed serving bowls. Divide the soup between the bowls and serve immediately.

1 Place the chicken strips, chopped ginger, chopped lemon grass and sliced chilli in a Chinese sand pot. Add the halved baby corn and the carrot sticks. Pour over the hot chicken stock and cover the pot.

COOK'S TIP
Rice noodles are available in a variety of thicknesses and can be bought in straight lengths or in coils or loops. They are a creamy white colour and very brittle in texture. Rice noodles are pre-cooked so they only require a very short soaking time – check the packet for exact timings. Vermicelli rice noodles are very fine and will only need to be soaked for a few minutes.

Energy 165Kcal/693kJ; Protein 13.3g; Carbohydrate 26g, of which sugars 3.1g; Fat 0.9g, of which saturates 0.2g; Cholesterol 26mg; Calcium 23mg; Fibre 1.4g; Sodium 852mg.

CREAM OF DUCK SOUP WITH BLUEBERRY RELISH

THIS DELICIOUS, RICH SOUP IS IDEAL FOR SMART OCCASIONS, AND IS SURE TO IMPRESS AT A DINNER PARTY. YOU CAN USE A WHOLE DUCK, BUT COOKING WITH DUCK BREASTS AND LEGS IS EASIER.

SERVES 4

INGREDIENTS
2 duck breasts
4 rindless streaky (fatty) bacon
  rashers, chopped
1 onion, chopped
1 garlic clove, chopped
2 carrots, diced
2 celery sticks, chopped
4 large open mushrooms, chopped
15ml/1 tbsp tomato purée (paste)
2 duck legs
15ml/1 tbsp plain (all-purpose) flour
45ml/3 tbsp brandy
150ml/¼ pint/⅔ cup port
300ml/½ pint/1¼ cups red wine
900ml/1½ pints/ 3¾ cups
  chicken stock
1 bay leaf
2 sprigs fresh thyme
15ml/1 tbsp redcurrant jelly
150ml/¼ pint/⅔ cup double
  (heavy) cream
salt and ground black pepper

For the blueberry relish
150g/5oz/1¼ cups blueberries
15ml/1 tbsp caster (superfine) sugar
grated rind and juice of 2 limes
15ml/1 tbsp chopped fresh parsley
15ml/1 tbsp balsamic vinegar

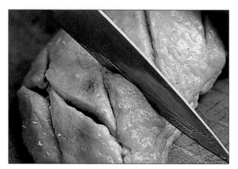

1 Use a sharp knife to score the skin and fat on the duck breasts.

2 Preheat a heavy-based pan. Place the duck breasts in the pan, skin sides down, and cook for 8–10 minutes, until golden. Turn and cook for a further 5–6 minutes.

3 Remove the duck from the pan and set aside. Drain off some of the fat, leaving about 45ml/3 tbsp in the pan. Add the bacon, onion, garlic, carrots, celery and mushrooms to the pan and cook for 10 minutes, stirring occasionally. Stir in the tomato purée and cook for 2 minutes. Remove the skin and bones from the duck legs and chop the flesh. Add to the pan and cook for 5 minutes.

4 Stir in the flour and cook for 1 minute. Gradually stir in the brandy, port, wine and stock and bring to the boil, stirring. Add the bay leaf, thyme and redcurrant jelly, then stir until the jelly melts. Reduce the heat and simmer for 1 hour.

5 Meanwhile, make the relish. Put the blueberries, caster sugar, lime rind and juice, parsley and vinegar in a small bowl. Very lightly bruise the blueberries with a fork, leaving some of the berries whole. Set aside until required.

6 Strain the soup through a colander, then through a fine sieve (strainer) into a clean pan. Bring to the boil, reduce the heat and simmer for 10 minutes.

7 Meanwhile, remove and discard the skin and fat from the duck breasts and cut the meat into thin strips. Add the meat strips to the soup with the double cream and season well. Bring just to boiling point. Ladle the soup into warmed bowls and top each serving with a dollop of the blueberry relish. Serve piping hot.

Energy 642Kcal/2673kJ; Protein 39.2g; Carbohydrate 14.2g, of which sugars 13.6g; Fat 35g, of which saturates 17.2g; Cholesterol 252mg; Calcium 83mg; Fibre 2.8g; Sodium 384mg.

DUCK BROTH <u>WITH</u> ORANGE SPICED DUMPLINGS

USING A DELICATE TOUCH WHEN BRINGING TOGETHER THE MIXTURE FOR THE DUMPLINGS WILL CREATE A LIGHT TEXTURE TO MATCH THEIR DELICIOUS FLAVOUR.

SERVES 4

INGREDIENTS

1 duckling, about 1.75kg/4–4½ lb, with liver
1 large onion, halved
2 carrots, thickly sliced
½ garlic bulb
1 bouquet garni
3 cloves
30ml/2 tbsp chopped chives, to garnish

For the spiced dumplings
2 thick slices white bread
60ml/4 tbsp milk
2 rashers (strips) rindless streaky (fatty) bacon
1 shallot, finely chopped
1 garlic clove, crushed
1 egg yolk, beaten
grated rind of 1 orange
2.5ml/½ tsp paprika
50g/2oz/½ cup plain (all-purpose) flour
salt and ground black pepper

1 Set the duck liver aside. Using a sharp knife, cut off the breasts from the duckling and set them aside.

2 Put the carcass into a large, heavy-based pan and pour in enough water to cover the carcass. Bring to the boil and skim the scum off the surface.

3 Add the onion, carrots, garlic, bouquet garni and cloves. Reduce the heat and cover the pan, then simmer for 2 hours, skimming occasionally to remove scum.

4 Lift the carcass from the broth and leave to cool. Strain the broth, and skim it to remove any fat. Return the broth to the pan and simmer gently, uncovered, until reduced to 1.2 litres/2 pints/5 cups.

5 Remove all the meat from the duck carcass and shred it finely. Set aside.

6 For the dumplings, soak the bread in the milk for 5 minutes. Remove the skin and fat from the duck breasts. Mince (grind) the meat with the liver and bacon. Squeeze the milk from the bread, then add the bread to the meat with the shallot, garlic, egg yolk, orange rind, paprika, flour and seasoning, and mix.

7 Form a spoonful of the mixture into a ball, a little smaller than a walnut. Repeat with the remaining mixture to make 20 small dumplings.

8 Bring a large pan of lightly salted water to the boil and poach the dumplings for 4–5 minutes, until they are just tender.

9 Bring the duck broth back to the boil and add the dumplings.

10 Divide the shredded duck meat among four warmed bowls and ladle in the broth and dumplings. Garnish with chives.

Energy 289Kcal/1214kJ; Protein 29.9g; Carbohydrate 19g, of which sugars 2.8g; Fat 13g, of which saturates 3.1g; Cholesterol 196mg; Calcium 63mg; Fibre 1.3g; Sodium 373mg.

MEAT SOUPS

Nourishing meaty soups are just the thing for warming you up on cold winter days. This section includes soups from all around the world — Irish Kidney and Bacon Soup, Mexican Beef Chilli with Nachos, Russian Pea and Barley Soup, and Japanese Miso Soup with Pork and Vegetables. For special occasions, try one of the delicious traditional Jewish soups — Beef and Lamb Broth, or Fragrant Beetroot and Vegetable Soup with Spiced Lamb Kubbeh.

COCK-A-LEEKIE WITH PUY LENTILS AND THYME

THIS ANCIENT SCOTTISH SOUP IS MADE WITH BOTH BEEF AND CHICKEN TO FLAVOUR THE BROTH. THE ADDITION OF PUY LENTILS GIVES THIS VERSION EVEN MORE EARTHINESS.

SERVES 4

INGREDIENTS

2 leeks, cut into 5cm/2in julienne
115g/4oz/½ cup Puy lentils
1 bay leaf
a few sprigs of fresh thyme
115g/4oz minced (ground) beef
2 skinless, boneless chicken breasts
900ml/1½ pints/3¾ cups good
  home-made beef stock
8 ready-to-eat prunes, cut into strips
salt and ground black pepper
fresh thyme sprigs, to garnish

1 Bring a small pan of salted water to the boil and cook the julienne of leeks for 1–2 minutes. Drain and refresh under cold running water. Drain again and set aside.

COOK'S TIP
To cut fine and even julienne strips, cut the leek into 5cm/2in lengths. Cut each piece in half lengthways, then with the cut side down, cut the leek into thin strips.

2 Pick over the lentils to check for any small stones or grit. Put into a pan with the bay leaf and thyme and cover with cold water. Bring to the boil and cook for 25–30 minutes until tender. Drain and refresh under cold water.

3 Put the minced beef and chicken breasts in a pan and pour over enough stock to cover them. Bring to the boil and cook gently for 15–20 minutes, or until tender. Using a slotted spoon, remove the chicken from the stock and leave to cool.

4 When the chicken is cool enough to handle, cut it into strips. Return it to the stock in the pan and add the lentils and the remaining stock. Bring just to the boil and add seasoning to taste.

5 Divide the leeks and prunes among four warmed bowls. Ladle over the hot chicken and lentil broth. Garnish each portion with a few fresh thyme sprigs and serve immediately.

Energy 275Kcal/1160kJ; Protein 32.3g; Carbohydrate 23.5g, of which sugars 7.4g; Fat 6.4g, of which saturates 2.4g; Cholesterol 70mg; Calcium 47mg; Fibre 4.1g; Sodium 82mg.

CELERIAC SOUP WITH BACON, CABBAGE AND HERBS

VERSATILE, YET OFTEN OVERLOOKED, CELERIAC IS A WINTER VEGETABLE THAT MAKES EXCELLENT SOUP. IT TASTES WONDERFUL TOPPED WITH A COMPLEMENTARY SEASONAL VERSION OF A SALSA.

SERVES 4

INGREDIENTS
  50g/2oz butter
  2 onions, chopped
  675g/1½lb celeriac,
    roughly diced
  450g/1lb potatoes, roughly diced
  1.2 litres/2 pints/5 cups
    vegetable stock
  150ml/¼ pint/⅔ cup single
    (light) cream
  salt and ground black pepper
  sprigs of fresh thyme, to garnish
For the cabbage and bacon topping
  1 small savoy cabbage
  50g/2oz/¼ cup butter
  175g/6oz rindless streaky (fatty)
    bacon, roughly chopped
  15ml/1 tbsp chopped fresh thyme
  15ml/1 tbsp chopped fresh rosemary

1 Melt the butter in a pan. Add the onions and cook for 4–5 minutes, until softened. Add the celeriac. Cover the vegetables with a wetted piece of baking parchment, then put a lid on the pan and cook gently for 10 minutes.

2 Remove the paper. Stir in the potatoes and stock, bring to the boil, reduce the heat and simmer for 20 minutes. Leave to cool slightly. Using a slotted spoon, remove half the celeriac and potatoes from the soup and set them aside.

3 Purée the soup in a food processor or blender. Return the soup to the pan with the reserved celeriac and potatoes.

4 Prepare the cabbage and bacon mixture. Discard the tough outer leaves from the cabbage. Roughly tear the remaining leaves, discarding any hard stalks, and blanch them in boiling salted water for 2–3 minutes. Refresh under cold running water and drain.

5 Melt the butter in a large frying pan and cook the bacon for 3–4 minutes. Add the cabbage, thyme and rosemary, and stir-fry for 5–6 minutes, until tender. Season well.

6 Add the cream to the soup and season it well, then reheat gently until piping hot.

7 Ladle the soup into warmed bowls and pile the cabbage mixture in the centre of each portion. Garnish with sprigs of fresh thyme.

VARIATION
Savoy cabbage is used for the topping in this dish, but other greens, such as kale or spring greens, would also be suitable.

Energy 462Kcal/1919kJ; Protein 12.3g; Carbohydrate 24.3g, of which sugars 7.3g; Fat 35.7g, of which saturates 20.4g; Cholesterol 97mg; Calcium 144mg; Fibre 4.3g; Sodium 954mg.

IRISH BACON BROTH

A HEARTY MEAL IN A SOUP BOWL. THE BACON HOCK CONTRIBUTES FLAVOUR AND SOME MEAT TO THIS DISH, BUT IT MAY BE SALTY SO REMEMBER TO TASTE AND ADD EXTRA SALT ONLY IF REQUIRED.

SERVES 6–8

INGREDIENTS

1 bacon hock, about 900g/2lb
75g/3oz/⅓ cup pearl barley
75g/3oz/⅓ cup lentils
2 leeks, sliced, or onions, diced
4 carrots, diced
200g/7oz swede (rutabaga), diced
3 potatoes, diced
small bunch of herbs (thyme, parsley, bay leaf)
1 small cabbage, trimmed and quartered or sliced
salt and ground black pepper
chopped fresh parsley, to garnish
brown bread, to serve

COOK'S TIP
Traditionally, the cabbage is simply trimmed and quartered, although it may be sliced if you prefer.

1 Soak the bacon in cold water overnight. Next morning, drain, put into a large pan and cover with cold water. Bring to the boil and skim off any scum. Add the barley and lentils. Bring back to the boil and simmer for 15 minutes.

2 Add the vegetables, some black pepper and the herbs. Bring back to the boil, reduce the heat and simmer gently for 1½ hours, or until the meat is tender.

3 Lift the bacon hock from the pan with a slotted spoon. Remove the skin, then take the meat off the bones and break it into bitesize pieces. Return to the pan with the cabbage. Discard the herbs and cook for a little longer until the cabbage is cooked to your liking.

4 Adjust the seasoning and ladle into serving bowls, garnish with parsley and serve with freshly baked brown bread.

Energy 276Kcal/1166kJ; Protein 26.6g; Carbohydrate 33.6g, of which sugars 8.4g; Fat 4.8g, of which saturates 1.6g; Cholesterol 13mg; Calcium 87mg; Fibre 4.8g; Sodium 765mg.

IRISH KIDNEY AND BACON SOUP

ALTHOUGH THERE IS A MODERN TWIST IN THE SEASONINGS, THE TWO MAIN INGREDIENTS OF THIS MEATY SOUP ARE STILL VERY TRADITIONALLY IRISH.

SERVES 4–6

INGREDIENTS

225g/8oz ox (beef) kidney
15ml/1 tbsp vegetable oil
4 streaky (fatty) bacon rashers
  (strips), chopped
1 large onion, chopped
2 garlic cloves, finely chopped
15ml/1 tbsp plain (all-purpose) flour
1.5 litres/2½ pints/6¼ cups water
a good dash of Worcestershire sauce
a good dash of soy sauce
15ml/1 tbsp chopped fresh thyme,
  or 5ml/1 tsp dried
75g/3oz/¾ cup grated cheese
4–6 slices French bread, toasted
salt and ground black pepper

1 Wash the kidney in cold, salted water. Drain, dry well on kitchen paper and chop into small pieces.

COOK'S TIP
Ox kidneys are tougher than veal or lamb, so they need to be cooked more slowly.

2 Heat the vegetable oil in a large pan over a medium heat. Add the chopped streaky bacon and sauté for a few minutes. Add the prepared kidney and continue cooking until nicely browned. Stir in the chopped onion and chopped garlic, and cook until the onion is just soft but not browned.

3 Add the flour and cook for 2 minutes. Gradually add the water, stirring constantly. Add the sauces, thyme and seasoning to taste. Reduce the heat and simmer gently for 30–35 minutes.

4 Sprinkle the cheese on to the toast and grill until it is bubbling. Pour the soup into bowls, and top with the bread.

Energy 379Kcal/1592kJ; Protein 23.7g; Carbohydrate 34g, of which sugars 3.2g; Fat 17g, of which saturates 7.1g; Cholesterol 184mg; Calcium 225mg; Fibre 1.6g; Sodium 1167mg.

RUSSIAN PEA, BACON AND BARLEY SOUP

THIS THICK AND WARMING SOUP, GROCHOWKA, MAKES A SUBSTANTIAL APPETIZER, OR IT MAY BE SERVED AS A MEAL IN ITS OWN RIGHT, EATEN WITH HOT CRUSTY BREAD.

3 Dry fry the bacon cubes in a frying pan for 5 minutes, or until well browned and crispy. Remove from the pan with a slotted spoon, leaving the fat behind, and set aside.

4 Add the butter to the frying pan, add the onion and garlic and cook gently for 5 minutes. Add the celeriac and cook for a further 5 minutes, or until the onion is just starting to colour.

SERVES 6

INGREDIENTS
  225g/8oz/1¼ cups yellow split peas, rinsed in cold water
  25g/1oz/¼ cup pearl barley, rinsed in cold water
  1.75 litres/3 pints/7½ cups vegetable or ham stock
  50g/2oz smoked streaky (fatty) bacon, cubed
  25g/1oz/2 tbsp butter
  1 onion, finely chopped
  2 garlic cloves, crushed
  225g/8oz celeriac, cubed
  15ml/1 tbsp roughly chopped fresh marjoram
  salt and freshly ground black pepper
  bread, to serve

1 Put the peas and barley in a bowl, cover with plenty of water and leave to soak overnight.

2 The next day, drain and rinse the peas and barley. Put them in a large pan, pour in the stock and bring to the boil. Turn down the heat and simmer gently for 40 minutes.

5 Add the softened vegetables and bacon to the pan of stock, peas and barley. Season lightly with salt and pepper, then cover and simmer for 20 minutes, or until the soup is thick. Stir in the marjoram, add extra black pepper to taste and serve with bread.

Energy 189Kcal/799kJ; Protein 11g; Carbohydrate 25.8g, of which sugars 1.8g; Fat 5.5g, of which saturates 2.8g; Cholesterol 13mg; Calcium 39mg; Fibre 2.4g; Sodium 190mg.

BACON <u>AND</u> CHICKPEA SOUP

THIS NUTTY SOUP IS DELICIOUS AND SO EASY TO MAKE. TAKE IT TO THE SOFA WITH A BOWL OF TORTILLA CHIPS AND DIP, CRUNCH AND SLURP YOUR WAY THROUGH YOUR FAVOURITE TELEVISION FIX.

SERVES 4–6

INGREDIENTS
  400g/14oz/2 cups dried chickpeas,
    soaked overnight in cold water
  115g/4oz/½ cup butter
  150g/5oz pancetta or streaky
    (fatty) bacon, roughly chopped
  2 onions, finely chopped
  1 carrot, chopped
  1 celery stick, chopped
  15ml/1 tbsp chopped fresh
    rosemary
  2 fresh bay leaves
  2 garlic cloves, halved

For the tortilla chips
  75g/3oz/6 tbsp butter
  2.5ml/½ tsp sweet paprika
  1.5ml/¼ tsp ground cumin
  175g/6oz plain tortilla chips
  salt and ground black pepper

1 Drain the chickpeas, put them in a large pan and cover with plenty of cold water. Bring to the boil and simmer for about 20 minutes. Strain and set aside.

2 Melt the butter in a large pan and add the pancetta or bacon. Fry over a medium heat until just beginning to turn golden. Add the chopped vegetables and cook for 5–10 minutes until soft.

COOK'S TIP
Packets of diced bacon are available in most supermarkets, and these are ideal for adding to soups.

3 Add the chickpeas to the pan with the rosemary, bay leaves, garlic cloves and enough water to cover completely. Bring to the boil, half cover, turn down the heat and simmer for 45–60 minutes, stirring occasionally. (The chickpeas should start to disintegrate and will thicken the soup.)

4 Allow the soup to cool slightly, then pour it into a blender or food processor and process until smooth. Return the soup to the rinsed-out pan, taste and season with salt and plenty of black pepper. Reheat gently.

5 To make the tortilla chips, preheat the oven to 180°C/350°F/Gas 4. Melt the butter with the paprika and cumin in a pan, then lightly brush the mixture over the tortilla chips. Reserve any leftover spiced butter.

6 Spread the chips out on a baking sheet and warm through in the oven for 5 minutes.

7 Ladle the soup into bowls, pour some of the reserved spiced butter over each and sprinkle with a little paprika. Serve with the warm tortilla chips.

Energy 996Kcal/4154kJ; Protein 31.4g; Carbohydrate 80.1g, of which sugars 6.6g; Fat 63.3g, of which saturates 30.1g; Cholesterol 126mg; Calcium 252mg; Fibre 14.3g; Sodium 1186mg.

MISO SOUP WITH PORK AND VEGETABLES

THIS IS QUITE A RICH AND FILLING SOUP. ITS JAPANESE NAME, TANUKI JIRU, MEANS RACCOON SOUP FOR HUNTERS, BUT AS RACCOONS ARE NOT EATEN NOWADAYS, PORK IS USED INSTEAD.

SERVES 4

INGREDIENTS

200g/7oz lean boneless pork
15cm/6in piece gobo or 1 parsnip
50g/2oz mooli (daikon)
4 fresh shiitake mushrooms
½ konnyaku or 125g/4½oz tofu
a little sesame oil, for stir-frying
600ml/1 pint/2½ cups second dashi
  stock, or the same amount of water
  and 10ml/2 tsp dashi-no-moto
70ml/4½ tbsp miso
2 spring onions (scallions), chopped
5ml/1 tsp sesame seeds

1 Press the meat down on a chopping board using the palm of your hand and slice horizontally into very thin long strips, then cut the strips crossways into stamp-size pieces. Set the pork aside.

2 Peel the gobo using a potato peeler, then cut diagonally into 1cm/½in thick slices. Quickly plunge the slices into a bowl of cold water to stop them discolouring. If you are using parsnip, peel, cut it in half lengthways, then cut it into 1cm/½in thick half-moon-shaped slices.

3 Peel and slice the mooli into 1.5cm/⅔in thick discs. Cut the discs into 1.5cm/⅔in cubes. Remove the shiitake stalks and cut the caps into quarters.

4 Place the konnyaku, if using, in a pan of boiling water and cook for 1 minute. Drain and cool. Cut in quarters lengthways, then crossways into 3mm/⅛in thick pieces.

5 Heat a little sesame oil in a heavy cast-iron or enamelled pan until purple smoke rises. Stir-fry the pork, then add the konnyaku or tofu and all the vegetables except for the spring onions. When the colour of the meat has changed, add the stock.

6 Bring to the boil over a medium heat, and skim off the foam until the soup looks fairly clear. Reduce the heat, cover and simmer for 15 minutes.

7 Put the miso in a small bowl and mix with 60ml/4 tbsp hot stock to make a smooth paste. Stir one-third of the miso into the soup; taste and add more if required. Add the spring onion and remove from the heat. Serve very hot in individual soup bowls, sprinkled with sesame seeds.

COOK'S TIPS
• Gobo is burdock root, and can be substituted with parsnip in this recipe.
• Mooli, also known as daikon, is a long, white vegetable which is a member of the radish family.
• Konnyaku is a gelatinous cake made from a relative of the sweet potato.

Energy 110Kcal/459kJ; Protein 16g; Carbohydrate 1.3g, of which sugars 0.9g; Fat 4.5g, of which saturates 1g; Cholesterol 32mg; Calcium 295mg; Fibre 0.4g; Sodium 573mg.

SWEET AND SOUR PORK SOUP

THIS VERY QUICK, SHARP AND TANGY SOUP IS PERFECT FOR AN INFORMAL SUPPER. IT IS JUST AS DELICIOUS WITH SHREDDED CHICKEN OR DUCK BREAST INSTEAD OF PORK.

SERVES 6–8

INGREDIENTS

900g/2lb pork fillet, trimmed
1 unripe papaya, halved, seeded, peeled and shredded
3 shallots, chopped
5 garlic cloves, chopped
5ml/1 tsp crushed black peppercorns
15ml/1 tbsp shrimp paste
30ml/2 tbsp vegetable oil
1.5 litres/2½ pints/6¼ cups chicken stock
2.5cm/1in piece fresh root ginger, grated
120ml/4fl oz/½ cup tamarind water
15ml/1 tbsp honey
juice of 1 lime
2 small red chillies, seeded and sliced
4 spring onions (scallions), sliced
salt and ground black pepper

1 Cut the pork into very fine strips, 5cm/2in long. Mix with the papaya and set aside. Process the shallots, garlic, peppercorns and shrimp paste in a food processor or blender to form a paste.

2 Heat the oil in a heavy-based pan and fry the paste for 1–2 minutes. Add the stock and bring to the boil. Reduce the heat. Add the pork and papaya, ginger and tamarind water.

3 Simmer the soup for 7–8 minutes, until the pork is tender.

4 Stir in the honey, lime juice, and most of the sliced chillies and spring onions. Season to taste with salt and ground black pepper.

5 Ladle the soup into bowls and serve immediately, garnished with the remaining chillies and onions.

Energy 229Kcal/963kJ; Protein 32.8g; Carbohydrate 11.1g, of which sugars 10.9g; Fat 6.2g, of which saturates 2.1g; Cholesterol 95mg; Calcium 37mg; Fibre 2.3g; Sodium 111mg.

KALE, CHORIZO <u>AND</u> POTATO SOUP
<u>WITH</u> FRENCH BREAD CROÛTONS

THIS HEARTY WINTER SOUP HAS A SPICY KICK TO IT, WHICH COMES FROM THE CHORIZO SAUSAGE.
IT IS WORTH BUYING THE BEST POSSIBLE CHORIZO SAUSAGE TO IMPROVE THE FLAVOUR.

SERVES 6–8

INGREDIENTS
    225g/8oz kale, stems removed
    225g/8oz chorizo sausage
    675g/1½lb red potatoes
    1.75 litres/3 pints/7½ cups
      vegetable stock
    5ml/1 tsp ground black pepper
    pinch cayenne pepper (optional)
    12 slices French bread, grilled
    salt and ground black pepper

1 Place the kale in a food processor
and process for a few seconds to chop
it finely.

2 Prick the sausages and place in
a pan with enough water to cover.
Simmer for 15 minutes. Drain and
cut into thin slices.

3 Cook the potatoes in lightly salted
boiling water for about 15 minutes or
until tender. Drain and place in a bowl,
then mash, adding a little of the cooking
liquid to form a thick paste.

COOK'S TIP
Chorizo sausage is usually sold whole or
cut into lengths or rounds.

4 Bring the vegetable stock to the boil
and add the kale. Add the chorizo and
simmer for 5 minutes. Add the paste
gradually, and simmer for 20 minutes.
Season with black pepper and cayenne.

5 Place bread slices in each bowl, and
pour over the soup. Serve, generously
sprinkled with pepper.

Energy 411Kcal/1740kJ; Protein 13.2g; Carbohydrate 69.3g, of which sugars 6.2g; Fat 11g, of which saturates 4.1g; Cholesterol 15mg; Calcium 140mg; Fibre 4g; Sodium 812mg.

SOUP OF TOULOUSE SAUSAGE WITH BORLOTTI BEANS AND BREADCRUMBS

A BIG-FILLER SOUP, THIS RECIPE IS BASED LOOSELY ON CASSOULET. FRENCH SAUSAGES AND ITALIAN BEANS CONTRIBUTE FLAVOUR AND SUBSTANCE, AND THE SOUP IS TOPPED WITH GOLDEN BREADCRUMBS.

SERVES 6

INGREDIENTS

 250g/9oz/generous 1¼ cups
  borlotti beans
 115g/4oz piece pancetta,
  finely chopped
 6 Toulouse sausages, thickly sliced
 1 large onion, finely chopped
 2 garlic cloves, chopped
 2 carrots, finely diced
 2 leeks, finely chopped
 6 tomatoes, peeled, seeded
  and chopped
 30ml/2 tbsp tomato purée (paste)
 1.27 litres/2¼ pints/5⅔ cups
  vegetable stock
 175g/6oz spring greens, roughly
  shredded
 25g/1oz/2 tbsp butter
 115g/4oz/2 cups fresh white
  breadcrumbs
 50g/2oz/⅔ cup freshly grated
  Parmesan cheese
 salt and ground black pepper

1 Put the borlotti beans in a large bowl, cover with plenty of cold water and leave to soak overnight.

2 Next day, place the beans in a pan, cover with plenty of cold water and bring to the boil, then boil for 10 minutes. Drain well.

3 Heat a large pan and dry fry the pancetta until browned and the fat runs. Add the sausages and cook for 4–5 minutes, stirring occasionally, until beginning to brown.

4 Add the onion and garlic and cook for 3–4 minutes until softened. Add the beans, carrots, leeks, tomatoes and tomato purée, then add the stock. Stir, bring to the boil and cover. Simmer for about 1¼ hours or until the beans are tender, then stir in the spring greens and cook for 12–15 minutes more. Season well.

5 Meanwhile, melt the butter in a frying pan and fry the breadcrumbs, stirring, for 4–5 minutes, until golden, then stir in the Parmesan.

6 Ladle the soup into six warmed bowls. Sprinkle the fried breadcrumb mixture over each portion. Serve with some warm crusty bread.

VARIATION
Toulouse sausage, which is flavoured with garlic, can be substituted with Polish kielbasa or Italian sweet sausage.

Energy 574Kcal/2405kJ; Protein 29g; Carbohydrate 47.7g, of which sugars 10.2g; Fat 31g, of which saturates 12.5g; Cholesterol 75mg, Calcium 281mg, Fibre 10.7g, Sodium 1179mg.

BEEF AND BARLEY SOUP

THIS TRADITIONAL IRISH FARMHOUSE SOUP MAKES A WONDERFULLY RESTORATIVE DISH ON A COLD DAY. THE FLAVOURS DEVELOP PARTICULARLY WELL IF IT IS MADE IN ADVANCE AND REHEATED.

SERVES 6–8

INGREDIENTS

450–675g/1–1½lb rib steak, or
   other stewing beef on the bone
2 large onions
50g/2oz/¼ cup pearl barley
50g/2oz/¼ cup green split peas
3 large carrots, chopped
2 white turnips, peeled and chopped
   into dice
3 celery stalks, chopped
1 large or 2 medium leeks, thinly
   sliced and thoroughly washed in
   cold water
sea salt and ground black pepper
chopped fresh parsley, to serve

1 Bone the meat and put the bones and half an onion, roughly sliced, into a large pan. Cover with cold water, season and bring to the boil. Skim if necessary, then simmer until needed.

2 Meanwhile, trim any fat or gristle from the meat and cut into small pieces. Chop the remaining onions finely. Drain the stock from the bones, make it up with water to 2 litres/3½ pints/9 cups, and return to the rinsed pan with the meat, onions, barley and split peas.

3 Season, bring to the boil, and skim if necessary. Reduce the heat, cover and simmer for about 30 minutes.

4 Add the rest of the vegetables and simmer for 1 hour, or until the meat is tender. Check the seasoning.

5 Serve in large warmed bowls, generously sprinkled with parsley.

Energy 167Kcal/705kJ; Protein 16g; Carbohydrate 21.4g, of which sugars 7.8g; Fat 2.6g, of which saturates 0.8g; Cholesterol 34mg; Calcium 54mg; Fibre 3.6g; Sodium 58mg.

MEXICAN BEEF CHILLI WITH NACHOS

STEAMING BOWLS OF BEEF CHILLI SOUP, PACKED WITH BEANS, ARE DELICIOUS TOPPED WITH CRUSHED TORTILLAS AND CHEESE. POP THE BOWLS UNDER THE GRILL TO MELT THE CHEESE, IF YOU WISH.

SERVES 4

INGREDIENTS

45ml/3 tbsp olive oil
350g/12oz rump steak, cut into
  small pieces
2 onions, chopped
2 garlic cloves, crushed
2 green chillies, seeded and
  finely chopped
30ml/2 tbsp mild chilli powder
5ml/1 tsp ground cumin
2 bay leaves
30ml/2 tbsp tomato purée (paste)
900ml/1½ pints/3¾ cups beef stock
2 x 400g/14oz cans mixed beans,
  drained and rinsed
45ml/3 tbsp chopped fresh coriander
  (cilantro) leaves
salt and ground black pepper

For the topping

bag of plain tortilla chips,
  lightly crushed
225g/8oz/2 cups Monterey Jack
  cheese, grated

1 Heat the oil in a large pan over a high heat and cook the meat all over until golden. Use a slotted spoon to remove it from the pan.

2 Reduce the heat and add the onions, garlic and chillies, then cook for 4–5 minutes, until softened.

VARIATION
Use Cheddar cheese instead of Monterey Jack if you prefer.

3 Add the chilli powder and ground cumin, and cook for a further 2 minutes. Return the meat to the pan, then stir in the bay leaves, tomato purée and beef stock. Bring to the boil.

4 Reduce the heat, cover the pan and simmer for about 45 minutes, or until the meat is tender.

5 Put a quarter of the beans into a bowl and mash with a potato masher. Stir these into the soup to thicken it slightly. Add the remaining beans and simmer for about 5 minutes. Season and stir in the chopped coriander. Ladle the soup into warmed bowls and spoon tortilla chips on top. Pile grated cheese over the tortilla chips and serve.

Energy 749Kcal/3135kJ; Protein 50g; Carbohydrate 54.1g, of which sugars 10.3g; Fat 37.2g, of which saturates 16.1g; Cholesterol 106mg; Calcium 609mg; Fibre 14.5g; Sodium 1473mg.

IRISH COUNTRY SOUP

Traditionally, buttered chunks of brown bread, or Irish soda bread, would be served with this hearty one-pot meal which is based on the classic Irish stew.

SERVES 4

INGREDIENTS

15ml/1 tbsp vegetable oil
675g/1½lb boneless lamb chump
  chops, trimmed and cut into
  small cubes
2 small onions, quartered
2 leeks, thickly sliced
1 litre/1¾ pints/4 cups water
2 large potatoes, cut into chunks
2 carrots, thickly sliced
sprig of fresh thyme, plus extra
  to garnish
15g/½oz/1 tbsp butter
30ml/2 tbsp chopped fresh parsley
salt and ground black pepper
brown or Irish soda bread, to serve

VARIATION
The vegetables can be varied according
to the season. Swede (rutabaga), turnip,
celeriac and even cabbage could be
added in place of some of those listed.

1 Heat the oil in a large pan, add
the lamb in batches and fry, turning
occasionally, until well browned all over.
Use a slotted spoon to remove the lamb
from the pan and set aside.

2 When all the lamb has been browned,
add the onions to the pan and cook
for 4–5 minutes, until the onions are
browned. Return the meat to the pan
and add the leeks. Pour in the water,
then bring to the boil. Reduce the heat,
then cover and simmer for about 1 hour.

3 Add the potatoes, carrots and fresh
thyme, and cook for 40 minutes, until
the lamb is tender. Remove from the
heat and leave to stand for 5 minutes,
then skim off the fat.

4 Pour off the stock into a clean pan
and whisk the butter into it. Stir in the
parsley and season well, then pour the
liquid back over the soup ingredients.

5 Ladle the soup into warmed bowls
and garnish with sprigs of fresh thyme.

Energy 453Kcal/1893kJ; Protein 36.5g; Carbohydrate 20.5g, of which sugars 6.2g; Fat 25.6g, of which saturates 11.3g; Cholesterol 136mg; Calcium 53mg; Fibre 3.7g; Sodium 185mg.

ROAST LAMB SHANKS IN BARLEY BROTH

SUCCULENT ROASTED LAMB SHANKS STUDDED WITH GARLIC AND ROSEMARY MAKE A FABULOUS MEAL WHEN SERVED IN A HEARTY VEGETABLE, BARLEY AND TOMATO BROTH.

SERVES 4

INGREDIENTS
  4 small lamb shanks
  4 garlic cloves, cut into slivers
  handful of fresh rosemary sprigs
  30ml/2 tbsp olive oil
  2 carrots, diced
  2 celery sticks, diced
  1 large onion, chopped
  1 bay leaf
  few sprigs of fresh thyme
  1.2 litres/2 pints/5 cups
    lamb stock
  50g/2oz pearl barley
  450g/1lb tomatoes, peeled and
    roughly chopped
  grated rind of 1 large lemon
  30ml/2 tbsp chopped fresh parsley
  salt and ground black pepper

1 Preheat the oven to 150°C/300°F/ Gas 2. Make small cuts all over the lamb and insert slivers of garlic and sprigs of rosemary into them.

2 Heat the oil in a flameproof casserole and brown the shanks two at a time. Remove and set aside. Add the carrots, celery and onion in batches and cook until lightly browned. Put all the vegetables in the casserole with the bay leaf and thyme. Pour in stock to cover, place the lamb shanks on top and roast for 2 hours.

3 Meanwhile, pour the remaining stock into a large saucepan. Add the pearl barley, then bring to the boil. Reduce the heat, cover and simmer for 1 hour, or until the barley is tender.

4 Remove the lamb shanks from the casserole using a slotted spoon.

5 Skim the fat from the surface of the roasted vegetables, then add them to the broth. Stir in the tomatoes, lemon rind and parsley.

6 Bring the soup back to the boil. Reduce the heat and simmer for 5 minutes. Add the lamb shanks and heat through, then season. Put a lamb shank into each of four large bowls, then ladle the barley broth over the meat and serve at once.

Energy 287Kcal/1199kJ; Protein 22.5g; Carbohydrate 19.5g, of which sugars 7.6g; Fat 13.1g, of which saturates 0.9g; Cholesterol 0mg; Calcium 35mg; Fibre 2.3g; Sodium 24mg.

LAMB <u>AND</u> VEGETABLE BROTH

THIS IS A GOOD MODERN ADAPTATION OF THE TRADITIONAL RECIPE FOR IRISH MUTTON BROTH, KNOWN LOCALLY AS BRACHÁN CAOIREOLA, AND IS DELICIOUS SERVED WITH WHOLEMEAL BREAD TO MAKE A FILLING LUNCH DISH ON A COLD WINTER'S DAY.

SERVES 6

INGREDIENTS
    675g/1½lb best end of neck of lamb
       on the bone (cross rib)
    1 large onion
    2 bay leaves
    3 carrots, chopped
    ½ white turnip, diced
    ½ small white cabbage, shredded
    2 large leeks, thinly sliced
    15ml/1 tbsp tomato purée (paste)
    30ml/2 tbsp chopped fresh parsley
    salt and ground black pepper

COOK'S TIP
Best end of neck (cross rib) is the rib
joint between the middle neck and loin.
It is the best cut to use for this soup.

1 Trim any excess fat from the meat.
Chop the onion, and put the lamb
and bay leaves in a large pan. Add
1.5 litres/2½ pints/6¼ cups water and
bring to the boil. Skim the surface
and then simmer for about 1½–2 hours.
Remove the lamb on to a board and
leave to cool until ready to handle.

2 Remove the meat from the bones
and cut into small pieces. Discard the
bones and return the meat to the broth.
Add the vegetables, tomato purée and
parsley, and season well. Simmer for
another 30 minutes, until the vegetables
are just tender. Ladle into warmed soup
bowls and serve piping hot.

Energy 167Kcal/696kJ; Protein 14.6g; Carbohydrate 10.5g, of which sugars 9g; Fat 7.6g, of which saturates 3.4g; Cholesterol 48mg; Calcium 58mg; Fibre 3.7g; Sodium 81mg.

BEEF AND LAMB BROTH

THIS TRADITIONAL JEWISH CHAMIM IS MADE WITH SAVOURY MEATS AND CHICKPEAS, BAKED IN A VERY LOW OVEN FOR SEVERAL HOURS. A PARCEL OF RICE IS OFTEN ADDED TO THE BROTH PART WAY THROUGH COOKING, WHICH PRODUCES A LIGHTLY PRESSED RICE WITH A SLIGHTLY CHEWY TEXTURE.

SERVES 8

INGREDIENTS
  250g/9oz/1 cup chickpeas,
    soaked overnight
  45ml/3 tbsp olive oil
  1 onion, chopped
  10 garlic cloves, chopped
  1 parsnip, sliced
  3 carrots, sliced
  5–10ml/1–2 tsp ground cumin
  2.5ml/½ tsp ground turmeric
  15ml/1 tbsp chopped fresh root ginger
  2 litres/3½ pints/8 cups beef stock
  1 potato, peeled and cut into chunks
  ½ marrow (large zucchini), sliced or
    cut into chunks
  400g/14oz fresh or canned
    tomatoes, diced
  45–60ml/3–4 tbsp brown or
    green lentils
  2 bay leaves
  250g/9oz salted meat such as
    salt beef (or double the quantity
    of lamb)
  250g/9oz piece of lamb
  ½ large bunch fresh coriander
    (cilantro), chopped
  200g/7oz/1 cup long grain rice
  1 lemon, cut into wedges, and a
    spicy sauce such as fresh chillies,
    finely chopped, to serve

1 Preheat the oven to 120°C/250°F/ Gas ½. Drain the chickpeas.

2 Heat the oil in a large flameproof casserole, add the onion, garlic, parsnip, carrots, cumin, turmeric and ginger and cook for 2–3 minutes. Add the chickpeas, stock, potato, marrow, tomatoes, lentils, bay leaves, salted meat, lamb and coriander. Cover and cook in the oven for about 3 hours.

COOK'S TIP
Add 1–2 pinches of bicarbonate of soda (baking soda) to the soaking chickpeas to make them tender, but do not add too much as it can make them mushy.

3 Put the rice on a double thickness of muslin (cheesecloth) and tie together at the corners, allowing enough room for the rice to expand while it is cooking.

4 Two hours before the end of cooking, remove the casserole from the oven. Place the rice parcel in the casserole, anchoring the edge of the muslin parcel under the lid so that the parcel is held above the soup and allowed to steam. Return the casserole to the oven and continue cooking for a further 2 hours.

5 Carefully remove the lid and the rice. Skim any fat off the top of the soup and ladle the soup into bowls with a scoop of the rice and one or two pieces of meat. Serve with lemon wedges and a spoonful of hot sauce or chopped fresh chillies.

Energy 385Kcal/1621kJ; Protein 25.6g; Carbohydrate 48.6g, of which sugars 5.3g; Fat 10.8g, of which saturates 2.7g; Cholesterol 24mg; Calcium 116mg; Fibre 5.4g; Sodium 54mg.

FRAGRANT BEETROOT AND VEGETABLE SOUP WITH SPICED LAMB KUBBEH

THE JEWISH COMMUNITY FROM COCHIN IN INDIA IS SCATTERED NOW BUT IS STILL FAMOUS FOR ITS CUISINE. THIS TANGY SOUP IS SERVED WITH DUMPLINGS MADE OF BRIGHT YELLOW PASTA WRAPPED AROUND A SPICY LAMB FILLING, AND A DOLLOP OF FRAGRANT GREEN HERB PASTE.

SERVES 6–8

INGREDIENTS
15ml/1 tbsp vegetable oil
½ onion, finely chopped
6 garlic cloves
1 carrot, diced
1 courgette (zucchini), diced
½ celery stick, diced (optional)
4–5 cardamom pods
2.5ml/½ tsp curry powder
4 vacuum-packed beetroot (beets)
   (cooked not pickled), finely diced
   and juice reserved
1 litre/1¾ pints/4 cups
   vegetable stock
400g/14oz can chopped tomatoes
45–60ml/3–4 tbsp chopped fresh
   coriander (cilantro) leaves
2 bay leaves
15ml/1 tbsp sugar
salt and ground black pepper
15–30ml/1–2 tbsp white wine
   vinegar, to serve
For the kubbeh
2 large pinches of saffron threads
15ml/1 tbsp hot water
15ml/1 tbsp vegetable oil
1 large onion, chopped
250g/9oz lean minced (ground) lamb
5ml/1 tsp vinegar
½ bunch fresh mint, chopped
115g/4oz/1 cup plain (all-purpose) flour
2–3 pinches of salt
2.5–5ml/½–1 tsp ground turmeric
45–60ml/3–4 tbsp cold water
For the ginger and coriander paste
4 garlic cloves, chopped
15–25ml/1–1½ tbsp chopped
   fresh root ginger
½–4 fresh mild chillies
½ large bunch fresh coriander
   (cilantro)
30ml/2 tbsp white wine vinegar
extra virgin olive oil

COOK'S TIP
Serve any leftover paste with meatballs or spread on sandwiches.

1 For the paste, process the garlic, ginger and chillies in a food processor. Add the coriander, vinegar, oil and salt and process to a purée. Set aside.

2 To make the kubbeh filling, place the saffron and hot water in a small bowl and leave to infuse (steep). Meanwhile, heat the oil in a pan and fry the onion until softened. Put the onion and saffron water in a food processor and blend. Add the lamb, season and blend. Add the vinegar and mint, then chill.

3 To make the kubbeh dough, put the flour, salt and ground turmeric in a food processor, then gradually add the water, processing until it forms a sticky dough. Knead on a floured surface for 5 minutes, wrap in a plastic bag and leave to stand for 30 minutes.

4 Divide the dough into 10–15 pieces. Roll each into a ball, then, using a pasta machine, roll into very thin rounds.

5 Lay the rounds on a well-floured surface. Place a spoonful of filling in the middle of each. Dampen the edges of the dough, then bring them together and seal. Set aside on a floured surface.

6 To make the soup, heat the oil in a pan, add the onion and fry for about 10 minutes, or until softened but not browned. Add half the garlic, the carrot, courgette, celery (if using), cardamom pods and curry powder, and cook for 2–3 minutes.

7 Add three of the diced beetroot, the stock, tomatoes, coriander, bay leaves and sugar to the pan. Bring to the boil, then reduce the heat and simmer for about 20 minutes.

8 Add the remaining beetroot, beetroot juice and garlic to the soup. Season with salt and pepper to taste and set aside until ready to serve.

9 To serve, reheat the soup and poach the dumplings in a large pan of salted boiling water for about 4 minutes. Using a slotted spoon, remove the dumplings from the water as they are cooked and place on a plate to keep warm.

10 Ladle the soup into bowls, adding a dash of vinegar to each bowl, then add two or three dumplings and a small spoonful of the ginger and coriander paste to each. Serve immediately.

Energy 210Kcal/881kJ; Protein 11.6g; Carbohydrate 22.1g, of which sugars 6.8g; Fat 9g, of which saturates 2.7g; Cholesterol 32mg; Calcium 55mg; Fibre 2.5g; Sodium 74mg.

INDEX

Architecture for the future

Architecture for the future

·TERRAIL·

Front cover illustration
Lyons Opera House,
France.
Jean Nouvel.

Frontispiece
Exhibition Hall,
Nagoya, Japan.
Itsuko Hasegawa.

Editors : Jean-Claude Dubost and Jean-François Gonthier
Cover design : Gérard Lo Monaco and Laurent Gudin
Art Director : Bruno Leprince
Editorial Assistant : Claire Néollier
English Text adapted by Peter Snowdon
Typesetting : Graffic, Paris
Origination : Litho Service T. Zamboni, Verona

© ÉDIGROUP/ÉDITIONS TERRAIL, PARIS 2004
25-27, Rue Ginoux - 75015 Paris - France
ISBN: 2-87939-028-1
Printed in France

CONTENTS

PERPETUAL MOTION

Foreword by Olivier Boissière

Prediction is a hazardous exercise. Even H.G.Wells and Aldous Huxley got it wrong. 1984 has come and gone. Big Brother is merely a ghostly memory and we are still waiting for our Brave New World.

It might seem paradoxical, naive, even pretentious to try and assess the future, but there are at least two good reasons for attempting to do so. First of all, architecture is itself an art of the future, a perpetual project whose plans are constantly being redrawn. The second reason is more concrete and more reassuring: architecture is a slow-moving art, closely dependent on economic, political and social factors, and on changing fashions. It is therefore quite legitimate to attempt to decipher premonitory signs, symptoms, and trends in contemporary architectures, from which we might cautiously infer long-term consequences.

Utopia and science fiction share two characteristics. One is a positive ambition to develop a specific vision of the world's and of mankind's future. The other is a propensity to edit out some fundamental aspect of reality, introducing in its place some purely imaginary condition: thus gravity may cease to exist, or the natural rhythm of the seasons come to a halt.

During what has been called its "heroic"[1] period, architecture embraced two overlapping utopias. The first, inspired by a new industrial impetus in the aftermath of the First World War, credited rationalised production with the supernatural power to create an ideal order which would utterly transform society, liberate creative forces, and give birth to a new man. The second – perhaps a mere illusion – was the idea that the architect, whose scope of activity would range from industrial design to town planning (from the dessert spoon to the city), would be the agent of such transformation, a literal *deus ex machina* capable of shaping a destiny for mankind: "Architecture or Revolution" as Le Corbusier ill-advisedly put it. The result was a spate of speeches and manifestos, of movements – De Stijl in the Netherlands, Constructivism in the Soviet Union – and schools, such as the Bauhaus in Weimar, and later Dessau, or the Vkhutmas in Moscow.

Conic intersection
Paris, 1975
Gordon Matta Clark (1943 - 1978)

An architectural intervention on the last 18th-century buildings in an area undergoing redevelopment. Through the cone, the Pompidou Centre, then under construction, was visible from a totally unexpected angle.

---

1. In general, this period is taken to run between 1910 and 1933. Cf. Peter and Alison Smithson, *The Heroic Period of Modern Architecture*, Thames& Hudson, London, 1981.

The most notorious heralds of this impending golden age were Van Doesburg and El Lissitzky, Walter Gropius and Le Corbusier[*]. A new vision was taking shape.

Vilém Flusser[2] aptly reminds us that our term "theory" derives from the Greek word for "vision" – *theoria*. A new theory was accordingly elaborated, which sought to do away with the "old architecture" and establish a new framework worthy of democracy triumphant. It aimed to transform both the city and life, freeing the forces of reason to build an ideal world. This universal ambition rapidly veered towards dogmatism. Le Corbusier's 'five points', for instance – free plan, horizontal strip windows, pilotis, roof-gardens, and free, non-load-bearing facades – were they not simply intended to replace the tenets of 19th-century treatises? Argument still rages, not as to their relative validity but as to their original intent: were such theoretical principles *constructional* or *aesthetic*? In 1932, the Americans Philip Johnson and Henry-Russell Hitchcock (the dandy and the critic) offered their response and sounded the knell of utopia by calling their exhibition at the New York Museum of Modern Art, "The International Style". When all was said and done, was it merely a question of style? Messianic modern architecture had had its day. The barque of love had foundered on the rocks of everyday life. Then came the invasion of Poland, Pearl Harbour, Stalingrad, the Holocaust and Hiroshima, the Berlin Wall and Vietnam, the loss of innocence and the fall from grace. The architect had to come to terms with the new world order: he was not to be the demiurge, the catalyst of social change he had dreamed of becoming, but merely an obscure hero with limited responsibilities. Rather than shaping life, he would design its context, giving form – where possible discreetly – to the *genius loci* and to the spirit of the age.

Objects fused together by heat from the bomb at Hiroshima
1945.

Today, if a utopian yearning still exists, it is a purely regressive phenomenon, represented by those few who still proclaim their nostalgic faith in a society free of concrete and metal, social tension and unemployment.

Within a few decades, both the 20th century and architecture have witnessed the demise of over-arching narratives, all-embracing ideologies and infexible dogmas. In a complex and contradictory world where reality is fragmentary, they have shed their illusions. A single, vast, inoperable theory has been replaced by a galaxy of small, usable, "tool-box"[3] theories tailored to projects limited in time and space. Deprived of a grand scheme, architecture has reappropriated a territory of its own, where the useful and the sublime have, somehoro, been reconciled.

And what of progress? It remains the central preoccupation for a significant number of architects, despite a popularly held view that its effects are highly questionable, if not directly nefarious. And rightly so! The veritable advent of modern architecture was marked by technical innovation – metallic structures, clad in concrete, traversed by lifts. Technology has transformed architecture irreversibly. A list of the milestones in this saga would clearly include Crystal Palace[*], Le Baron Jenney's steel-framed building in Chicago[4], the Eiffel Tower, the Flat Iron building in New York, and the now demolished hangar at Orly by Freyssinet. To which might well be added

2. Vilém Flusser, philosopher and theoretician, in *World Architecture* n°27, 1993.
3. Michel Foucault and Gilles Deleuze, in *L'Arc*, 1972.
4. *Home Insurance Building*, 1885.

* For names and terms followed by an asterisk, see glossary.

the Crimean War assembly-kit field hospital designed and built by the great engineer Isambard Kingdom Brunel[*] for the intrepid nurse Florence Nightingale, whose component parts were dismantled, recycled and sold off after hostilities had ceased.

It is therefore hardly surprising that architects have been enthralled by the fantasy of technical progress. This century counts a number of brilliant innovators, architects-cum-engineers, and engineers-cum-architects, such as the American Buckminster Fuller, the Frenchman Jean Prouvé, the Italians Morandi and Nervi, the Mexican Felix Candela, and Britain's Ove Arup, Peter Rice and Tony Fitzpatrick[*]. Working alone or in partnership, they explore the limits of constructional technique, constantly on the look-out for new materials, carrying out *ad hoc* transfers of technology from space research or polymer chemistry. They play a vital role in boosting performance levels, lightening structures, and freeing up large, flexible spaces. Champions of constructive truth or willing victims of the machine aesthetic, these technological crusaders might well have pursued low-key, somewhat marginal careers had it not been for the founding of Archigram[*] in the early 1960s. In a short-lived blaze of activity, the effects of which are still felt today, this exhuberent young group of designers introduced an explosive blend of the best in the British engineering tradition with the extravagance of the fashion world, the blare of advertising, and the imminent sexual revolution, propelling architecture into the MacLuhan galaxy. The Pompidou Centre remains the most fully-achieved demonstration of the Archigram approach although it is now quite dated: in today's automated, miniaturised world, this type of technical expressivism is on the wane. A new preoccupation, that of form, is emerging among the high-tech generation. But was the absence of form not already a kind of form in itself?

Victor Hugo had predicted the death of architecture, believing that the spread of the written word would deprive the former of its code-bearing role. Were the late 19th century and the budding industrial revolution the swan song of this art form? Never in its history had architecture experienced such unbridled eclecticism, such a riot of ornamentation. Young, modern architects were nauseated by the turn-of-the-century surfeit of ornate motifs, Viennese frills, and Art Nouveau circumvolutions. The Viennese architect Adolf Loos[*] denounced ornamentation as a crime; sobiety was the order of the day. Armed with the new, definitive conviction that beauty was use, they developed a rigorous rationalism, in which a puritanical respect for geometrical form was barely tempered by a taste for colour, where possible primary. It is to be noted that this approach was the fruit of a dominant, yet by no means exclusive school of thought: the champions of functional architecture like Gropius and Mies Van der Rohe[*], before presiding over the fortunes of the Bauhaus, had been enthusiastic members of the Novembergruppe[*], whose members pusued a highly imaginative and expressionistic style and which survived long after those two masters had made their U-turn. Nor could the use of form by the Russian Constructivists have properly been called ascetic.

The post-war spread of the International Style signalled its decline: the pursuit of "pure" architecture mercilessly exposed mediocrity. Few could match Mies Van der Rohe and mute curtain-wall facades were soon a worn-out cliché. The rehabilitation of form was heralded by Robert Venturi[*].

The Eiffel Tower under construction 1889.

In two seminal works – two "gentle manifestos" – *Complexity and Contradiction in Architecture* and *Learning from Las Vegas*, Venturi revalorized an architecture that was rich, inclusive and "impure", deriving its references both from history and from an emerging, vibrant, popular culture. By pinpointing street life, commercial advertising, and shopping malls as the crucibles of urban vitality, Venturi was, perhaps unwittingly, among those responsible for bringing architecture back down to earth, and for putting an end to the discipline's relative autonomy. Then came the Ronchamp* chapel in the French Jura, which astonished the public (and was a subject of great perplexity for the young James Stirling*). Le Corbusier, apostle of the "machine for living in", author of the "ode to the right angle", had produced this complicated, generous, sensual building, full of folds and curves. Architecture was awakening from a long sleep; it shook itself and, gazing around, realised that the world was changing. It rediscovered its affinities with the visual arts and their evolution over the past half-century. Suprematism, Concrete Art and Expressionism were reappraised. Neo-Dadaism, Pop Art, Minimal and Conceptual Art were embraced. It became clear that an infinite variety of possibilities had replaced monopolistic conformity as the contemporary aesthetic. Technology has removed all barriers. Cultural homogenisation brought about by the free flow of information has paradoxically engendered the assertion of identity and difference. The proliferation of images has invested the semantic field with a new importance, thus proving Victor Hugo wrong, and allowing architecture once more freely to encapsulate the spirit of its time and to embody the *genius loci*. By ignoring geography and pursuing the *tabula rasa* as an obsession, modern architecture had ended up by confusing context and world, nature and public gardens. The energy crisis and a new ecological awareness brought it back down to earth. Think globally, act locally: such is the watchword of a whole generation, one which also ponders the type of relationships it can establish with a natural world that has been profoundly altered by industrial society. A new sensitivity to natural phenomena and the ways in which they can be harnessed by technology is emerging, filtering the heat of the sun and taming the wind, creating a relationship that is at once economical and sensual. Beautiful *and* useful?

"Light is", proclaimed the great American architect Louis Kahn. He had in mind divine, natural light, the distant gleam of the stars. He pretended not to know, or to consider as insignificant, that man in his infinite ingenuity had invented electricity. More than a century after its appearance, electricity continues to fascinate. Produced nowadays from a wide variety of sources, its multi-coloured light pervades our cities and their architecture.

One day in 1925, the Italian physicist and Nobel prize winner, Guglielmo Marconi, transmitted a radio signal from his boat in the Mediterranean that, by a single pulse, flooded the City Hall in Sydney with light. Our late 20th-century architects should spare him a kindly thought. For a handful of them are striving to create just such a miraculous aesthetic, as they explore the fields of electronics and communication, investigate networks and fibre optics, and connect up to video screens and computers. The architecture they hold out as a promise, and of which we have already been offered glimpses, is made of images, swirling clouds, holograms and

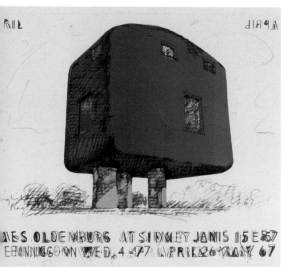

Building in the shape of an electric plug
1967.
Gouache.
Claes Oldenburg

insubstantial veils. It is an immaterial architecture, a conjurer's architecture revealing the futility and anxiety of a society in a state of continuous flux.

The texts and images which follow highlight a wide range of questions and possible answers. Through them, a vision of the future is slowly taking shape.

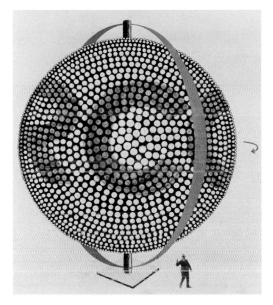

Project for a luminous advertizing sphere
1924.
Herbert Bayer

Project for Peace Pavilion
Universal Exhibition, Paris, 1937.
Laprade and Bazin

1. ATTITUDES

"Not happiness for all, but happiness for each of us".
Boris Vian

The end of our century has been marked by the collapse of ideology and the demise of grand theoretical ambition. Architecture too has had its share of would-be universal principles, of unique and definitive solutions to the fate of humankind, of dogmatic excess. But this is no longer a time for all-embracing manifestos, whose weaknesses are all too quickly exposed by reality.

Faced with a world that is both complex and unpredictable, architectural thinking has become both more modest and more pragmatic. Rather than elaborating grand theories, the emphasis is on foregrounding given situations, small-scale predicaments and specific attitudes. A "soft" approach. The age of proselytism is past. Theory is now the "tool box" of the philosophers Foucault and Deleuze. It is necessarily active, and its activity may be what saves it from delusions of its own importance.

The texts in this section demonstrate the diversity of preoccupations and perspectives that prevails in the profession today. They raise some central questions about architecture, the world, and the relationship between the two: the role of the avant-garde (Peter Cook); the threat to modernity (Daniel Libeskind); the event as the structuring element in the project (Bernard Tschumi); the renewal of the phenomenology of perception (Arakawa and Gins); war as a context for architecture (Lebbeus Woods); and strategies for confronting an elusive reality (François Roche).

This mosaic of reflections represents, of course, only one small part of the wide range of ideas that are at work in architecture today. ■

Opposite
National Studio for Contemporary Art
Tourcoing, France.
Bernard Tschumi

PETER COOK

London, Great Britain

In optimistic, swinging London, in the early sixties, the emergence of Peter Cook and Archigram* was a revolution of the same order as pop and the miniskirt. Archigram took all the ideas that had been debated throughout the fifties by the Independent Group*, a group combining artists and critics, – took them literally, and tried to give them form, drawing on the conventions of the cartoon strip. Over the space of ten years, Archigram was to invent a hedonistic architectural vision of the future that paid homage to technology, the media and consumer society. In doing so, it determined (particularly in the work of Cedric Price*) the archetypes of British high-tech.

Since that time, Peter Cook has continued to create his own architecture, based on flexible programmes and an ecological awareness. Visually, his work has become more gentle and more expressive, as it has made space for nature and for colour.

Notes on an Avant-Garde Architecture
Essay

At this moment in history we are supposed to be wary of the role of the avant-garde, perhaps because it was predominant in the early part of the century and therefore at the wrong time for us in terms of acceptable historical cycles, or perhaps because it threatens the neat structure of architectural categorization by its maverick patterns of play.

The avant-garde often set itself against the procedures of the day, as well as its icons. At its best, however, it attempted to explode the entire system of relationships: dismantling the language of criticism, the tonal scale, the frame, or the medium of transmission while affronting the eye, mind, or ear with more than a mere alternative. Perhaps the major weakness of much architectural avant-gardism is its habit of integrating itself back into the mainstream at too early a point. While this is understandable in that architecture is a social and useful art, it is puzzling in light of the plethora of drawn architectural statements of the last few years. Even without being partisan as to style or content, one can say that very few architectural projects attend to the question of fundamental composition or the aesthetics of the chain of events, although literature, music, and dance have been involved in just such a revolution within the same period. Daniel Libeskind, in his ability to sum up gambits that are clearly related to both mathematics and music, Coop Himmelblau in their consistent attempt to "dart" across all the carefully documented niceties of task, place, and space by capturing the instantaneous, the first gesture – each in their own way displays a fearlessness and, more

Office Building
Hamburg, Germany.

15

significantly, a wish to bypass (or is it reinvent?) the tyranny of additive and circumstantial thinking in architecture. In this sense, they are surely in the tradition of the best of the avant-garde. We can examine their work on the level of a captured dynamic, whether or not the actual artefacts have a symbolic dynamic. Essentially, they contribute to the re-creation of the culture of architecture by concentrating upon its process.

Sudden lurches of architectural magic do occur in a particular place, and the spirit of the individuals concerned is bound up with their view of themselves in that place and of that place. In the nineteenth century we could find great cities of action - Glasgow, Buffalo, Berlin - where architecture could run along beside the audacities and aspirations of the city and therefore include a disproportionately large quantity of inventive (and opportunistic) building. Other cities, emerging as replacements of Vienna, Rome, or St. Petersburg, craved cultural recognition. Sometimes they strove to define sophistication by adopting a high style, as in the case of Brussels and Art Nouveau. In the twentieth century it has become a more furious and less monumental trade, one of money, power, and influence, with the architecturally interesting cities distributed unevenly. Any examination of these cities has to take into account the particular city's aspirations, its patronage structure and how that may be manifested, and – to use that word again – its "spirit."

The greatest cities do not fit comfortably into this scheme. New York is too supportive of the idea of measurable (and provable) success to easily handle the new at the point of pain, preferring to wait until creative clones have been bred. Paris is too much in love with the memory of its position as the cradle of the artistic avant-garde to be able to do more than host visiting virtuosi – hence the programme of Grands Projets. (It remains to be seen whether these will act as a catalyst for any creative architectural life within the Paris studios themselves.) At the same time, London is experiencing one of its periodic fits of philistinism, encouraged by the Prince of Wales; any evidence of strange or inventive work is viewed as part of the tradition of English eccentricity and therefore amusing but harmless (meaning, of course, not worth bothering about).

Yet such cities possess more than their fair share of influence. Air travel and the accumulation of academies, publishing houses, and world-networked professionals feed the insidious (though creative) institution of architectural chitchat. This in itself becomes a useful structure within which to shock, amaze, and tantalize, generating a vicious competitiveness that favours the energetic and ambitious while forcing a certain conformity on potentially original work.

What is important in determining the essential difference between most "spirited" architecture and work that has coarsely been termed "post-modern", is the question of space, physical ambition, and rhetoric. The post-modern condition most often depends on figuration, profile, automation, and a com-positional manner more akin to graphic design than to three-dimensional design. What links the opportunistic design of the nineteenth century, modernism and the new explosive architecture lies outside these constraints. The new work also does not need quotation to gain our interest. In some senses it is more primeval, inherently tantalized by the challenge of capturing space and welding substance; it reminds one of the effort involved and then revels in some of the distortions and diversions possible along the way. The fascination, for instance, that Toyo Ito and Itsuko Hasegawa have with layering

Way Out West
Berlin, Germany.
Elevation from the square.

semi-transparent skins and then drawing analogies between them and the natural phenomena of clouds or forests remains a primeval wish to be associated with the basic observable elements of nature.

The distance of their city, Tokyo, from the rest of the world in which twentieth-century architecture is discussed and exchanged forces a self-consciousness that manifests itself in two ways. The first is the awareness of layers and layers of accumulated sophistication that involve craft, myth, placement, illusion, and manners. The other is a delight in the newness and the sheer availability of the fruits of the twentieth century. Hasegawa can only have experienced joy in landing large domes and metallic hills and forests in a dreary part of Tokyo's outer suburbia, in the same way that Masaharu Takasaki must have revelled in placing his egg-like form and its attendant antennae into the bourgeois area of Shinjuku in Tokyo. Of course, we can soften the argument by remembering that Tokyo is essentially a city of bricolage, where there are frequent shifts of reference, grain, intensity, and substance. Nonetheless, it remains the most potentially ripe ground for new and experimental architecture.

In the ostensibly different conditions of Los Angeles, the most catalytic factor remains that of the place itself as if the threat of descent into the sea and the avoidance of acknowledging a centre were a mandate for anti-architecture. The exaggerated beach town has created gems and Frank Gehry has inherited the vigour with which West Coast artists have reacted to the special mixture of light and landscape, escapism and invention. He is a cultural figure, raising the status of building in the city; a coercive figure, creating a virtual school; and an ambassador for the West Coast, working by invitation and commission across the coast and deep into Europe.

As the mode of controlled bricolage is transferred to other talent, we can ask what is especially powerful about the Angelino model. Surely it is that essentially twentieth-century quality of equal value and equal acquisition. The plethora of forms and materials that can be incorporated into buildings in that city seems to force architects to really think hard. No longer can they fall back on the dictates or manners of the street, the cornice line, or the consistency of infill. Architects as different as Morphosis and Aks Run succeed in establishing new and original values as well as forms for the relaxed city.

Equally inventive in its use of regional inspirations – and in progression beyond them – is the recent architecture of Spain where present practitioners have created a sophisticated architectural culture in Barcelona that embraces Oscar Tusquets at its more theatrical extreme and Piñón and Viaplana at its more contemplative. Their offspring, Carme Pinós and Enric Miralles do, however, draw from far more than a regional set of influences. The atmosphere of Barcelona is by nature tough and critical.

It remains to be seen how the global discussion of values and forms will affect that country, which is now politically and economically in a mood for expansion. In terms of the architectural mainstream, it is possible to compare Spain with Holland. In both there is a greater percentage of good architects than in other European countries, but is there a genuinely new spirit?

It may well be that the architectural initiative of the next twenty years will come from a country or a city that has hitherto been considered on the periphery. We need only consider the important roles played by Sweden in the 1940s, Brazil in the 1950s, and Spain at this moment, and then contemplate their previous obscurity. Perhaps the hotbed of a "post-tech" architecture will

Way Out West Berlin
Berlin, Germany.
Detail of the section.

be Australia (with its remarkably inventive band of architects, who seem to pick up on the technical tradition of metal buildings in the Australian outback with increasing sophistication), or perhaps the Czech Republic or Hungary (with their sophisticated European background that has been wound up like an unused spring), or Canada. The candidate for such a role will most likely be "first-world," since highly developed buildings are expensive.

Opposite
Way Out West
Berlin, Germany.
Location plan.

Left
Section.

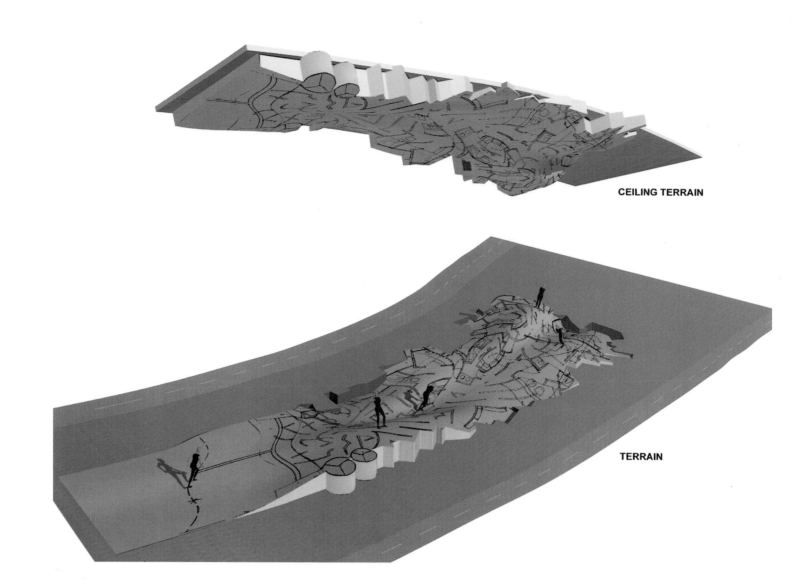

CEILING TERRAIN

TERRAIN

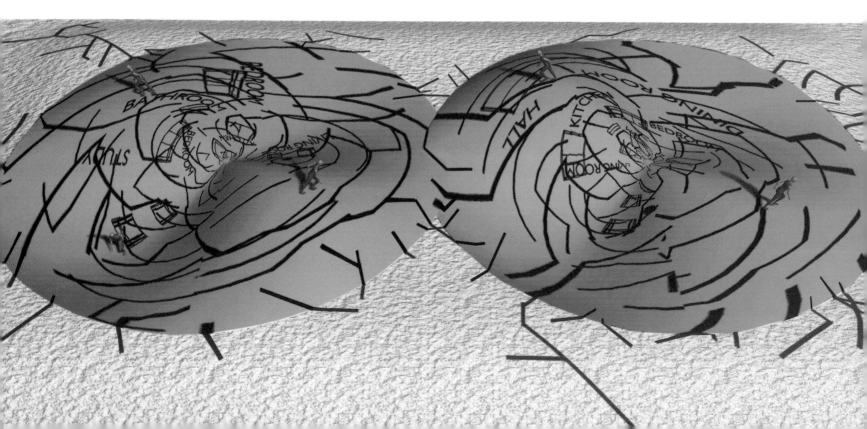

ARAKAWA AND MADELINE GINS

New York, USA

Left
Reversible Destiny Housing

Above
Ceiling terrain and terrain.
Below
Model.

Time was the major preoccupation of Arakawa's work as a painter in the 1960s. Today, the installations he produces in collaboration with Madeline Gins are ways of exploring both philosophical and aesthetic issues. The standard conditions of perception are overturned by poetically explosive systems which seek to transcend the categories of space, the material and the immaterial, the sensorial and the non-sensorial, so as to defeat time through the invention of a reversible destiny.

Reversible Destiny Houses

The first Reversible Destiny House and the Reversible Destiny Office are located at Gifu in Japan. A provisional agreement has been reached for the construction of Reversible Destiny Middle-Income Housing.

- It may take a few hours to go from the living room to the kitchen.
- Terrain predominates over plan.
- The only destiny worth talking about is a reversible one.
- Houses will consist primarily of entrances.
- Walls will be entered.
- Complex conversations will be carried on between the body and the terrain. It will be a moot point from moment to moment which of them will take the lead.
- The house will be valued for the instability it provides.
- Labyrinth and house will be cross bred.
- Every labyrinth will have its centre removed and the frustrations that it offers re-worked.
- Distinctly different re-worked labyrinths (or collections of labyrinth-derived patterns of wall segments) will be used one above the other in contradistinction to one another.
- It will not be possible to take an unambiguous step.
- An area with a ten-foot ceiling height may contain from two to nine distinctly different layers of labyrinth-derived segmenting.
- A kitchen may be an exact replica of the garden it faces.
- There will be parts of the kitchen or living room that will reappear in the bedroom and in the bathroom.
- Some rooms will make reappearances but with oppositely pitched terrains.
- Nothing will be allowed to stand on its own.
- There will be a superabundance of references, a surfeit of landing sites.
- The underside of things will always be ready at hand.

– Whenever possible the rising of structures up off the ground will be taken step (or, rather, less-than-step) by step so as not to have perception led by "the abrupt."

– Use and convenience will be re-invented.

– It may take several days to find everywhere in the house that the dining room is.

– The modern will become rococo along specific lines and volumes for parsing experience.

– Communal settings will provide double and triple horizons.

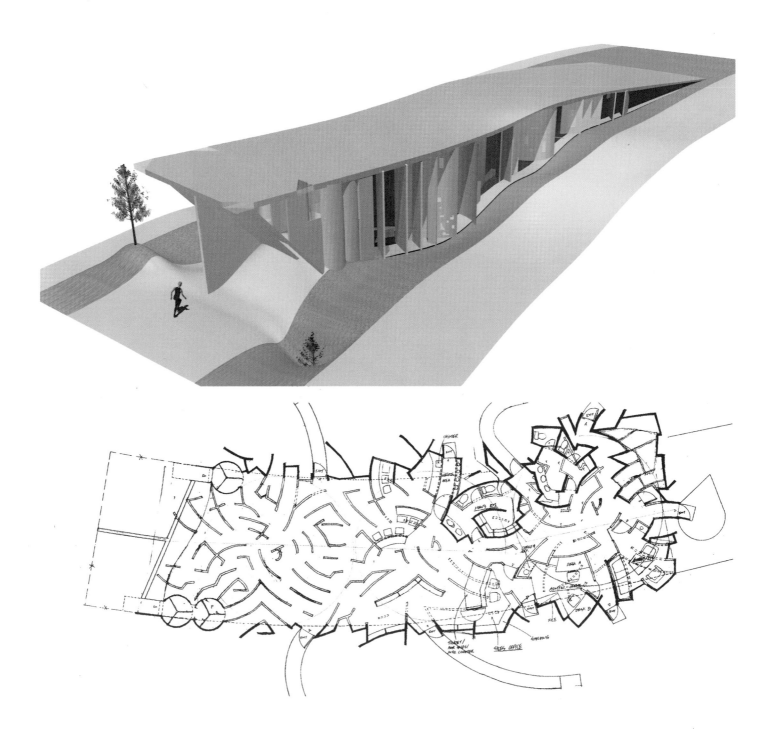

– Liverpool and Antarctica will be joined and used as a model.
– Some houses will be small versions of their own (or of different) villages.
– [In an office] it will be possible to enter the men's room before entering it.
– Residents will begin by relying as much on their houses as on themselves and will eventually come to rely more on their houses than on themselves.
– The episodic will become as hallucinatory and non-hallucinatory.
– The house will relieve one of having to have personality.
– A house may become a substitute for a life.

Arakawa and Madeline Gins

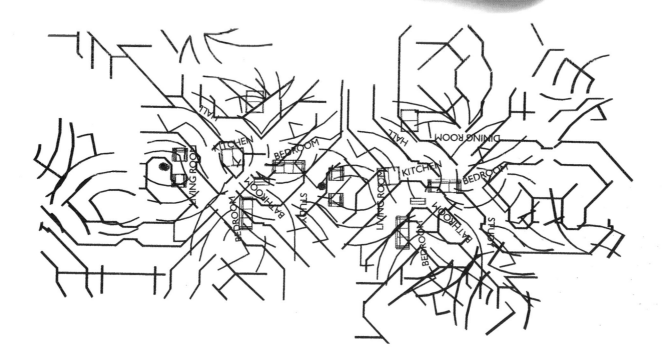

DANIEL LIBESKIND

Berlin, Germany

Daniel Libeskind was born in Poland, and qualified as an architect at the Cooper Union School in New York, before going on to study the history and theory of architecture at the University of Essex in England. During the eighties, he emerged as a unique figure in his field, searching for a language that could renew the meaning of architecture by drawing on sources as disparate as music, mathematics and history. His drawings and models, with their complex angular geometry, have contributed to the revival of architecture as drama.

No subject could have lent itself better to an exploration of the darker side of human experience, than the construction of a Jewish Museum as part of the Berlin Museum complex. The building, which is currently being completed, will be an eloquent, dignified and rigorous response to this historic tragedy.

Letter from Berlin
Essay

Today in Germany one constantly hears a particularly depressing comment about architecture and planning: "It's over." What's over? Some would have you believe that the time when vision and dream mattered is over, that the time in which the fatality of the past was transformed into something new by the courage to build has ended. Building is perhaps the only art that is essentially optimistic. For no one can construct the city and its buildings without feeling that they will usher in a better future. Yet today pessimism and a loss of nerve thwart the desire to embrace the future as a challenge. The ghosts of the past are now invoked in an authoritarian mood determined to undermine the extraordinary achievements of post-war Germany.

Since the end of World War II Germany has played a leading role in architecture and urban planning, striving to create fresh environmental alternatives and technically innovative ways of living through building. This tradition of expanding possibilities through realizing dreams has been associated with Germany ever since the great experiments in architecture and planning, beginning with the Werkbund, the Bauhaus, and the Siedlung developments and continuing through the post-war building exhibitions. Invoking poetic rationality Josef Paul Kleihues demonstrated in the recent IBA projects in Berlin that planning can incorporate diverse elements from around the world into the rich mosaic of the city.

Is this legacy about to end? Certain forces now seek to deny the preeminent role that innovative architecture and urban planning have played in

Opposite
Extension to the Berlin Museum, with the Jewish Museum
Berlin, Germany.
View of the model.

Germany. I believe that the continuity of its tradition of hope is today threatened by reactionary tendencies that seek to eliminate the awareness that Germany has produced truly great visions, buildings, and cities, and that its energy has given real substance to the very premise of European culture.

Some months ago I sat in a hall in Magdeburg at a conference devoted to the planning and building of the newly opened areas in the former DDR. I listened as planners and architects from the East were given the new ABCs that would make them successful in the reunited Germany. The proposed set of rules called for a rigid and reactionary order that employs a seductive simplicity in attacking complex problems; in short, there was to be iron discipline during a time of transition.

The delegates were instructed on the various points of the new order: no new ideas were needed in architecture or urban planning, no dreams, no thoughts, no vision – only silence and conformity. As I sat there amidst the architects and planners of the former DDR, listening with an increasing sense of dismay, I felt a sense of outrage that what was being advocated was a reactionary call to order: be silent, don't dream, relinquish vision, forget individual creativity, follow the rules of the game if you want to build.

This dogmatic and antidemocratic view of society has begun to affect and transform the architectural climate of Germany. Even more distressing is the fact that it is representative of what is now happening in Berlin – not only theoretically but practically in building. Architecture in Berlin is now subjected to a staggering degree of regimentation and control, which is disguised by a rhetoric of order. Arbitrary constraints under the guise of rationalism now exist, which even able architects such as Philip Johnson, Arata Isozaki, and Richard Meier cannot overcome. Six months ago Philip Johnson delivered a public apologia in Berlin for his scheme for the Business Centre at Checkpoint Charlie, explaining that no other modern city would have been able to force him to do such a boring and mediocre design. Without commenting on the aesthetics of these architects, the point is clear: if leading and successful architects find it impossible to produce architecture that would match the great architectural legacy of Berlin, then what hope is there for the younger generation?

It is enough to look at the winning projects in the last three years of competitions in Berlin to see how these new rules are transforming the fascinating diversity of Berlin into banal uniformity. With few exceptions, those buildings now under construction round the city represent an unimaginative regurgitation of bureaucratic administrative formulas subsumed under the banner of rationalism. The style is simple, quick, and sterile, tolerating no deviation in form or material. It provides the perfect background for the emergence of the one-dimensional individual, the individual without qualities.

Berlin is a fascinating montage of conflicting histories, scales, forms, and spaces – a rich mix of substance and imagination. The current criteria of the Senatsbau administration of Berlin are not just basic guidelines to guarantee responsible future development but are authoritarian and repressive edicts. The planning framework no longer covers simple measures or parameters for construction, but actually interferes with the materials, forms, expression, and, finally, the message of architecture. In using stone facades, gable roofs, punched-in windows, invariable grids, unrelenting symmetries, and closed blocks, the buildings and streets conform to one bureaucrat's idea of the good. Recently the winner of the Alexanderplatz competition stated that the city can no longer be built with glass, concrete, and steel, but must be rebuilt in the eternal material of granite.

Life in a pluralistic society involves tremendous vitality and the necessary diversity of experience and views of reality. One of the aspects that made me feel welcome in democratic Germany was the condition of openness that confirmed a fundamental respect for the individual, for initiative, for the different, for the other. Yet today this precious state no longer exists. An intolerance, a fundamentalism, a truly destructive hostility toward the new has crept into the present discourse of architecture and urban planning. A strong polarization based on power and control attempts to further the illusion of unanimity through exclusion.

The belief that architecture has fallen into the wrong hands - capitalist investors, the media, artist-architects, and ignorant people - is itself part of the crisis being decried. What is being demanded is a definitive transformation of the city from an all-too-human institution to a perfectly controlled and singular image. Such a nihilistic analysis of history reduces the complexity and mystery of the city to a diagrammatic and lifeless entity.

Glass Pavilion
Exhibition of the Deutscher Werkbund,
Cologne, 1914.
Bruno Taut

Planning decisions should be concerned with creating a vital city that looks toward the future. The city is a great spiritual creation of humanity, a collective work that develops the expression of culture, society, and the individual in time and space. Its structure is intrinsically complex; it develops more like a dream than a piece of equipment. The impact of the spiritual, the individual, and the creative cannot be relegated to some outdated past. As long as there are human beings, there will be the possibility of dreaming the impossible and achieving the possible, which is the very essence of humanity.

The dimension of the city is a fundamental structure. As Peter Behrens said: "Architecture, too, strives towards infinity; but more than any other art it is the art that, because of its techniques and purpose, remains bound to tangible materials ... it remains tied to Earth but seeks a spiritual link to the universe." If the creative space of architecture is reduced to some abstract formula of "redoing simple plans and strong elevations" then there is no more possibility for architecture, only for critics who read buildings and build readings. Is the urban realm to be reduced to a nullity by these heartless materialists and spiritless technocrats?

Simple-minded analyses of society, the economy, politics, and architecture cannot deal with the problems of density, ecology, and reconstruction of cities. It is no answer to rummage through the debris of history in order to cartoon some moment within it for further exploitation. In selecting for Berlin and the newly opened lands particular points in history from the nineteenth century, or from the Art Deco period, or even the Third Reich itself, there is a pretence that one can choose one's history as simply as a breakfast cereal.

Any architect or historian might have a preferred period of history. But that is very different from abusing history in order to suppress and politically legislate against other histories and against the present. An architect working in an open society has the responsibility to struggle with the conflicting interpretations of history expressed within the city. To produce meaningful architecture is not to parody history but to articulate it; it is not to erase history but to deal with it. One must take, for example, the existing context in the former DDR seriously, not because one likes the ill-conceived buildings, but because its history and its people must be respected.

The richness and historical heritage of German architecture cannot be purged of everything that is thought to pollute it. The explicit belittlement and dismissal of the art of architecture is a radical denial of the tradition that extends from before Karl Friedrich Schinkel and Peter Behrens and goes beyond Mies Van der Rohe. It includes significant architects such as Hans Scharoun, Bruno Taut, Erich Mendelsohn, and Hans Poelzig. The policy of anti-modernity is a policy against culture itself.

An unethical architecture, whether politically or economically motivated, is unacceptable and deplorable because it is profoundly anti-humanistic – an embodiment of the ideal of mass conformity. The old trick of lumping humanity into a single mass of submissive users in the name of the one and only truth is malignant and dangerous. Those who decry the lack of order only testify to their own confusion and lack of talent. The phrase "the myth of innovation" implies a comparison with those who saw the whole humanistic basis of the 20th century as a myth to be debunked. Something is wrong when architecture is conceived as no more than a technique for adjusting the *Kleinbürger* so completely to the times that he or she no longer feels a desire for anything but silence. The claim that the cities of Sienna and St. Petersburg are products of monotony and repetitiveness is ridiculous since these cities share a unity based on a shared spiritual belief rather than on technocratic legislation.

The desire for a universal national style coupled with the privileging of handicraft is not a refinement of architecture in our time but a dead end. No one involved in architecture can possibly be deluded into believing that contemporary industry and technology will suddenly give way to stone masons hewing obediently according to clear patterns. The present ecological crisis necessitates a serious rethinking of building in relation to materials and functions. The facile cosmetics of corporate architecture are not needed, nor is the banal formalism of 22-metre-high blocks (24 yds) with courtyards and internal green space. Instead we must be concerned with the architectural and human quality of buildings. Mies Van der Rohe's famous adage "God is in the details" has been deliberately misinterpreted. Now technique and details have themselves become gods.

Although we must question and criticize the obvious crass commercialism and pretentious excesses of the 1970s and 1980s, the solution to the complex problems that exist, in Germany and elsewhere, is not to be found by looking fifty years into the past, nor by advocating repetitive anonymity in the future. The answer is not to suppress individual creativity, nor abandon tolerance and diversity. One must never forget or forfeit the universal sanctity of thought and its expression. The architect must be more than a mouthpiece for the prevailing opinion. His soul must have a part in the creative struggle. The intelligence, desire, and ambition of people everywhere should not be underestimated in the task of creatively mastering the challenge of today.

National Gallery
Berlin 1962-1967.
Mies Van der Rohe.

Landsberger Allee
Berlin, Germany.
View of the competition model.

Landsberger Allee and Ringstrasse, Berlin, Germany

The Landsberger Allee project won first prize in 1994 in an international urban design competition. The scheme represents a radical departure from the conventional imposition of rigid block structures. The plan is based on an overall ecological organization which takes into consideration the existing social fabric. It is an approach that is neither traditionally contextual nor a simple replay of the dream of a *tabula rasa*. It proposes an open urban strategy which would immediately produce dramatic architectural interventions, transformations and improvements, both in residential and in working areas.

The entire zone has been conceived as a gateway to the twenty-first century and the forces of change. The Landsberger Allee itself, one of the grandest monumental boulevards of the former GDR, is transformed into a street whose rhythm is related, both visually and architecturally, to the surrounding region.

The future of such areas can no longer be determined by narrow individual interests based on ideology and dogma. They must be seen in the context of the full spectrum of social, political and cultural complexities by which the future is related to the past through the present.

The Berlin Museum with the Jewish Museum

The Jewish Museum won first prize for Daniel Libeskind in an international competition in 1989, and is due to open in 1996. The project seeks to show how the history of Berlin is inseparable from that of its Jewish citizens – two histories which have been tragically intertwined. There were three fundamental aspects to be addressed: the impossibility of representing the history of Berlin without including the history of its Jewish population; the

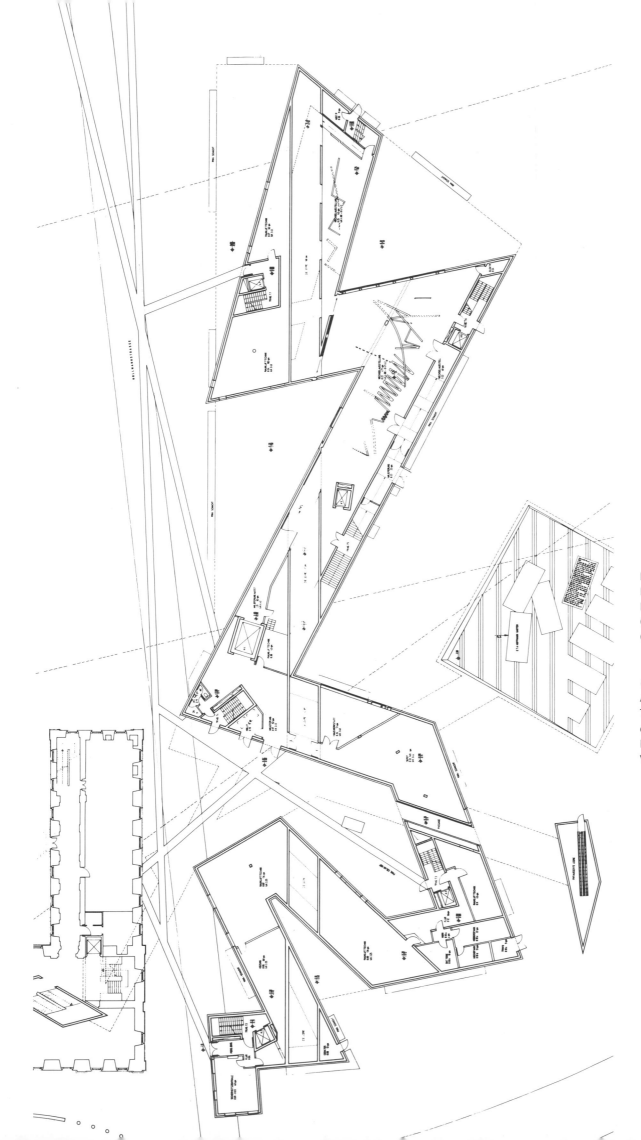

Extension to the Berlin Museum, with the Jewish Museum
Germany.
Ground floor plan.

Opposite
Above
The Jewish Museum under construction.
Below
View of the model.

need to find an architectural project that would physically incorporate the fact of the absence of Jewish life in the city after the Holocaust; and, on an urbanistic level, the need to shed light on the relationship between place and memory in the once divided city.

The new Museum is entered through the old Baroque building. Visitors go down into a basement, where they discover an intersection where three "roads" meet. The first short road leads to a cul-de-sac which forms an acute angle with the Holocaust tower: in this structure will be deposited the last signatures of all those Jews who were deported from the city and murdered. The second road leads to the E.T.A. Hoffman garden, which is composed of pillars symbolizing Jewish exile and emigration. Along the last road, which is also the longest, will be displayed those religious artefacts of the Jewish community that have survived. This road leads the visitor back to the main galleries by a staircase.

At the heart of the building, then, is an empty space: an impenetrable structure, criss-crossed by empty bridges leading from one galery to another. Visitors are led around this space of absence, which testifies to the eradication of Berlin's Jewish community.

BERNARD TSCHUMI

New York, USA
Paris, France

During the seventies, Bernard Tschumi was one of the first to introduce material from other disciplines into architecture: texts (the James Joyce garden), cinema (a plan based on the ballet scene from *Frankenstein*), and journalism (defenestration as an architectural experience) in his series of witty and provocative manifesto pieces, the *Manhattan Transcripts*.

With projects such as the Parc de la Villette in Paris or the Groningen video gallery, he has continued to assert the precedence of event over architectural context, defining architecture as "a pleasurable and sometimes violent confrontation between space and activity".

The Architecture of the Event
Essay

Architecture has always been as much about the event that takes place in a space as about the space itself. In today's world where railway-stations become museums and churches become nightclubs, we must come to terms with the complete interchangeability of form and function, the loss of traditional or canonical cause-and-effect relationships as sanctified by modernism. Function does not follow form, form does not follow function, or fiction for that matter. However, form and function certainly interact, if only to produce a shock effect.

If "shock" can no longer be produced by the succession and juxtaposition of façades and lobbies, maybe it can be produced by the juxtaposition of events that take place behind these façades in these spaces.

If "the respective contamination of all categories, the constant substitutions, the confusion of genres," as described by critics of the right and the left alike (from Andreas Huyssens to Jean Baudrillard), is the new direction of our times, it may well be used to one's advantage, to the advantage of a general rejuvenation of architecture. If architecture is both concept and experience, space and use, structure and superficial image (nonhierarchically), then architecture should cease to separate these categories and should merge them into unprecedented combinations of programmes and spaces. "Cross-programming," "transprogramming," "disprogramming": these concepts stand for the displacement and mutual contamination of terms.

My own work in the seventies constantly reiterated the thesis that there was no architecture without event, without action, without activities, without functions; architecture was to be seen as the combination of spaces, events and movements, without any hierarchy or precedence among these concepts. Needless to say, the hierarchical cause-and-effect relation between function and form is one of the great certainties of architectural thinking – it lies behind that reassuring *idée reçue* of community life that tells us that we live in houses "designed to answer to our needs" or in cities planned as machines to live in. And the cosy connotations of this *geborgenheit* notion go against both the real "pleasure" of architecture, in its unexpected combinations of terms, and the reality of contemporary urban life, in its most stimulating, as well as unsettling, facets. Hence, in works like the *Manhattan Transcripts*, the definition of architecture could not be form, or walls, but had to be the combination of heterogeneous and incompatible terms.

The incorporation of the terms "event" and "movement" was no doubt influenced by situationist discourse and the '68 era. "Les événements," as they were called, were events, not only in action, but also in thought. Erecting a barricade (function) in a Paris street (form) is not quite equivalent to being a flaneur (function) in that same street (form). Dining (function) in a university hall (form) is not quite equivalent to reading or swimming in it. Here, all hierarchical relationships between form and function cease to exist.

This unlikely combination of events and spaces was charged with subversive capabilities, for it challenged both the function and the space: such confrontation parallels the Surrealists' meeting of the sewing machine and the umbrella on the dissecting-table. We find it today in Tokyo, with its multiple programmes scattered throughout the floors of the high-rise buildings: department-store, museum, health-club, railway-station, putting-greens on the roof. And we will find it in the programmes of the future, where airports are also simultaneously amusement-arcades, athletic-facilities, cinemas, and so on. Regardless of whether they are the result of chance combinations or of the pressures of ever rising land prices, such non-causal relationships between form and function, or space and action, go beyond poetic confrontations of unlikely bedfellows.

Foucault, as was recalled in an excellent recent book by John Rajchman, expanded the use of the term "event" in a manner that went beyond the single action or activity. He spoke of "events of thought." I would suggest that the future of architecture today lies in the construction of such events. For Foucault, an event is not simply a logical sequence of words or actions, but rather "the moment of erosion, collapse, questioning or problematization of the very assumptions of the setting within which a drama may take place - occasioning the chance or possibility of another, different setting" (Rajchman). The event is seen here as a turning-point, not an origin or an end (as opposed to propositions such as "form follows function").

After Foucault, Derrida expanded on the definition of "event," calling it "the emergence of a disparate multiplicity" in a text about the folies of the Parc de la Villette. I had constantly insisted, in our discussions and elsewhere, that these points called folies were points of activities, of programmes, of events. Derrida elaborated this concept, proposing the possibility of an "architecture of the event" that would "eventualize," or open up, what in our history or tradition is understood to be fixed, essential, monumental.

Derrida had also suggested earlier that the word "event" shared roots with "invention." I would like to associate it with the notion of "shock," a shock that in order to be effective in our mediated culture, in our culture of images, must go beyond the definition of Walter Benjamin and combine the idea of function or action with that of image. Indeed, architecture finds itself in a unique situation: it is the only discipline that by definition combines concept and experience, image and use, image and structure. Philosophers can write, mathematicians can develop virtual spaces, but architects are the only ones who are the prisoners of that hybrid art where the image hardly ever exists without combined activity.

It is my contention that far from being a field suffering from its inability to question its own structures and foundations, architecture is the field where the greatest discoveries will take place in the next century. The very heterogeneity of the definition of architecture – space, action and movement – makes it that event, that place of shock, or that place of the invention of ourselves. The event is the place where the rethinking and reformulation of the different elements of architecture (many of which have resulted in, or added to, contemporary social inequities) may lead to their solution. By definition, it is the place of the combination of difference.

Of course, it is not by imitating the past that this will happen. It is also not going to happen by simple commenting through design on the various dislocations and uncertainties of our contemporary condition. I do not believe it is possible, nor that it makes sense, to design buildings that formally attempt to blur traditional structures, i.e. that display forms that lie somewhere between abstraction and figuration, or somewhere between structure and ornament, or that are cut up, dislocated for aesthetic reasons. Architecture is not an illustrative art; it does not illustrate theories.

You cannot design a new definition of the city and its architecture. But you may be able to design the conditions that will make it possible for this nonhierarchical, nontraditional society to happen. By understanding the nature of our contemporary circumstances and the media processes that go with them, architects are in a position to construct conditions that will create a new city and new relationships between spaces and events.

Architecture is not about the conditions of design, but about the design of conditions. Or, to paraphrase Paul Virilio, our object today is not to fulfil the conditions of construction, but to achieve the construction of conditions that will dislocate the most traditional and regressive aspects of our society and simultaneously reorganize these elements in the most liberating way, where our experience becomes the experience of events organized and strategized through architecture. Strategy is a key word today in architecture. No more masterplans, no more locating in a fixed place, but a new heterotopia. That is what our cities are striving towards, and here we architects must help them by intensifying the rich collision of events and spaces.

Tokyo and New York only appear chaotic; in reality, they mark the appearance of a new urban structure, a new urbanity. Their confrontations and combinations of elements may provide us with the event, the shock, that I very much hope will make the architecture of our cities a turning-point in culture and in society.

Folies in the Parc de La Villette
Paris, France.

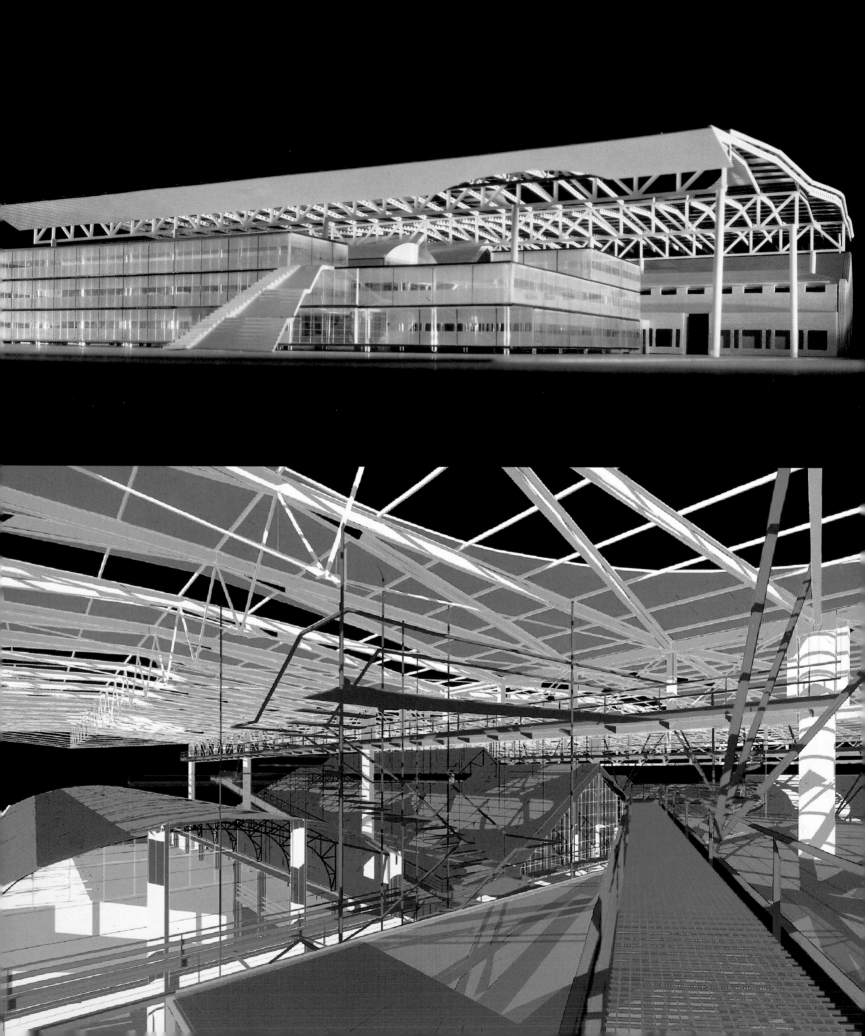

National Studio for Contemporary Arts, Tourcoing, France

The complex is intended to be precise and rational in its conception, yet richly poetic in its spatial diversity. The great steel roof, traversed by "clouds" of light, floats above the old tiled roofs, creating a new plane of reference, an artificial sky ("artifi-ciel"). Not only does this huge roof generate the new poetic space of the "in-between", but it provides a pragmatic solution to problems of climate, energy and information. The scale and presence of this horizontal space relativizes the concepts of inside and outside in relation to the old building. The "in-between" iself becomes a concept, condensing different fields of investigation: teaching, performance, and research; art and cinema; music and image. This multi-functional space, which is intended to "cover" the event (whether it be a congress, a concert, an athletics meeting, or an exhibition, not to mention their thousands of visitors), is one possible model for the new "urban" spaces of the 21st century.

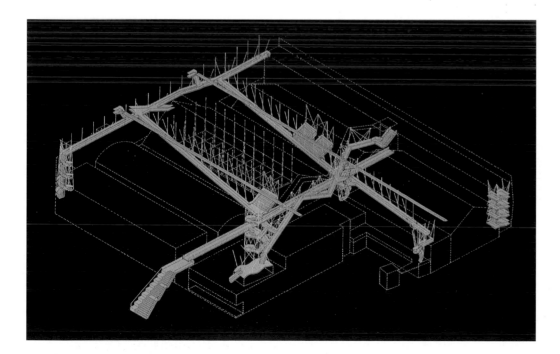

National Studio for Contemporary Arts
Tourcoing, France.
Axonometric showing the circulation paths.

Opposite

Above
View of the model.
Below
Interior perspective.

LEBBEUS WOODS

New York, USA

Lebbeus Woods stood out as an original figure against the backdrop of futile post-modernism that enshrouded New York in the 1980s. He reinvented architecture by integrating time and wear into his projects. His vision of building was realistic, not to say pessimistic. His manifesto-projects were bathed in an expressionistic atmosphere as they sought to describe a mechanistic world at the limits of science fiction: an ageing, run-down universe, brought to the verge of ruin. In the 1990s, his work has taken a political turn, provoked by the war between Serbia and Bosnia. Woods' recent projects put architecture on a war footing.

War and architecture, Bosnia Freestate
Essay

Architecture has always attempted to codify, by the definition of an analogous spatial order, the best of what any society possesses, from the material and technological to the intellectual and poetical.

Present society offers a richer, more complex and in many ways more conflicting and paradoxical spectrum of choices than any before it. As a result, demands are made on architecture to provide an analogous, accommodating structuring of space. However, there has been a qualitative change in the historical mission of architecture, owing chiefly to the increasing complexity of social relationships and interactions, but also to the radical collapse of time in which social exchange takes place. It will no longer be sufficient for architecture merely to accommodate or express ideas and events, for this requires a historical distance or objectivity that no longer exists. Rather, architecture can only participate in social transformations, becoming more dynamic, fluid and even more kinetic than it has ever been before.

Social institutions are increasingly polarized into those supporting choice for as many people as possible, and those working against it. The projects presented here attempt to define new types of spatial order, corresponding to the paradoxical and conflicting events and ideas that continue to shape human society.

The Wall, Bosnia Freestate is conceived for a besieged state with a history of being on the periphery of contending empires and absorbing them into a model multi-cultural society. At the same time, it proposes a type of heterarchical urban and architectural order that results from the accumulation of small-scale elements not designed to be together, using new principles of spatial construction and organization. It functions on the principle of absorbing and transforming the enemy's land-based attacks by the complexity of

41

its construction. Its complex, discontinuous series of spaces once entered cannot be easily exited, and the lack of a spatial hierarchy prevents any form of mass military action. Small-scale encounters lead inevitably to less hostile forms of exchange and the combatants and their camp followers gradually build up a complex urban network – a city – in the space between contending nation-states.

Zagreb Free-Zone comprises a series of structures that appear in the streets of a newly-forming state seeking a transition from centralized state

The Wall, Bosnia Freestate
Drawing.

The Wall, Bosnia Freestate is a massive structure that defends the territory of a people who have suffered a medieval form of aggression with modern weapons.

socialism to an as-yet-undefined form of open society. The structures have no pre-determined meaning or function, and yet contain spaces with a potential for inhabitation. Their non-Cartesian form, however, frustrates conventional ways of inhabitation, and, at the same time invites and facilitates the invention of new ones. They comprise a city-within-a-city, a free-zone, that corresponds to communities emerging in the world today which are based on the increase of personal choice and responsibility through non-traditional uncontrolled forms of exchange.

FRANÇOIS ROCHE

Paris, France

A period as a member of the punk movement and a sojourn as a hermit in the desert are among the stages that make up the unusual career of François Roche. Roche graduated as an architect in 1987. He first began to be noticed in France in the early 1990s, thanks to his combative public pronouncements. Turbulent and polemical, he was an unsettling presence in the staid, insecure world of French architecture, whose dreams had been brought down to earth in no uncertain manner, now that the "Grands Travaux" state building programme was completed. Roche is both pragmatic and irreverent. He has no time for rules and conventions which seem to him out of place or out of date. He reaffirms the social function of architecture, and seeks to refocus attention on domains which are distinctly less glorious than the monumental constructions of the preceding decade. For Roche, the role of architecture is to confront the challenge of housing and public space, in a society that is prey to considerable social problems.

The shadow of the chameleon
Essay

I know people who are born into truth. I am not like them. Some have a creed, a mission, a philosophy, others plagiarize counterfeit ideologies. I do not belong to either camp. What I am interested in are the multiple, complex choices that are opened up, once architecture has put off its princely autonomy, and at last agrees to learn from those areas of experience to which it had tried to dictate. But do not think I want to take pride in seeing while all around me are blind. Sight is worth nothing, if it is not shared.

Architects have invariably represented the domination of man over nature, of the city over the ecosystem, of the built over the un-built. In the end, land has served as at best, a found object, at worst, an alibi, there to be exploited. Our profession has become isolated, egotistical and self-absorbed, restricting its activity to stylistic exercises and in-fighting. The architecture which was born out of utopian dreams never managed to cast off its perverse sclerosis, its halo of progressivist prediction and a better future...

In a system whose only preoccupation is with its own image, few suspect that the architectural object has imploded to such an extent that it is useless to try and cling to what it was or what it should be. Situated at the intersection of political interests, economic, territorial and social tensions, spurred on by continuous technological and industrial change, it is eternally condemned to be torn apart by competing demands. And yet there is no justification for drawing the eclectic conclusion from this state of affairs, and siding blindly with

omnipresent chaos. On the contrary, the greater the confusion, the more urgent are the ethical and political choices which would be capable of reviving the processes of meaning and stemming the wastage that surrounds us today.

The interpretation of Place and Context should be the very essence of the architectural act.

Creeds and individualisms should be contorted, infiltrated and inserted in and against that which they were seeking to destroy.

Stylistic effects, intelligently reworked, should be sensitive to existing territorial conditions: to climate, wind, wear and tear, the seasons, the built and the un-built, time and raw materials, reduced to their bare essentials.

At last we should learn how to do LESS so that we can work WITH.

We must reinvent an architecture that would be animistic, sensual, primitive, political, an antidote to blind and hyper-active modernity, both lucid and optimistic in the face of anxiety as our planet burns; we must reinvent architecture, not in order to launch a new style, a new school, a new theoretical hegemony, but so as to redefine the basis of our profession, in today's conditions.

Whether landscape is urban, suburban, natural or cultivated, it has its own topographical, emotional and climatic codes. It is through these places and these contexts that we must work. Clearly, their constitution can only be discovered by spending time in them, sometimes only by living with them... The "genetic code of territoriality" is not a recipe that can be printed out, a politically-correct label for yuppies in search of an ideology, but a process of entering into contact, which must be enacted afresh for each intervention.

Do not get me wrong: there is nothing pastoral or fashionably green about the approach I advocate. It is not a return to nature for the Sunday supplements, vegetarianism as architectural alibi. The process of infiltration must employ means that match the scale of the territories to be confronted. The re-education of our own vital instincts that will follow must be equally radical.

This plea for an architecture of time and wear, of sensuality and of meaning, that is both territorial and human, would have no substance, if it could not draw on new skills and techniques in cartography, geology, the reasoned assessment of preconditions and the evolution of technologies. The aim is not to produce a contemporary version of the sterile, reheated recipes of the Academy, but fresh fruit and fresh vegetables, fresh meat and fish. An architecture at the cutting edge of art – and history – at the end of this century.

Its skin must be light-sensitive to its immediate context. Its basic functions must be rethought. In this way, architecture can limit its tendency to glorious isolation, and learn to respond to variations in climate, atmosphere, topography and custom. It must sum up nothing that it has not already transformed.

It is imperative that we stay close to what can revive our sense of responsibility, both for the sake of our own survival, and for that of our union with the elements. In the end, isn't the Aristotelian world of appearances and artefacts just as valid as the world of ideas and concepts? All we need to do is come to terms with the real, which is still, despite everything, our only haven, so that our work can intercede for us between our desires and the world they were supposed to dominate.

Opposite
Renovation of building n°48
Sarcelles, France.

Above
Cross-section.
Below
Perspective

Left
Elevation.

2. PERFORMANCES

"I may be of lower than average intelligence; but I am well-informed."
R. Buckminster Fuller

Since the dawn of the industrial revolution, technology and science have played an increasingly important role in building. From the Crystal Palace* to the Eiffel Tower, from the skyscraper to the geodesic dome, architecture has attempted to overcome the constraints of solidity and gravity by using ever more delicate structures, larger spans, higher performance materials. The ensuing pact with the engineers and the search for maximum efficiency gave rise to a puritanical attitude to form that, seen as the direct result of necessary constraints, was cold and neutral: beauty as efficiency.

But it soon became obvious that rigorous procedures could produce other, very different kinds of work and that technology had the potential to create new, original forms.

There is no doubt that the Lem that NASA sent to the moon in 1969 came as a shock to the purists: how could the most advanced technology have produced such a shaggy object?

The projects presented here prove, if such proof were needed, that high-tech and the continuing search for technical innovation and performance are compatible with a genuinely free imagination. ■

Opposite
Torre de Collserola
Barcelona, Spain.
Sir Norman Foster

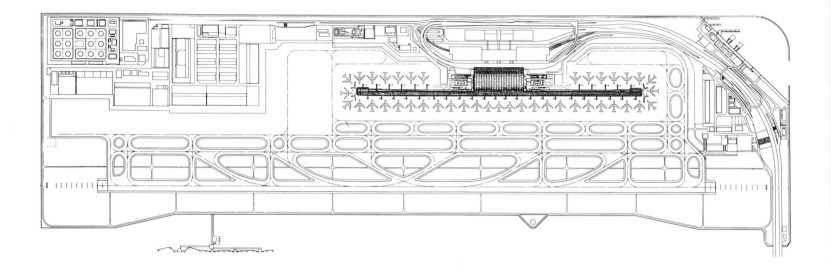

RENZO PIANO

Genoa, Italy
Paris, France

Renzo Piano belongs to a tradition of architects who are above all builders, for whom the primacy of materials and their deployment leads to the patient and detailed search for the solution that is best adapted to each particular problem. Whence the constant, craftsman-like inventiveness of his architecture. From the Pompidou Centre in Paris (1971-77) which made him famous, to his experiments with local workshops for renovating old buildings, from his prototype car for Fiat to the steamships he designed for a Californian collector, Renzo Piano has always been faithful to his own lights. In his work, the quiet perfectionism of his "trade" counts for so much more than the spectacular gesture.

Kansai International Airport

In order to protect the coastal enviroment and to avoid both pollution and the protests of ecologists, Kansai Airport was constructed on an artificial island 4.37 km x 1.25 km (4,779 yds x 1,367 yds), situated 5 km (a little more than 3 miles) out into Osaka Bay.

It was Renzo Piano's passion for this unique project which helped him to win the competition. The transition from the magical state of air travel to the realities of arrival on the island suggested playing on the relation between nature and technical efficiency. This idea is realised in concrete terms as two natural planted "valleys", one of which separates the runway from the terminal, and the other the terminal from the roadways leading to the town. These two valleys echo the serenity of the bay and its islands.

The form of the terminal itself was derived from the study of airflow dynamics. New methods of computer-assisted analysis which enable the visualization of airflow patterns, implied a more supple structure and provided the basis for the creation of new irregular forms, possessing a complex mobility. The fluid curves of the terminal building are intended to recall the forms of aeroplanes.

There is no facade in the traditional sense of the term. Land and architecture are gently integrated one with the other. The interior space and the embarcation piers are designed for maximum transparency. The passengers are thus in contact with the reality of runway and machine. The special character of the building derives from this balance between nature and technology.

Opposite
Kansai International Airport, Japan.

Above
Master plan.
Below
Aerial view of the island.

Kansai International Airport Japan.
Computer analysis of air flows on which the form of the roof is based.

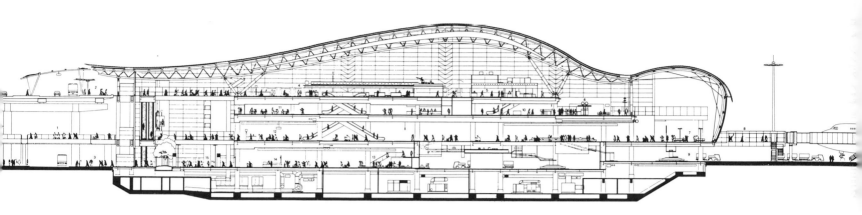

Kansaï International Airport,
Japan.

Above
Cross section of the main terminal building.
Below left
Elevation, runway side.
Below right
Interior.

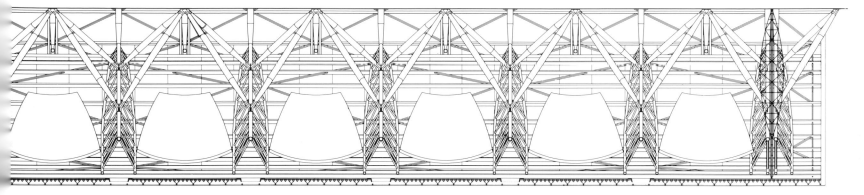

Above
Longitudinal axonometric of the structure.
Below
Check-in area.

Overleaf
The terminal at night.

NICHOLAS GRIMSHAW

London, Great Britain

After studying architecture at Edinburgh University, Nicholas Grimshaw was an outstanding student at the Architectural Association in London, where he obtained his diploma in 1965. His early partnership with Terry Farrell was dissolved when the latter decided to embrace post-modernism. Grimshaw, on the other hand, has always been driven by his determination to explore the resources offered by industrial modes of production, and to design buildings which feel incontrovertibly "right". Whence the sense of restraint that pervades all his most characteristic projects. He has often been called on to design working spaces (the Vitra factory in Weil am Rhein, the Financial Times printing works). The attention he pays to the "human" aspect of such buildings moderates any tendency to technical expressivism. Yet his monumental structure for Waterloo Station in London is undeniably spectacular in the huge curve it defines to follow the line of the tracks. As for the Berlin stock exchange, the very scale of the project seems to have led the architect to address new urban and architectural problems.

Berlin Stock Exchange, Germany

The project for the Ludwig Erhard Haus, which will house the Berlin stock exchange and communications centre, and which is due to be completed in 1997, was conceived in response to three specific criteria. First, in order to avoid an excessively tall building, it was necessary to use all the available ground area on the irregularly-shaped site. Second, a direct relationship was to be established between the inner life of the building and the life of the city outside. Third, the public spaces were to be arranged along a gently curving inner "street".

The project was also designed to achieve low energy consumption, reasonable running costs and extremely low pollution levels.

The offices on the upper floors are organized around two unheated triangular atria, which serve to temper the continental climate of Berlin and to bring natural light into the very heart of the building. The inner streets and atria combine to produce a spectacular array of changing perspectives.

Waterloo International Terminal, London, Great Britain

The functions of the Waterloo International Terminal are analagous to those of an airport, and it has most of the services and facilities one would associate with such a building. Yet it is still very much a railway station, a heroic edifice erected on a city-centre site and hemmed in by constraints, less than ten minutes from Trafalgar Square : the first monument of a new era in rail transport.

Berlin Stock Exchange,
Germany.
Aerial view of the model.

Opposite
Computer-generated perspective.

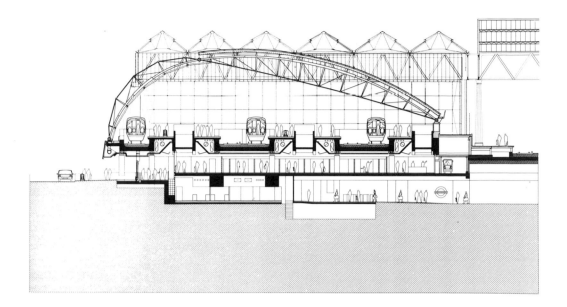

Waterloo International Terminal Station
London, Great Britain.

Above
Cross-section.
Below
Interior.

Opposite
View of the roof.

The roof provides both the greatest technical challenge and the high-point of the drama. It runs for 400 m (437 yds) in a sinuous tapering line determined by the topography of the site and the layout of the tracks. Its strangeness – the asymmetry of its forms – is not wilfully aesthetic, but is determined by the position of a track which runs along the western boundary of the site. The form's inflexion is necessary to create enough height beneath it for a train to pass. Trains approach the terminal from this side. The facade is clad in glass and its form is emphasized by the external structure. It functions as an enormous window onto Westminster and the Thames for arriving passengers.

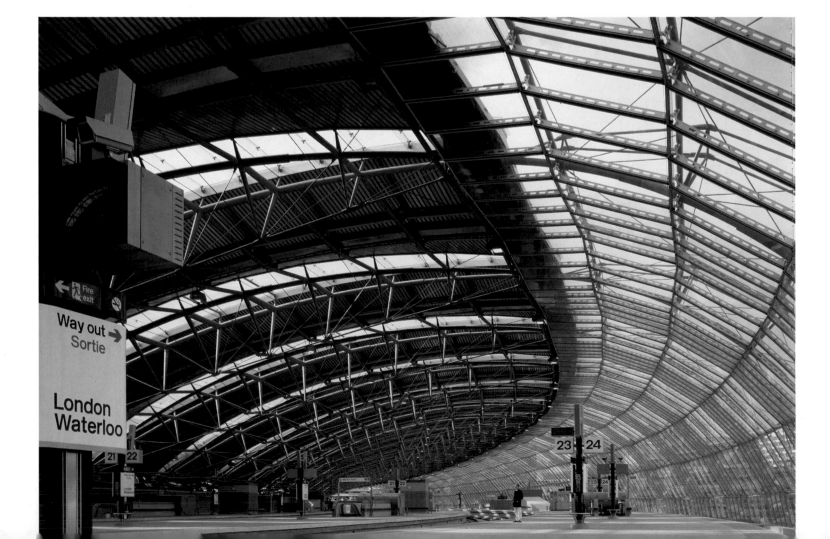

SIR NORMAN FOSTER

London, Great Britain

Over the last twenty years, Sir Norman Foster has created many architectural landmarks: the museum-hangar of the Sainsbury centre, the Swindon Renault factory, both in Great Britain, and the tower of the Hong Kong and Shanghai Bank in Hong Kong, are among the masterworks of the closing decades of the century. Sir Norman is certainly the purest of the so-called "high-tech" architects, and has made the most persuasive case for faith in technical progress. He has collaborated – and continues to collaborate – with the best engineers: Buckminster Fuller, Jean Prouvé, Tony Fitzpatrick. His buildings feature subtle articulations and finely-drawn structures. They create vast, well-lit spaces, in their search for formal expression: a puritanical aesthetic which owes much to zen, both the zen of archery and that of motorcycle maintenance.

Torre de Collserola, Barcelona, Spain

This telecommunications tower was built to coincide with the Olympic Games. It is a symbol of Barcelona's determination to ally itself with modernity through the creation of a "monumental technological element". The tower rises to 288 metres (315 yds) above ground level, 440 metres (481 yds) above sea level. There is a public gallery and a glass elevator. Its distinctive shape is now a dominant presence, high above the city and its bay.

Reichstag, New Parliament, Berlin, Germany

The Reichstag has had a troubled history from the outset. It was built amid arguments between the architect Wallot and Chancellor Bismarck, burnt down in 1933, and remained abandoned until the sixties when Paul Baumgarten renovated it for sporadic use.

With the reunification of Germany and the decision to transfer the German Parliament from Bonn to Berlin, an open competition for its redevelopment was organized. Sir Norman Foster and Partners were the outright winners, with a design that was both monumental and subtle. A new roof over the original edifice was to define a raised plaza surrounding the building, which would give direct access to the first-floor level. The plenary chamber is circular in form and partially sunk below ground level.

This scheme has since been considerably modified, and the new roof has been abandoned in favour of a plan to rebuild the original cupola – the very cupola which caused Wallot so many problems. Sir Norman has put forward several different propositions for its reconstruction. If the project succeeds, it will be both a monument in its own right, and a symbol of the new Berlin.

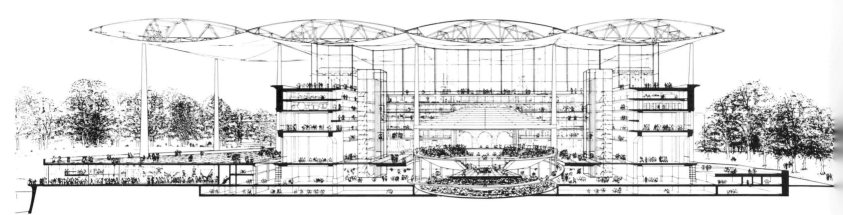

Schnitt Nord-Süd

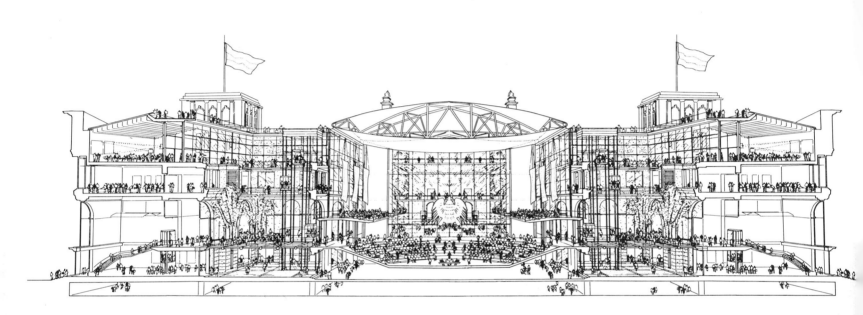

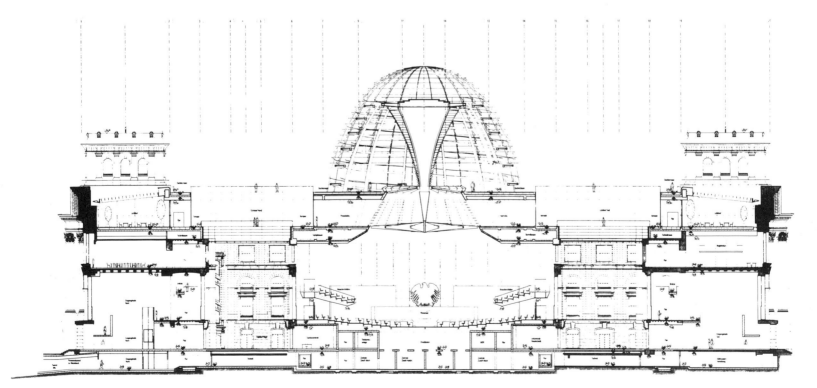

Schnitt CC

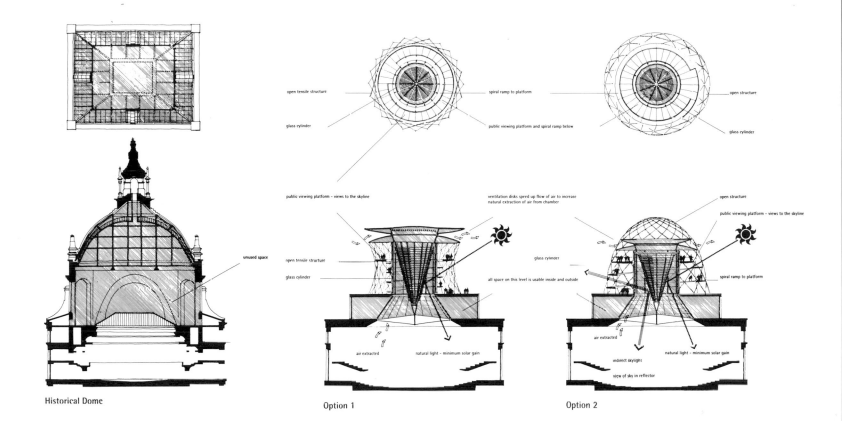

open tensile structure — spiral ramp to platform — open structure

glass cylinder — public viewing platform and spiral ramp below — glass cylinder

public viewing platform – views to the skyline — ventilation disks speed up flow of air to increase natural extraction of air from chamber — open structure — public viewing platform – views to the skyline

open tensile structure — glass cylinder — glass cylinder — spiral ramp to platform

unused space — all space on this level is usable inside and outside

air extracted — natural light – minimum solar gain — air extracted — indirect skylight — natural light – minimum solar gain — view of sky in reflector

Historical Dome

Option 1

Option 2

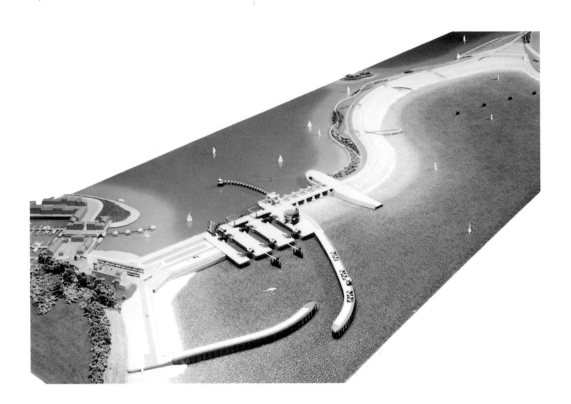

ALSOP & STÖRMER

London, Great Britain

William Alsop trained at a time when British architecture was still in the shadow of Archigram* and the quasi-mythical figure of Cedric Price*. Alsop first achieved recognition in the early 1980s with bizarre high-tech projects that reflected his colourful and outlandish imagination. In his buildings, Alsop tries to marry technical rigour to the expressive freedom of the plastic arts. Thus he "paints" his designs before he draws them. His buildings in Hamburg and Marseille are major urban landmarks, thanks to their powerful, dynamic and highly-coloured presence.

Cardiff Barrage, Cardiff, Great Britain

For the Cardiff barrage, Alsop & Störmer deployed all their skills in both architecture and landscape design, to turn what might have been merely a utilitarian piece of civil engineering into a gigantic work of art. The barrage carries a new road running into the centre of Cardiff, via the dockside of the Victorian suburb of Penarth. The structure curves across the valley; en route, the user discovers a series of architectural "events", whether he is travelling by car or on foot. Brightly coloured structural elements, groves of specially selected plants, picnic areas, fishing piers, and even an artificial island close to the inland side. The aim is to create an architectural drama that will appeal to a wide cross-section of the public, and that will act as a focus for tourists, as well as for the local population.

Le Grand Bleu, Marseille, France

The Grand Bleu is the Regional Government Headquarters for the Department of the Bouches-du-Rhône. The simplicity of its structure – two rectangular sections, administrative blocks and an assembly hall in the shape of a cigar, all joined together by bridges and suspended walkways – creates a series of unexpected spaces and experiences. As they pass through the atria that punctuate the building, employees and members of the public discover the sky above and the activity of the great hall below. The materials employed are simple ones – concrete, glass, wood and steel. But they are used to create a zoomorphic expressionism, which can take even the most jaded visitor by surprise.

Opposite
Above
Cardiff Barrage
Cardiff Bay, Great Britain.
Aerial view of the model.
Below
Visitors' Pavilion.

Le Grand Bleu, Regional Government
Headquarters of the Bouches-du-Rhône
Marseille, France.

Opposite
Atrium and walkways.

Right
Cross-section.
Below
General view.

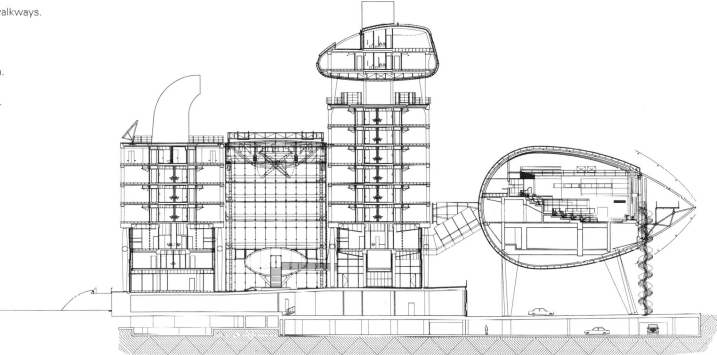

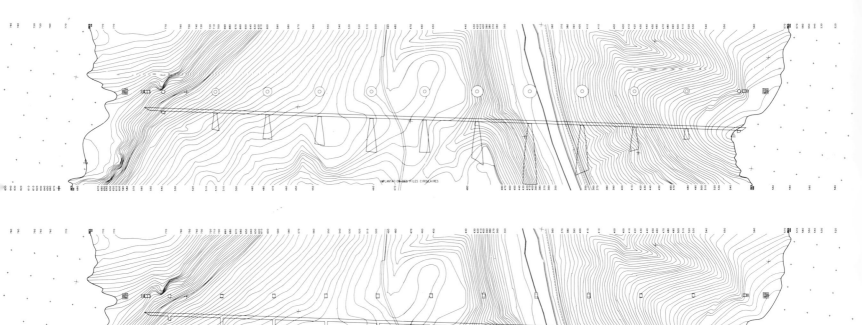

IMPLANTATION DES PILES CIRCULAIRES

IMPLANTATION DES PILES RECTANGULAIRES

JACQUES HONDELATTE

Bordeaux, France

Jacques Hondelatte occupies a special place in the French architectural world. Once he had finished his studies, he chose to settle in Bordeaux, a city that, since the war, has been home to a whole generation of talented modernist architects. There, he acquired a reputation for unusual, innovative projects – a 70 m (77 yds)-long house, an inward-looking student hostel clad in shiny metal – that were the product of an original approach in which imagination and text were more important than accurate plans ("I draw", Hondelatte has said, "once the project is completed").

This freedom of approach excludes neither logic nor technical innovation. It is this vision which enables him to go beyond traditional limits, as in his bold proposal for the Millau viaduct, which seems to have resulted from an improbable collaboration between the two Morandis (the painter and the great engineer).

Viaduct over the Tarn, Aveyron, France

For the point where the A75 motorway is to cross the Tarn Valley, linking the Causse Rouge to the north with the Larzac plateau to the south, a viaduct was chosen, in order to meet constraints of both economy and efficiency. This solution also has the advantage of avoiding an invasive road network.

There can be no question of camouflaging a construction that is 2,600 metres (2,843 yds) long and which rises 270 metres (295 yds) above the floor of the valley. The result must therefore be conceived as a work of art, whose presence will inevitably have an enormous impact on the landscape. Jacques Hondelatte was well aware of this, and studied all the various possibilities, rejecting first of all any that involved piers or pylons which would rise above the level of the surrounding hills (on the model of the Golden Gate Bridge in San Francisco). He also refused to exploit the opportunity to erect some ultimate monument to modernity, and indulge in a brilliant and flashy technological tour de force.

Instead he chose a "single, simple, regular" construction, with uniform spans and beam lengths. The fundamental decision was to have the two traffic lanes one above the other, within a thick, hollow beam, to be made either of concrete or of steel. The dimensions of the roadway and those of the piers have been chosen on the basis of analogy, so as to fuse together rather than articulate separately the different parts of the structure.

The substantial winds that will buffet the viaduct led to the choice of thin rectangular shafts at the head. Further study of circular constructions (silos, radio towers) also inspired a variant form, with circular piers on simple foundations, like soft cones or giant bottles, that blend into the forms of the neighbouring causses.

3. FORM EXPLODED

"...and remember that people have peculiar tastes."
Lou Reed.

Heroic Modernism was under the illusion that it could replace the treatises and patterns of "the old architecture" with a new set of prototypes (Le Corbusier's "five points" replacing the column, the pediment and the entablature).

However, the freedom of form in architecture that has been in evidence for the past two decades goes against this hypothesis. It has various possible origins: the exhaustion of traditional symbols, advances in construction techniques, and the exploration of form by artists opening up the possibility of unprecedented inventions... The complex world revealed through the increased availability of images has also played a role in founding the new awareness of a multiplicity of cultures all affirming their identities and their differences.

Once the age old questions of stability and convenience had been resolved, the architect found himself free to give expression to and to reinvent form itself, rather than a language with a fixed, codified vocabulary and grammar. Architecture is coming to terms with a loss of gravity, in both senses of the word.

The following pages illustrate the plethora of forms, some harking back to the avant-gardes of the past, others emerging from some improbable planet, UFOs, lonely, orphaned objects that may well have no posterity. ■

Opposite
Nationale-Nederlanden Office Building
Prague, Czech Republic
Frank O. Gehry

Views of the model.
The corner site of the Nationale-Nederlanden Office Building is adjacent to an unusually shaped public square and calls for a twin tower scheme that makes a smooth transition from one street to the next, while at the same time creating a strong visual focus.
This massing strategy also establishes a sculptural dialogue appropriate to the urban context. The main exterior facade, overlooking the river bank, responds to the rich textures and scale of the adjacent row of houses.

CHRISTIAN DE PORTZAMPARC

Paris, France

Christian de Portzamparc belonged to the May 1968 generation that broke violently with the Beaux-Arts tradition. He was a supporter of the "return to the city" movement and was wary of Modernism in its most dogmatic form. The "Hautes Formes", a housing development in Paris, brought him to the attention of the general public. The buildings that date from the early eighties display a rather rigid formalism which he has left behind in his mature work: the Cité de la Musique at La Villette and the hotel opposite at the Porte de Pantin in Paris prove his loyalty to his urban commitments, the freedom he has acquired with form and his mastery of technique and vision.

Cité de la Musique, Parc de La Villette, Paris, France

The Cité de la Musique is a "suite" in the musical sense, a series of paths, of places that are discovered by wandering through them. "In architecture, as in music, things are perceived in a time sequence, in duration. I am very attached to the fact that architecture should encourage movement: we go from one place to another because we want to discover something." The design of the auditorium permits new relationships between the audience and the musicians, and the optimal use of space for different types of music: symphonic, chamber music, recitals. Colour is of paramount importance throughout the Cité. For example, in the auditorium lighting is provided in the three primary colours which a computer programme can combine into limitless variations. Thus, the auditorium can take on all the colours of the rainbow and the changing colours can be programmed to "play" in sequence.

Crédit Lyonnais Tower, Lille, France

The design for the Crédit Lyonnais tower is the exact solution to an equation with several unknows: to build a 50 m (55 yds) bridge over the TGV train station with a fixed budget; to rise 120 m (131 yds) into the air at at least one point and yet not exceed 15,000 sq.m. (17,943 sq.yds) in area; to orient the buiding towards the south of the city; and to create for it its own specific form.

Cité de la Musique
Parc de La Villette, Paris, France.

Opposite
Housing, Fukuoka
Japan.

Overleaf
Cité de la Musique
Parc de La Villette, Paris, France.

Above
General view,
Parc de La Villette.
Below
Auditorium.

Extension to the Palais des Congrès, Paris, France

The extension to the Palais des Congrès corresponds to a double aim: to improve the functioning and performance of the existing building and to improve the quality of the site as part of the city. The new facade must therefore be designed to catch the attention of people in passing cars: it has to be clearly defined and simple, immediately accessible but also subtle when viewed over time. Finally, it has to has to serve as a huge notice board to advertize the programme of activities.

Bandaï Cultural Complex, Tokyo, Japan

The Cultural Complex has been designed as a form to receive and diffuse light. By day, the play of changing light and sculptural planes gives the building a strong presence on the avenue. At dusk, a programme of coloured lighting bathes the edifice in a mysterious atmosphere.

Opposite
Crédit Lyonnais Tower
Lille, France.

The orientation of the upper floors passes from north-south to east-west through a progressive deformation of the tower that opens onto the south and the city of Lille.

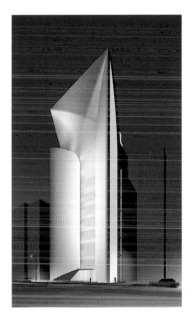

Bandaï Cultural Complex
Tokyo, Japan.
View of the model.

Left
Extension to the Palais des Congrès
Paris, France.

The huge opening in the diagonal plane itself brings light into the entrance and the diagonal functions as a canopy. In this opening a cone symbolizes softness: the outside curves round to become the inside. A horizontal plane cuts through the diagonal plane, serving as an immense support for texts and images, a lectern for the city.

79

KIYOSHI SEY TAKEYAMA

Osaka, Japan

Kiyoshi Sey Takeyama's aim is to create relationships between incomplete things and events, to give structure to isolated phenomena in a world which is fragmented, discontinuous, and incomplete. His work, often using symbolic ideas, has both solidity and stillness, while at the same time emphasising discontinuity and fragmentation as positive values – because, ultimately, "we have no alternative but to live and act in such a context."

The Future of the City
Essay

The city is a fabric woven from "memories". Architecture is an incubator for time. The technologies that have allowed human life to prosper in the past were methods of time preservation. Books have preserved time for thought. Photographs, recordings, films, videos, have preserved time in various ways by light or sound. In a similar way, works of architecture have materialized the programme of each age, thus presenting time in many different ways. Architecture is a "memory factory".

One of the features of "incomplete form" is its interaction with other forms, like the electron exchanging ions. Another is its capacity for architectural expression which reflects our consciousness. To define the "present", we can only describe it in an incomplete way. The invention of communication technologies has made all sorts of information accessible to us. But these technologies have broken down the information into bits and pieces. Conversely, we could say that society, by adopting fragmentary information, has made it possible for communication technologies to progress rapidly. We no longer dream of a self-sufficient utopia with a common treasury of information. We must seek our own place in the midst of the flood of incomplete, fragmentary, broken bits and pieces of information. At present, and in the future, we can see the world only in terms of a continual discontinuity of incomplete events. The incompleteness of information, and the incompleteness of human existence embody a "present", where various "times" coexist.

The media, which are the products of human invention, have changed our consciousness and given us a new vision of the world. As long as architecture is a representation of our consciousness of space, the architecture that represents the "present" cannot avoid being incomplete. For only in an incomplete form can the future become present.

Opposite
Shuto-cho Pastoral Hall
Yamaguchi, Japan.

Above
View of the building and access to the exterior auditorium.
Below
View of the foyer.

Shuto-cho Pastoral Hall,
Yamaguchi, Japan.

Opposite
Above
Outside Auditorium.
Below
Inside Auditorium.

Below
Section showing the two auditoriums.

Shuto-cho Pastoral Hall, Yamaguchi, Japan

This Pastoral Hall is designed for the performance of classical music and to be the focal point for cultural activities in the park surrounding it. For Takeyama, architecture is the stylization of the earth and its contours, and although technology has made it possible to rise above the earth's surface, it is still the fundamental meaning and nature of architecture to work with the contours of the planet. An awareness of "creating contours" penetrates the entire design of the park. A promenade has been designed that is not solely the means to an end, but also a process, a place for wandering with no purpose. The contours of the promenade are intended to provoke interaction between those who have come for a specific event and those who are lost in silence, or in music.

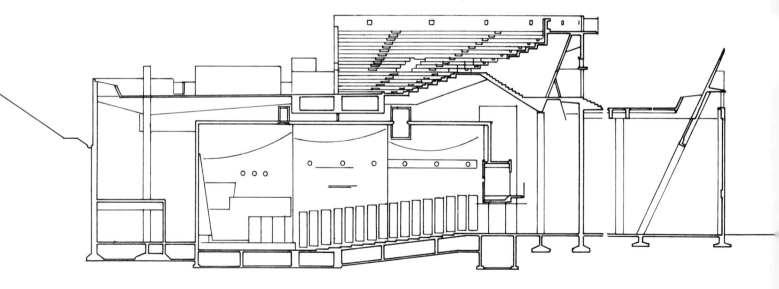

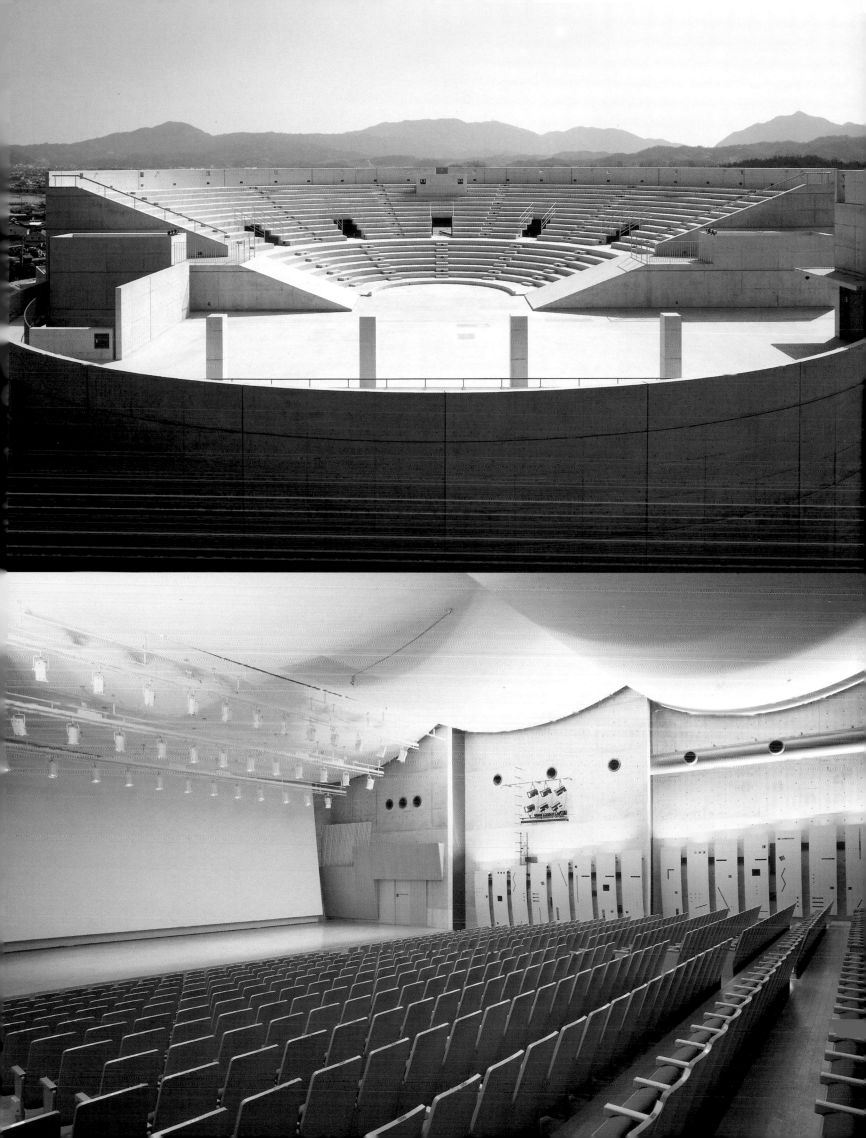

Candie Saint-Bernard
Paris, France.

Right
Gymnasium.

Below
View of the housing.

Opposite
Above
West elevation.
Below
View of the zinc facades.

provide housing, with the added benefit that some apartments straddle the two waves and can thus make use of two levels staggered to the west.

The incongruous forms that make the whole complex seem out-of-scale are domesticated by the traditional zinc of roofs and facades and their regular openings.

For the gymnasium and the sports facilities, the materials and colours chosen are harsh: rough concrete, grey and black textures. The result is aesthetically brutal and direct, but tempered by sensitive details and by the freshness of the black and white fresco by Enzo Cucchi.

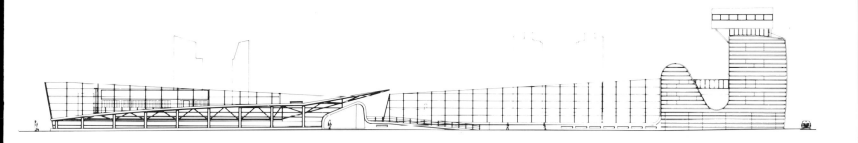

ODILE DECQ AND BENOÎT CORNETTE

Paris, France

Odile Decq and Benoît Cornette first came to public notice with their work for the Bank of Brittany in Rennes (1990). Since then, their reputation has grown as practitioners of a dynamic, metallic architecture, clearly inspired by the punk movement. Their projects emphasize movement, three-dimensionality and asymmetry in opposition to monumental stasis, frontal presentation and symmetry. Their aesthetic is kinetic, even cinematic, in the way in which it plays with ideas of speed and procession.

Carrières-sur-Seine Viaduct and
Motorway Control Station, Nanterre, France

On the one hand, a viaduct that links an underground junction and a motorway bridge; on the other, a building: the control station for the motorway network. Above, the motorway with its noise, its speed, the smell of petrol; below, a landscaped park along the Seine, the end of the green corridor that runs along the historical axis of Paris. Between the two, a pilot building. Located in a network of flows and fluidity, this project is a place of passage with its own dynamic equilibrium.

The three main elements of the viaduct, the roadway, supports and piers are clearly disassociated from one another. Thus, the functional autonomy and the structural role of each of the elements are clearly identifiable and the construction's appearance is considerably simplified. The continuity of the park is thus preserved and the green area is not imprisoned within a wall of motorway.

Better still, the position of the control station also preserves the physical continuity of the park.

Rather than placing the control station like a barrier in the middle of the park, it has been raised off the ground and attached to the underside of the motorway bridge. The area under the building is no more than a shadow on the green park. Thanks to this miracle of levitation, the control station in no way forms part of the park, but clearly belongs to the motorway system, of which it constitutes the pilot's cabin.

But the control station is submarine as well as air-borne. It is immersed in the flow of traffic that continuously rushes past. Only the supervisor's box protrudes. This volume is inserted between the two roadways that make up the motorway bridge, rising above the traffic with its antenna raised towards the sky, thus marking the entrance to the capital and the nerve centre of the motorway control system.

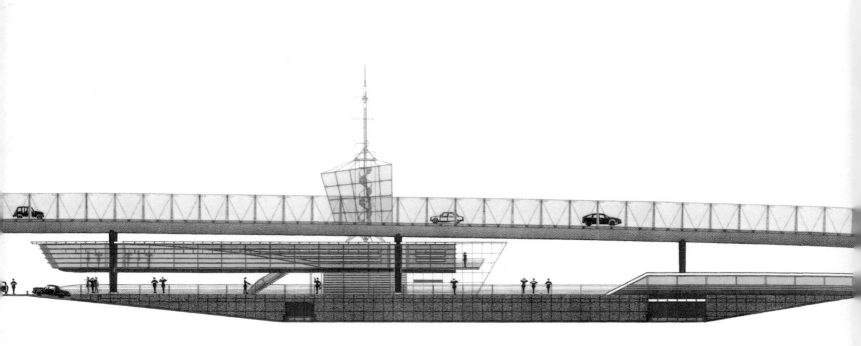

Motorway Control Station
Nanterre, France.

Above
Elevation.
Centre
Cross section.
Below
General plan.

Opposite
Colour perspective.

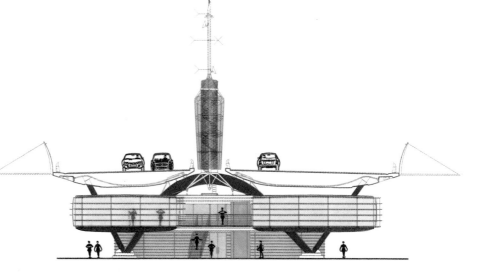

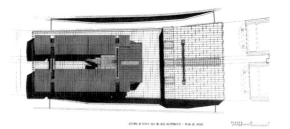

GÜNTHER DOMENIG

Graz, Austria

Günther Domenig began by flirting with the ideas of megastructure that were fashionable in the 1960s. He went on to play an active part in the school of young Austrian architects known as the School of Graz. An office building that appeared to be the result of a catastrophe, a high-tech masterpiece that had passed through an earthquake – the Central Savings Bank in Vienna (1979) – sealed his reputation.

Domenig has set out to explore new territory for expressionism. His menacing figures in concrete and steel evoke Atlantic bunkers or the space ship of the film *Alien*. They make a strong and unsettling statement.

Opposite and overleaf
Stone House
Steindorf, Austria.
General views.

Stone House, Steindorf, Autriche

Architecture and landscape
Architecture and the site
Architecture and the idea
The one site
grass and stone
The other site
open and soft
The subjective dimensions of the site
The site as memory
The site as experience
The site as representation
The site as self-representation

Hills rise from the ground
rocks burst through
They are separated by an abyss
The rocks are metal
and the hills are walls
Spaces and paths
leading below the water table

cut through them.
Deep down in the basement
the spiral staircase
the arrow
and water emerging from the ground
in the stationary
and in the floating
rocks dreams also
come piggy-back
The abyss is where one walks
the cube where one meets
the wedge where one eats.
The low path under the water
to the water
the high path
to the water
and into the water
Breaking out
getting ready
to break through

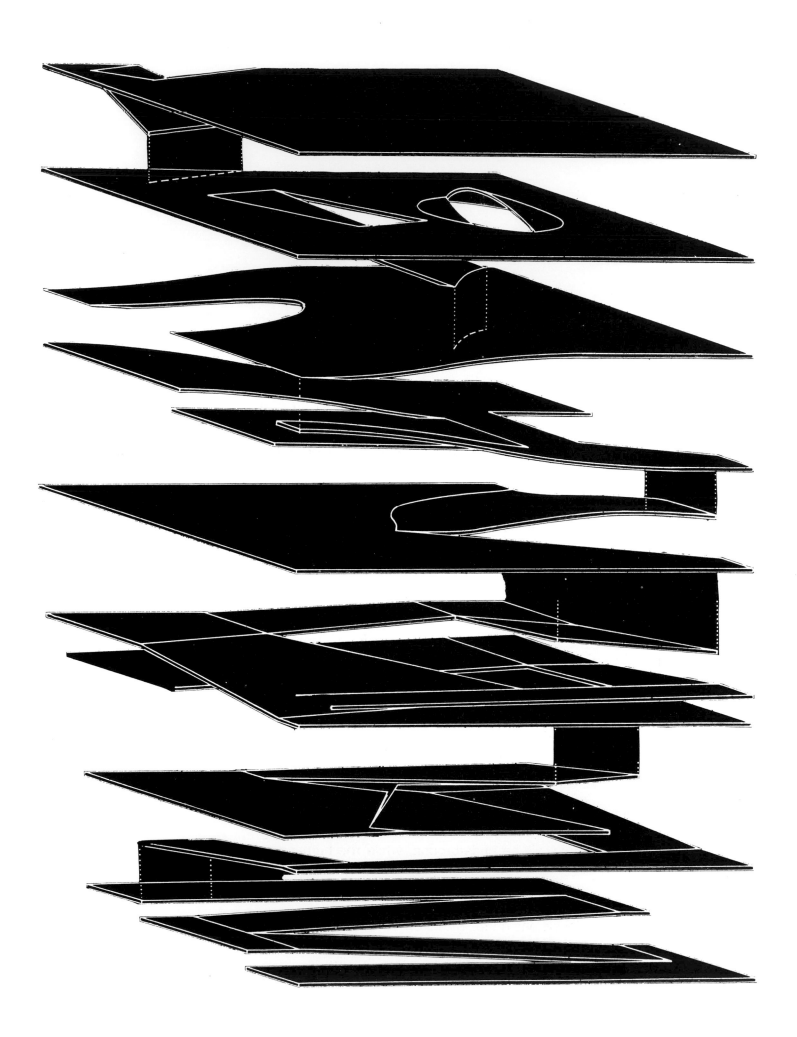

OMA – REM KOOLHAAS

Rotterdam, Netherlands

Rem Koolhaas and OMA (Office for Metropolitan Architecture) established their reputation in the 1970s through a series of provocative manifesto-projects, culminating in a book which proclaimed the need for a "culture of congestion": *New York Delirium*.

These projects were inspired by the determination to return to a modernity that had somehow managed to survive on the other side of the Atlantic, thanks to an overwhelming culture of optimism. "The richest ideas are to be found lying in the dustbin of history", Koolhaas said later. "If there is a method to be employed in this work [architecture], then it is that of systematic idealization, the automatic over-estimation of the existing state of affairs, a speculative onslaught which [...] will be unleashed even on what is most mediocre".

Rem Koolhaas's talents are obvious in his dance theatre in The Hague, the Alva house, the Rotterdam Kunsthalle and the Lille Conference Centre. His next great challenge will be the libraries for the Jussieu university campus in Paris, for which he won the competition in 1992.

The Two Libraries, Jussieu campus, Paris, France

The Jussieu libraries will not be a building, but a network. Conceived at the hub of the campus, they will gather there like a residue, plain, empty, sandwiched between their base and the existing buildings.

So as to make its presence felt again, we have imagined in this project that the surface of the ground area is flexible, a sort of communal flying carpet, which we have folded up to create a pile of platforms. These platforms will complete the grid patterns of the Jussieu site.

The essential problem of the present gound plan is its dispersion. By reconfiguring it in this way, its substance can be concentrated. So as to take best advantage of the site, the two libraries will be situated according to a relationship that is "inversely proportional" to the platforms and the reading rooms. Thus, the science library will be underground, while the humanities library will rise above the plaza which leads to the metro station to the south and to the river Seine to the north. The plaza will advance into the building like a double helix to form the reception area.

Instead of simply piling up levels one on top of the other, the planes of each floor will be modified to connect them both to the floor above and the floor below. Thus a continuous path leads through the whole building, like the loops of an interior boulevard, offering both access and visibility. The visitor is like Baudelaire's *flâneur*, an observer who is seduced by the world of books, information and "urban situations" through which he strolls.

Opposite
The Two Libraries, Jussieu
Paris, France.
The form is a pile of platforms that are cut out and unfolded in a continuous strip.

The Two Libraries, Jussieu,
Paris, France.

Above
North facade (facing the Seine), east facade
(facing the Jardin des Plantes), south
facade (facing the Jussieu campus) and
west facade (facing the Institute of the
Arab World).
Below
Sections.

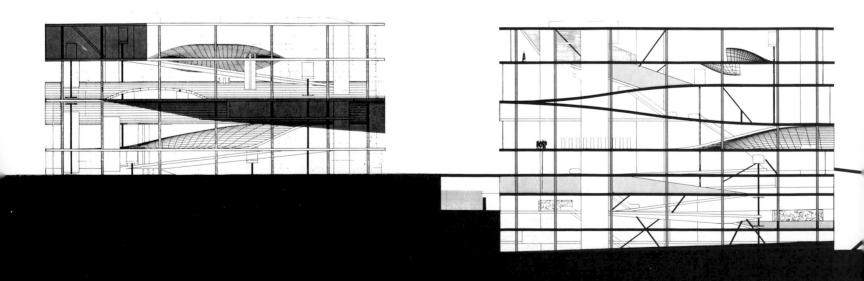

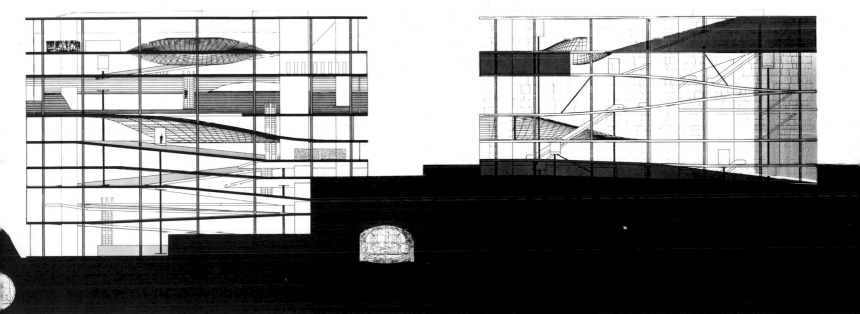

The Two Libraries, Jussieu campus
Paris, France.

Above
Interiors (studies).
Above right
Structural model.
Below
Unfolded section and level plans
with circulation paths.

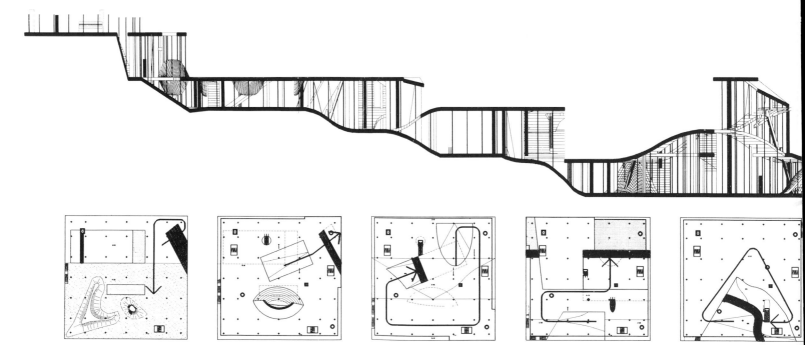

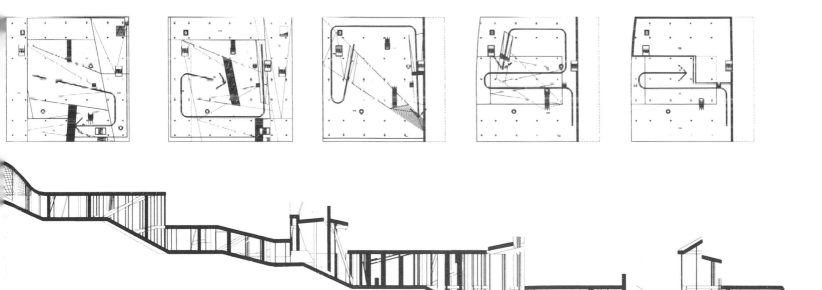

ZAHA HADID

London, Great Britain

Zaha Hadid comes from Irak, but has long made her home in London, where she graduated from the Architectural Association*. She first came to public notice with OMA in 1978, for her entry in the competition for the parliament building in The Hague. Her earliest projects were influenced by Malevich and Supremacism, and she has retained her taste for a weightless architecture, created by displacing large plane surfaces in an ethereal space. Her winning project in the 1983 competition for "The Peak" in Hong Kong was exemplary in this respect. She has disarmed envious critics with the success of her built projects – in Japan, or near Basle, with the fire station she designed for the furniture manufacturer and architecture "collector", Vitra. It is no longer possible to cast doubt on the appropriacy of her methods and the spatial wealth of her painterly designs.

Art and Media Centre, Düsseldorf, Germany

The Düsseldorf Art and Media Centre project provided the impetus for the redevelopment of the old Düsseldorf harbour area. Rising from the river, an enormous metallic triangle pierces the wall, to form an entrance ramp to the street and a sloping plaza below. The adjoining ground planes crack open to reveal technical studios to the north, shops and restaurants to the south. Below ground, the technical service aeras are compressed into a wall part of which rises above ground, curving round to form a 320-seat cinema. On the street side the wall has tiny, linear incisions in its concrete elevation; while on the river side, individual floors are articulated by varying depths of cantilever. One floor breaks completely free, leaving a void which becomes a terrace; then, on reaching an adjoining block, it turns into a solid black box.

The advertising agency is an even more fragmented series of slabs, set perpendicular to the street. It is a minimalist glass box surrounded by a family of sculptured supports and heavy, triangular, transfer structures.

Vitra Fire Station, Weil am Rhein, Germany

The whole building is petrified movement, expressing the tension of being on the alert all the time, and the potential to burst into action at any moment. The walls seem to slide past each other, while the large sliding doors literally form a moving wall.

The fire station also functions as a screening device in front of neighbouring buildings, thus complicating the identity of the Vitra complex. Space-defining and screening functions were the point of departure for the architectural concept: a linear, layered series of walls. The activities of the fire station occupy the spaces between these walls, which open, tilt on break in two, according to functional requirements.

Cardiff Bay Opera House, Cardiff, Great Britain

The building concept of the Cardiff Bay Opera House is based on the architectural expression of the hierarchy between serviced and servicing spaces: the auditorium and the other public and semi-public performance and rehearsal spaces are threaded like jewels on a string of rationally aligned support accommodation. This band is then wrapped around the perimeter of the site like an inverted necklace where all the jewels turn towards each other, creating a concentrated public space between them, accessible to the public from the centre, while serviced from the back around the perimeter.

Vitra Fire Station
Weil am Rhein, Germany.

Opposite
Above
The exterior at night.
Below
Interior.

Below
Concept drawing.

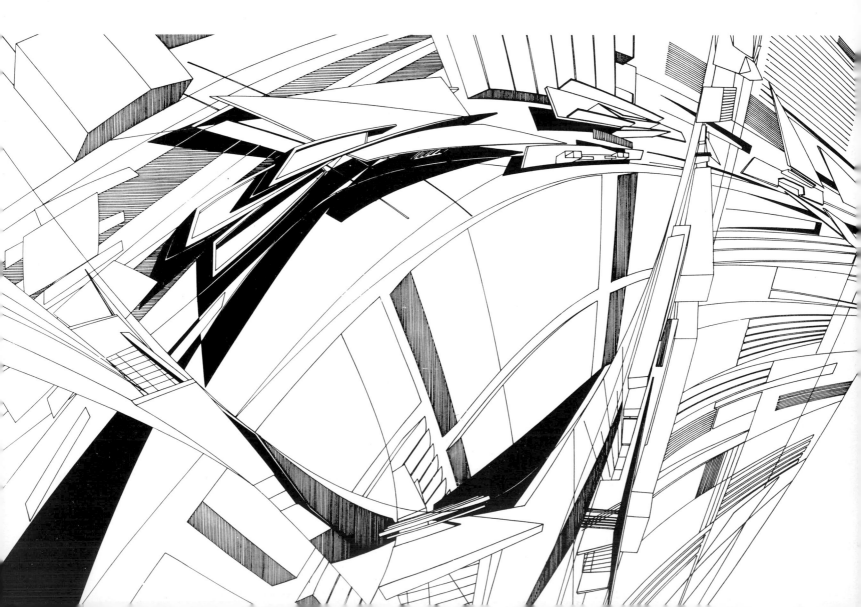

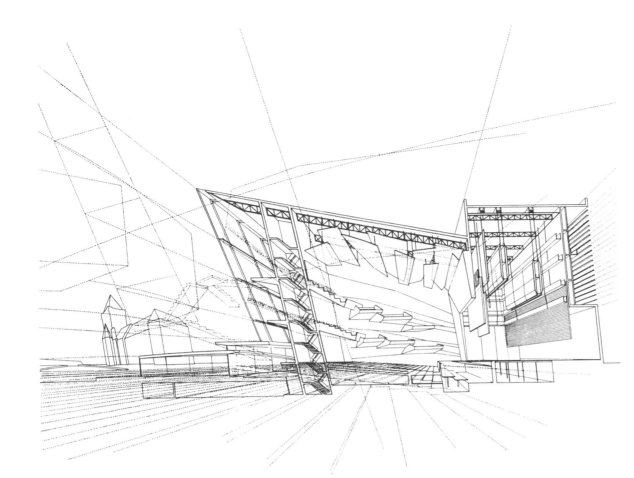

Cardiff Bay Opera House
Cardiff,
Great Britain.

Above
Section.
Below
View of the model.

Opposite

Above
Overall plan
Below
Aerial view of the second
model.

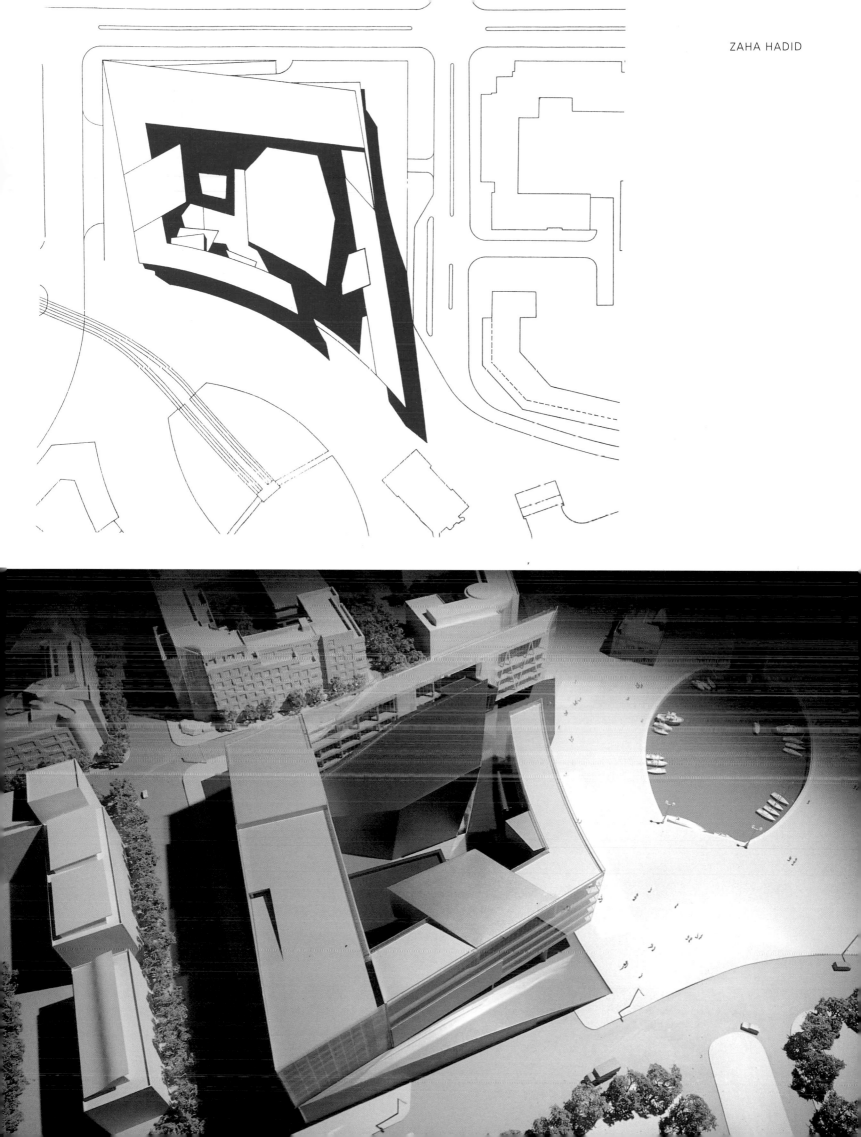

COOP HIMMELBLAU

Vienna, Austria
Los Angeles, California, USA

In the late 1960s, Vienna was suddenly invaded by psychedelic space capsules, giant inflatables and self-sufficient bubbles, a participative, subversive, pneumatic and hedonistic architecture that, once again, was destined to change our lives. The main protagonists in this adventure were Missing Link*, Haus Rucker Co* and Coop Himmelblau.

Once these dreams of a spatial Eden had evaporated, Coop Himmelblau recentred their activities on developing a provocative and abrasive architectural style. Their aim is weightlessness, and their means are the inversion of the interior/exterior distinction. But all their taut cables and protruding antennae cannot entirely hide their highly sophisticated technical achievements.

A Future of Splendid Desolation
Essay

The architectures of the future have already been built.

The solitude of its squares, the desolation of its streets, the devastation of its buildings characterize the city of the present and will characterize the city of the future as well. Expressions like "safe and sound" are no longer applicable to architecture.

We live in a world of unloved objects, relics of an urban civilisation. We have these objects, and we use them daily to our advantage. Today's architecture reinforces this discrepancy, until it becomes schizophrenic.

Reactionary architecture tends to conceal the problems rather than create the necessary new urban awareness.

Today's architecture must be defined as a medium of expanding vitality.

Contemporary architecture will be honest and true, when streets, open spaces, buildings and infrastructures reflect the image of urban reality, when the devastation of the city is transformed into fascinating landmarks of desolation. Desolation not as a result of complacency but as a result of the identification of urban reality will encourage the desires, the self-confidence and the courage necessary to take hold of the city and to alter it.

The important thing won't then be the grass you can't walk on, but the asphalt you can.

Of course, you will have to discard everything that may obstruct this "emotional act of using". The false aesthetic, which sticks like smeared make-up to the face of mediocrity, the cowardice of antiquated values, the belief that everything that is disquieting can be beautified. The autocrats whose motto is "efficiency, economy and expediency".

Architects must stop thinking only of how to accommodate their clients.
Architects have to stop pitying themselves for the bad company they keep.
Architecture is not a means to an end.
Architecture does not have to function.
Architecture is not palliative. It is the bone in the meat of the city.
Architecture gains meaning in proportion to its desolation.
This desolation comes from the act of using, it gains strength from the surrounding desolation.
And this architecture brings the message:
Everything you like is bad.
Everything that works is bad.
Whatever has to be accepted is good.

UFA Cinema Complex, Dresden, Germany

The UFA Cinema Complex unites three districts of Dresden into one continuous urban landscape. Its triangular form is seen as a transparent glass envelope which, like an aquarium, houses a liquid space filled with free-floating, dynamic entities. The external facades are made up of multiple screens through which the people inside can be seen moving around amid changing patterns of light and colour.

The Groningen Museum, Netherlands

The design concept for the new Groningen Museum of Art is based on the idea of unfolding positive and negative space. The section mass evokes a series of broken volumes with the different strata revealed along the sectional lines. The breaks in the skin allow the inside to come out as well as the outside to fold inwards. The building has been described as volumes placed in a light-space, volumes of light cutting through mass.

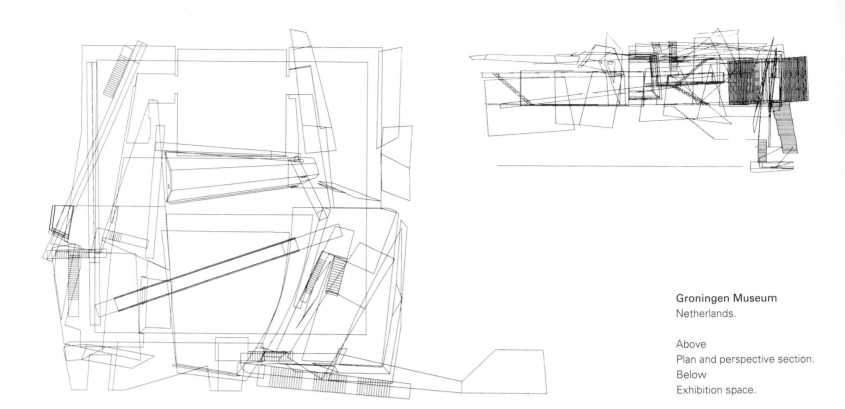

Groningen Museum
Netherlands.

Above
Plan and perspective section.
Below
Exhibition space.

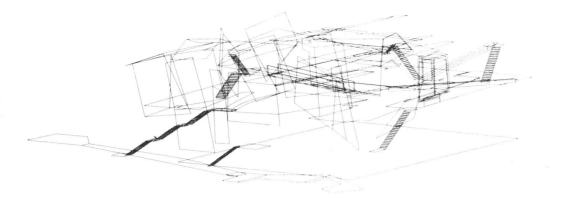

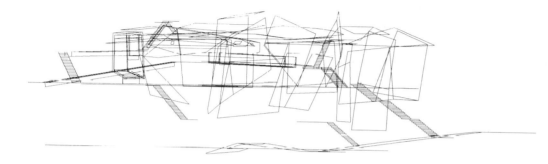

Above
Computer-assisted perspective sections.
Below
Exhibition space.

Overleaf
South-west facade.

ENRIC MIRALLES MOYA

Barcelona, Spain

Enric Miralles has been at the forefront of the new wave of contemporary Spanish architecture which combines the rigour and restraint of the modernist tradition with formal invention, material sensuality and contextual sensitivity. His work seems to break down the barriers between architecture and landscape, so that the man-made and the natural gradually merge and fuse.

New Entrance to Takaoka Railway Station, Japan

The aim of the new entrance is to articulate the way to the station by creating a landmark at the end of the avenue leading to it, and to restore to the square in front of the station the symmetry that was destroyed by a traffic layout that ignored all design and planning criteria. The architect describes his preoccupations as follows:

"The road leads to a square... The necessity of information... Trains and services... We wanted a facade which would take into account all the light and all the urban elements of a railway station complex... Communication links, display boards, wires, rails... As well as roofed-over areas where you can buy tickets or wait for the bus, safe from the weather."

Meditation Pavilion, Unazaki Gorge, Japan

The Meditation Pavilion in the Gorge of Unazaki was designed to make a traditional excursion spot even more attractive. A bridge, a small park and an old pilgrims' path have been linked to form an ensemble that is at one with the rugged beauty of nature.

"The snow which collects in the hollows will form artificial mountains and, later on, small fast-flowing streams of rain water... The transparent surfaces will mirror the contours of the mountains, the water of the river, the fish and the birds..."

Opposite
New Entrance to Takaoka Station
Japan.

The perspective of the new station entrance creates a focal point at the end of the avenue. It consists of lightweight elements, columns and rails, with electronic displays, showing all the necessary information for travellers. Groups of aluminium rails bearing the illuminated lettering run along the facade. They are supported by columns of concrete and steel. In front of the entrance, the columns draw close to form a forest. Some of them pierce through the roofs which are covered with metal or glass.

Perspective of the structure of the rails.

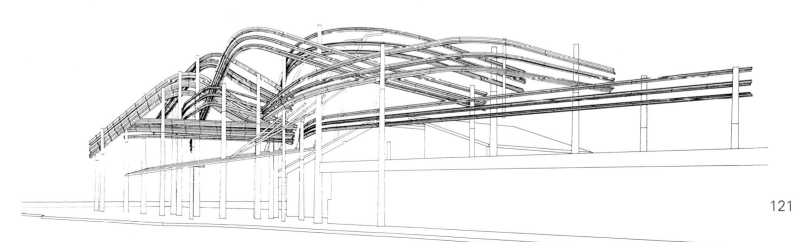

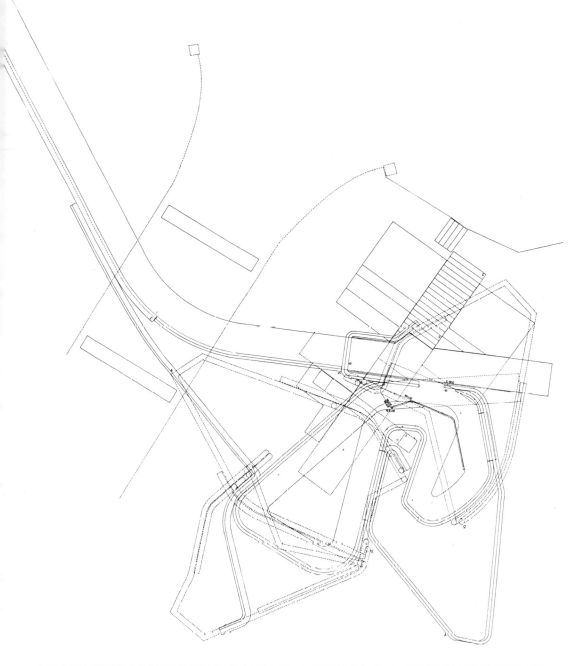

Meditation Pavilion
Unazaki Gorge, Japan.

Above
Overall plan.

Opposite and below
View of the pavilion.

The pavilion is anchored in the steep mountain slope and hangs out over the abyss, supported by pillars arranged in pairs. The frame consists of steel girders and is filled in with glass and wooden panels. Steel frames, covered with bamboo shoots, form a screen, creating a feeling of intimacy. The roof in glass and zinc sheeting consists of a number of elements set off against one another at different angles and in varying shapes and materials.
Design criteria were:
Search for the best location for the pavilion.
Establishment of the best route for travellers.
Exploring the scenic landscape.
Architecture as the preparation for a moment of meditation and inner peace, of fusion with an almost virgin landscape.
Showing due respect by careful analysis of the genius loci.
Exploring every turn in the path.
Understanding the gigantic changes in scale which the bridge introduces into the landscape.

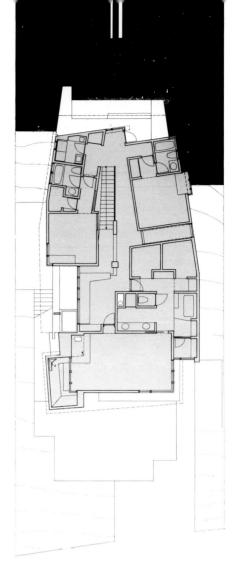

FRANKLIN D. ISRAEL

Los Angeles, California, USA

Born in New York, Frank Israel studied at Yale and Columbia, winning the 1973 Rome Prize. His early life was nomadic, as he moved between a period at the American Academy in Rome, and his position as a "senior" architect with Llewelin-Davies, the agency that was responsible for the major urban development projects of the Shah of Iran. In 1977, "exiled from his own town", it was almost inevitable Israel should settle in Los Angeles. There he taught, was involved in the cinema and, under the influence of Frank Gehry, returned to architectural practice. His work since then has played on the sensuality of materials and colours (in an Angelino tradition closer to Schindler than to Neutra), composing object landscapes, micro-cities that fluctuate between tension and relaxation.

Drager House, Berkeley, California, USA

The Drager House replaces the original 1926 house which was destroyed by forest fires in 1991. The new design takes full advantage of the topography of the site, whether backing onto the existing slope of the hill or hollowing it out. Its volume is more modest than that of its predecessor, but the surface area created is greater. The articulation of the different levels is emphasized by terraces and external staircases. Frank Israel here demonstrates his sensitivity to place, giving his own free interpretation of the San Francisco Bay vernacular style. Instead of the omnipresent natural shingle, he uses a copper substitute to enwrap the taut volumes in a willful structure of trapezoid planes, that serve to shade the extensive areas of glazing.

Weisman Pavilion, Brentwood, California, USA

In spite of his many donations in recent years, Frederick Weisman still owns an important collection of contemporary art which his house was no longer large enough to exhibit. So he decided to house it in a new pavilion designed by Frank Israel, a simple structure on two levels built into the hillside.

The lower level, which is accessed from the garden under a porch that also forms a balcony for the gallery, contains the storerooms and studios. The upper level comprises a tall rectangular gallery with a sloping roof, its wooden structure being fully visible.

Two small masterpieces by craftsmen contribute to the effect of this understated building: the porch/balcony that rises up out of the garden facade like some spaceship invented by Jules Verne, and the staircase in wood and metal that leads to the garden from the gallery.

Drager House
Berkeley, California, USA.

Above
Third-floor plan.

Opposite
From the south west.

Below
By night.

Weisman Pavilion
Brentwood, California, USA.

Opposite
The porch/balcony.

Above
Garden facade.
Below
The gallery and the staircase
leading to the garden.

ERIC OWEN MOSS

Los Angeles, California, USA

Born in Los Angeles, Eric Owen Morris was educated at the University of Southern California (UCLA), then made a detour via Berkeley and Harvard, before returning to set up his practice in his home town. Like Frank Gehry, he is acutely sensitive to the specificities of Los Angeles – its loose structure, its contextual vagaries, its heterogeneity of materials. But that is as far as the comparison goes. Frank Gehry's interpretation of this incomplete city is relaxed, not to say disenchanted. But for Moss, the quality-free environment of the suburbs is an exceptional catalyst. He deploys banal, even incongruous materials (chipboard, vitrified clay tubing) with a maniacal precision to create complex geometries and superbly refined forms.

Samitaur 1, Culver City, California, USA

The building site for Samitaur I is subject to multiple zoning regulations: it's cut off at the top by a height limit; at the bottom by a truck clearance requirement; at the perimeter by the City Fire Department who wouldn't allow the new building above to extend over existing buildings. So the zoning rules defined the limits of an orthogonal block, within which the architect provided certain anomalies, in the form of voids in the block.

There are two primary anomalies, where trucks and cars enter the road under the structure, and where they exit. A conference space and a lounge/bathroom area also constitute exceptions within the block. New steel legs dance around old roll-up doors, while driveways and windows allow existing buildings to operate as before.

Samitaur 1
Culver City, California, USA.
Detail of the model.

Opposite
Two views of the model.
The office space is supported on steel legs that straddle the road.

Below
Axonometric.

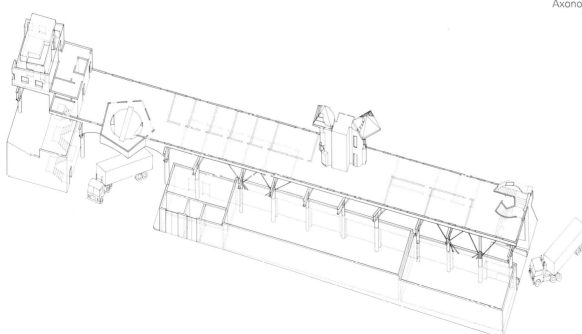

The Box
Culver City, California, USA.

Right
Plans of staircases, the conference room and the roof .

Opposite
Axonometric.

The Box – reception/deck/conference area – is one material and one colour, an almost black cement plaster inside and out. No material distinctions are made from roof to wall and none from inside surface to outside. The Box has three parts. The first is an almost cylindrical reception area, which cuts into the roof of the existing wood shed. Behind the reception area is an exterior stair that leads to a second level roof deck supported on the exposed trussed system below, and suspended over the cylinder. The zone between square deck and round roof cut is glazed, lighting the reception space below. Up the exterior stair, a door between levels 2 and 3 connects an interior stair to the Box itself, a private third-floor conference space.

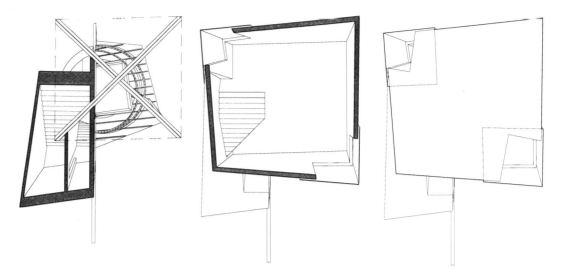

The Box, Culver City, California, USA

The formal expression of the Box – a private third-floor conference space added to an existing building – works by arguing with the simple, orthogonal box shape, both as a traditional precept, and as an amended object which extends the box idea.

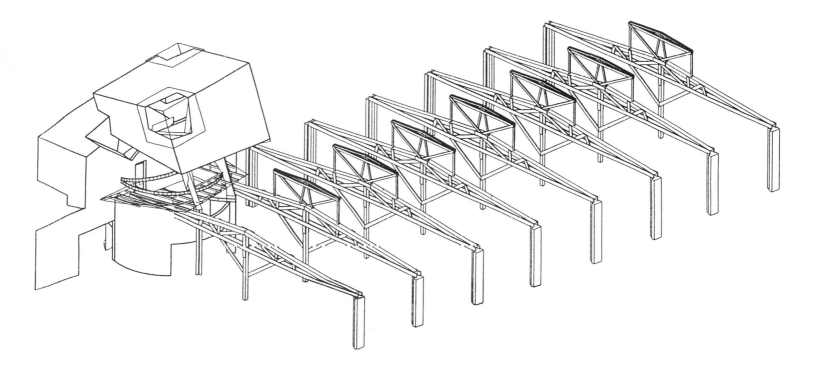

FRANK O. GEHRY

Los Angeles, California, USA

Frank Gehry is an insatiable exporer of the forms and materials available to the contemporary architect. Since the early 1970s, he has been producing work that is strong, proteiform, open to new inventions. His first Angelino constructions – the Ron Davis studio (1972), the Gehry house (1978) – are remarkable for their economy of means, their casting against type of materials, their relaxed execution, their simple yet often skewed geometry and their dramatic perspectives. In his more complex large-scale projects, he uses fragmentation to break up any single sense of scale, and produce an accretion of "small one-room buildings", as at the Loyola Law Faculty in Los Angeles.

His international reputation brought him to Europe, where he built an almost expressionistic museum for Vitra on the outskirts of Basle. The Frederick Weisman Museum in Minneapolis marks a turning point in his work, which Gehry himself has likened to Matisse's discovery of paper cut-outs.

Opposite
Weisman Art Museum
Minneapolis, USA
The galleries.

Weisman Art Museum, Minneapolis, USA

The University of Minnesota Museum is intended to draw together a campus that spreads along both banks of the river Mississippi. It is located at one end of the Washington Avenue road bridge, to which it is directly connected by a pedestrian ramp.

The museum space follows a logical sequence: on the main floor, entered from the foot bridge, are the galleries, the auditorium and the permanent collections; beneath them are the service areas, studios and car park; while the "tower" that rises above the galeries houses the administrative offices.

Gehry is always passionate in his attention to light, mixing artificial and natural sources. Here, the natural light comes from three "chimneys" which have been sited to ensure that no ray of light should ever directly strike the picture rails. Whence the turbulent outlines of the building's external form, whose chaos is emphasized by the large plates of bright stainless steel which look out towards the far bank of the river.

Guggenheim Museum, Bilbao, Spain

The Guggenheim Museum in Bilbao is intended to fit in with the existing proportions of the town, and with the traditional construction materials to be found along the river front. The sculptural form of the roof serves to unify the different buildings. The impressive scale of the central atrium allows it to house monumental installations and spectacular one-off events. Equipped with a powerful computer network, the museum is ready to cope with innovations in electronic art forms and performances using the new media.

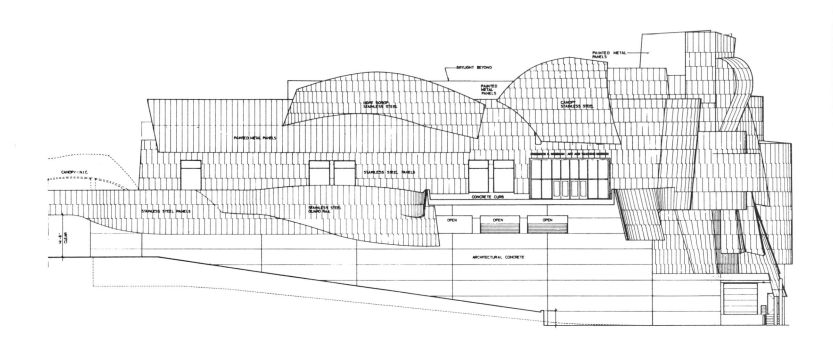

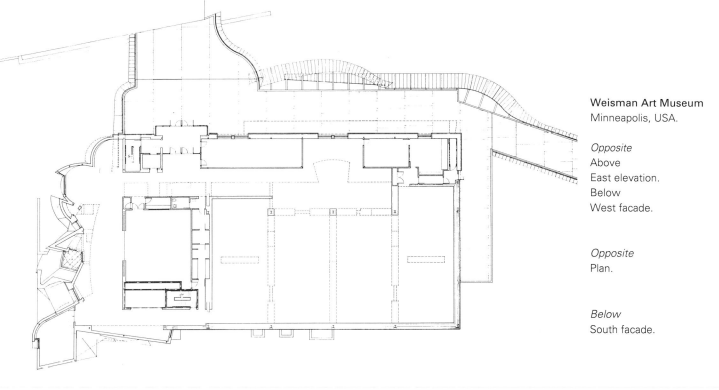

Weisman Art Museum
Minneapolis, USA.

Opposite
Above
East elevation.
Below
West facade.

Opposite
Plan.

Below
South facade.

Guggenheim Museum
Bilbao, Spain.

Above
Roof plan.

Below
View of the river facade.

Opposite
Above
Ground floor plan.
Below
General view of the model.

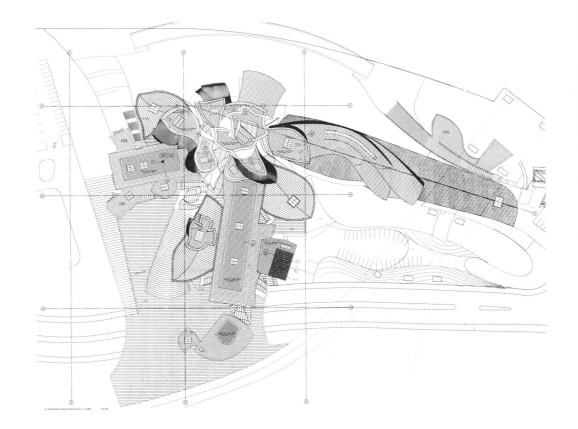

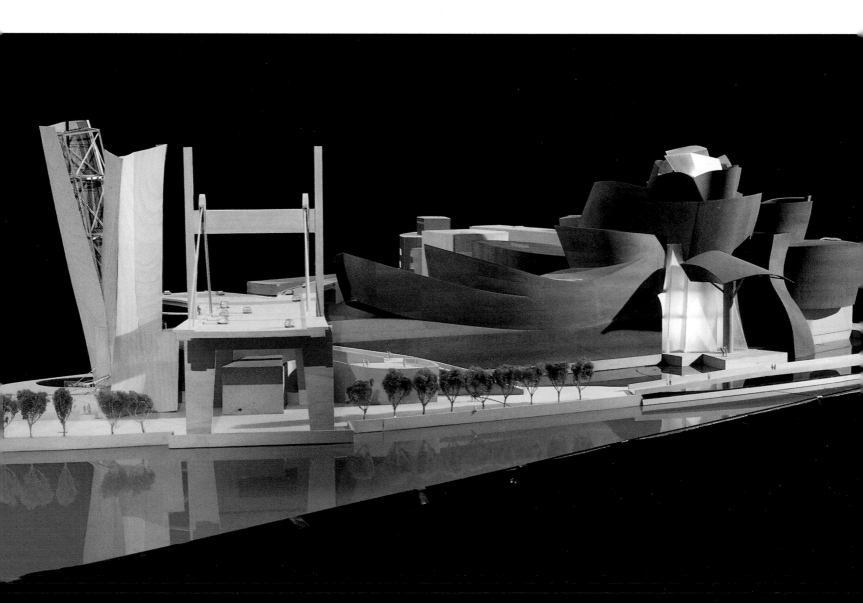

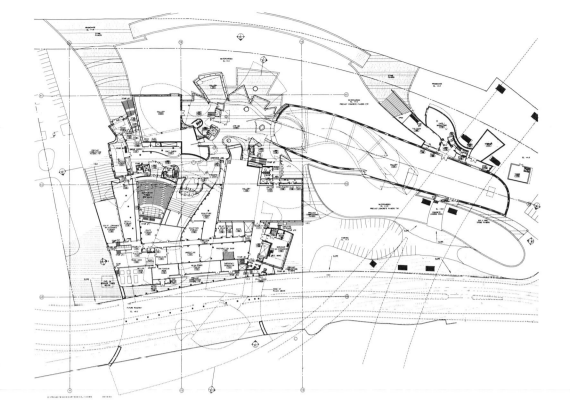

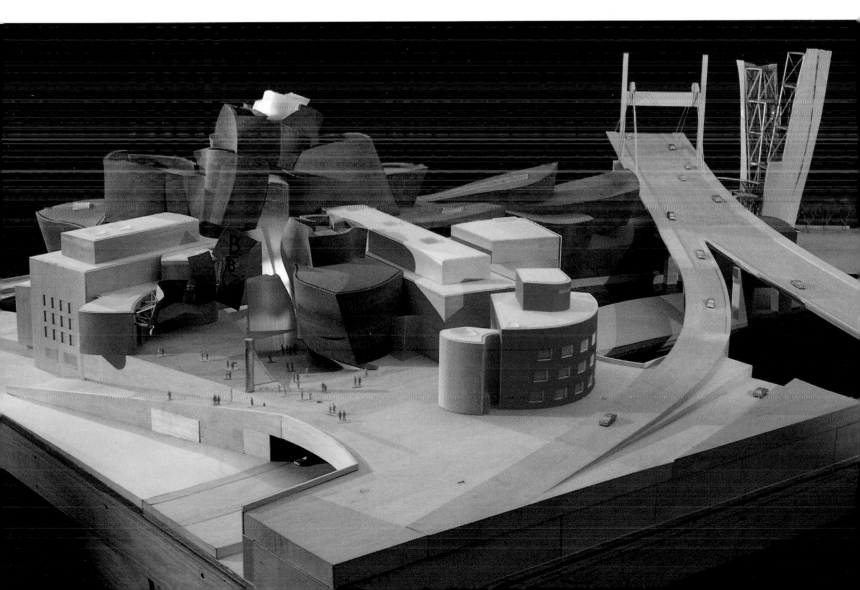

4. A SECOND NATURE

"You know, I think we should put mountains here.
Otherwise, where will the people fall from?
And what if we add a staircase?
Yodellayheehoo."
Laurie Anderson

Ever since the Enlightenment, the loss of nature has haunted the city dweller's conscience. The cruelty and dangers of nature have been forgotten in favour of an idyllic and harmonious image, of nostalgia for a lost paradise or a rediscovered Arcadia based on a new peaceful relationship between man and the elements.

At the end of the 20th century, urbanisation has reawoken this consciousness. For the architect, who deals with the real world, these rejuvenated preoccupations with ecology have taken on a pragmatic form that expresses itself in two opposing ways:

– either by restoring the relationship between nature and the human environment that has been compromised: we introduce nature into the city;

– or by questioning the true nature of nature (and thus of artifice) in the light of the questions posed by the apostles of "virtual reality". "After all" Itsuko Hasegawa has said, "all artefacts produced by man have their origin in nature."∎

EMILIO AMBASZ

New York, USA

Well-known both as a product designer and as an architect, Emilio Ambasz's distinctive approach stems from his special interest in the nature of materials and his reinterpretation of natural environments through technology. His tendency to design series of highly-defined, technologically sophisticated objects connected to each other by a narrative thread, points to the influence of his work as a product designer. But his characteristic explorations of the ground plane as a three-dimensional space in itself are specifically architectural.

Opposite
House for Leo Castelli

Green cities: ecology and architecture
Essay

A green town is man created architecture that is in harmony with nature and the earth to provide a friendly space for human beings. There is a great tradition in urban planning, starting in the late nineteenth century, towards creating garden cities. The most outstanding among many enlightened practitioners was Ebenezer Howard. He proposed the creation of garden cities which became the forerunners of those suburban communities which have developed around London. Later, similar minded movements introduced this idea to the United States where a number of such garden city communities were developed. Naturally, these American communities were modified versions of the original British models, reflecting the availability of land as well as the beginning of an automobile-determined society. In essence, they were the forerunners of what we now know as the American suburbs.

Recently there has been a growing inquiry into the new American phenomenon referred to as "Edge-Cities" wherein new suburban communities, having sprung fully grown on the edge of larger cities, are born fully empowered politically, capable as well as willing to contest the supremacy of the nearby large city. In all cases, suburbs and "Edge-Cities" are attempts at finding urban solutions that will be spiritually, as well as economically, fulfilling. To date we have evidence that none of the models built so far has satisfactorily succeeded. Moreover, we have great evidence that many of the new cities created from zero to become capitals, such as Brasilia and Ahmedabad, have been resounding failures. It is only man's infinite capacity for adaptation that lets them limpingly survive.

Therefore, there is a need to develop new models. Today's electronic means make it possible for a very large number of professions to perform their tasks from home, or from satellite offices, without the need of direct presence at headquarters. By the same token, it is no longer necessary for headquarters to be established in large cities in order to draw on a pool of talent, since now the pool of talent can be obtained nationwide. This is far from fostering the notion that any social group can prosper without having direct physical contact. That would be an unwise foundation on which to build an idea, but it is also true that such physical contacts can be organized productively and designed to come about where needed, and not be just the result of casual vicinity.

Ideally, a new town should begin operation with a population ranging from 10 to 35 thousand inhabitants. This will provide the critical mass necessary to support a number of social activities.

We propose to create a new town which is a Green Town. We have had examples of suburban towns where the house sits in the centre of the garden. We propose to go beyond the house in the garden to have "the house AND the garden." In some countries we have seen enlightened legislation aimed at having the "green surrounding the grey," that is to say, gardens surrounding the buildings. What is daringly proposed here is that we should have the "green OVER the grey." I have spent the last twenty-five years of my professional life making proposals to create buildings which give back to the community as much of the green as possible. In some cases I have been able to give back one hundred per cent of the land in the form of gardens which occupy the same area as the ground which the building covers.

A building of this nature should be accessible to the whole community, used by the members of the community at large as well as by the corporation members who pay for it. The architectural formula of putting the "green over the grey," or the "soft over the hard," shows a very simple but profound way of creating new urban settlements which do not alienate the citizens from the vegetable kingdom, but rather, create an architecture which is inextricably woven into the greenery, into nature.

I have worked on this idea, piece by piece, over the last twenty years. My method of work has been to create first a "catalogue," a typological sampling, of the different types of buildings which would be needed to house the diverse needs of such a new Green Town. These buildings have been designed according to the principles of the "green over the grey" and of giving back to the community as much as possible of the land covered by the building. Some of these buildings have been built, and there are others which have not yet come to fruition for reasons mainly having to do with the present economic recession.

The idea of Green Towns is a magnificent opportunity for a country, such as Japan, to give its own unique answer to the problem of society's urbanization process as it passes from a secondary and tertiary type of economy onto a quaternary level, concerned with the creation and utilization of information.

Phoenix Museum of History, Arizona, USA

The Phoenix Museum of History – a pilot project in an ambitious redevelopment programme – restores to the city virtually all the land that a more traditional design would have taken away. Triangular wall sections functioning like buttresses in the indigenous adobe architecture protrude into the central courtyard and leave openings that allow light to flood into the gallery space behind. The two sides meet in a circular double-height lobby where visitors experience the sensation of descending deep within the earth.

Fukuoka Prefecture International Hall, Japan

The design for the Fukuoka Prefectural International Hall extends an existing park through a series of low terraced gardens that climb the full height of the building's south side, culminating in a belvedere that offers a breathtaking view of the city harbour. Park and building work together to return to the city the land they occupy, by doubling the size of the existing public space while also creating a powerful symbolic structure at the centre of Fukuoka.

Worldbridge Trade and Investment Center, Baltimore, Maryland

The Worldbridge Trade and Investment Centre comprises an office complex that looks like the result of an orchestrated eruption of the earth's surface and an exhibition hall in the form of a carefully-wrought cavity. Together they are composed from a graduated pile of organically-shaped plates. In the office complex, gardens are placed where one plate extends beyond the next. The monumental atrium – a truncated cone – is dramatically lit from above by an oculus. At the base of the interior space, a two-storey bowl opens onto a landscape of rock, moving water, and abundant plant life. The sunken exhibition hall offers a sense of spaciousness through the controlled use of vegetation and the introduction of natural light through its hollow core.

Overleaf

Above left
Fukuoka Prefecture International Hall
Japan.
View of the model.
Below left
Section.

Above right

Worldbridge Trade and Investment Center
Baltimore, Maryland, USA.
View of the model.
Below left
Section.

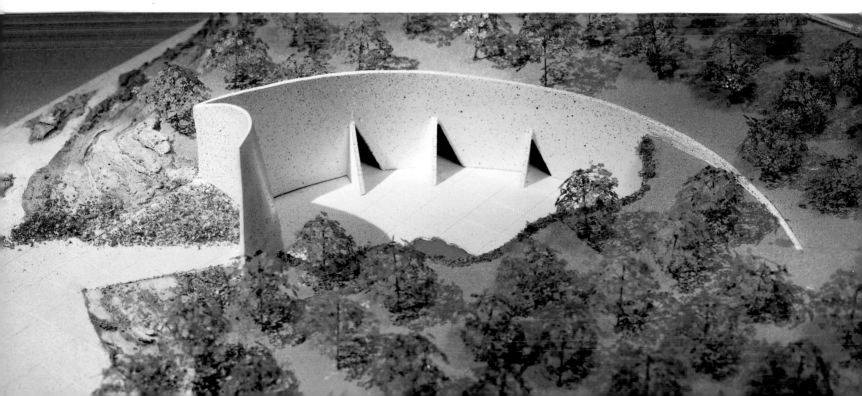

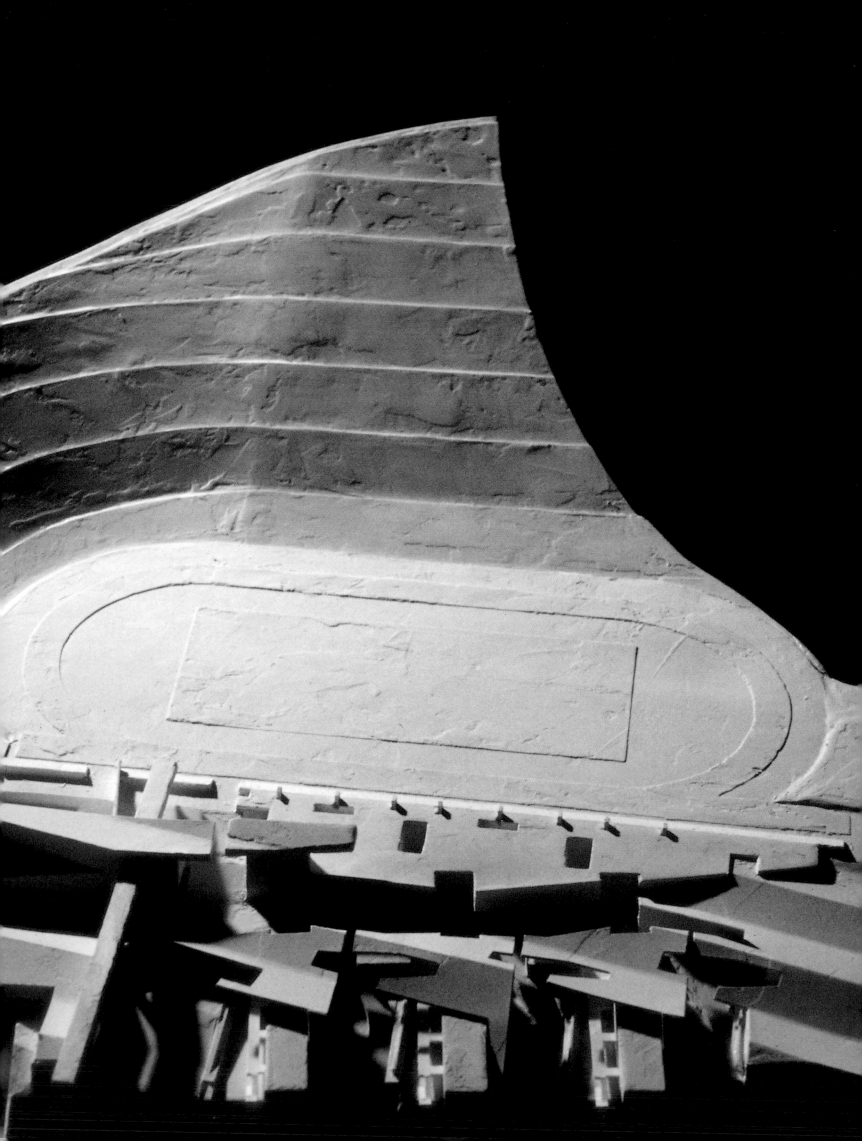

MORPHOSIS

Los Angeles, California, USA

Founded in 1974 by Thom Mayne and Michael Rotondi, and now run by Thom Mayne alone, Morphosis belongs to an Angelino architectural tradition which seeks to create new relationships between man and nature in a given urban context. Its work is rooted in forms where deconstructionist allusions can be found alongside a strong sense of drama. This aesthetic is exemplified in Kate Mantilini's Restaurant and the underground extension to the Cedars Sinai Hospital.

Diamond Ranch High School, Pomona, California

Diamond Ranch High School focuses on the desire to take advantage of the natural beauty of the site by integrating the playing fields and the buildings with the surrounding hillsides. The aim is to create a dynamic built environment to foster maximum social interaction between students, teachers, administration and the community. It should also provide a flexible teaching environment.

The intention was to create a building that would be perceived as "at one with the site" rather than "on top of the site." By reshaping the topography with outdoor playing fields, public spaces and a continuous undulating surface, Morphosis attempted to create a cohesive ensemble of building and landscape. In a similar manner, the building is integrated with its users through the courtyards and a pedestrian street which encourages interaction while fostering flexibility within the learning community. The project is also presented as a tangible way of preserving nature.

Opposite
Diamond Ranch High School
Pomona, California, USA.
View of the model

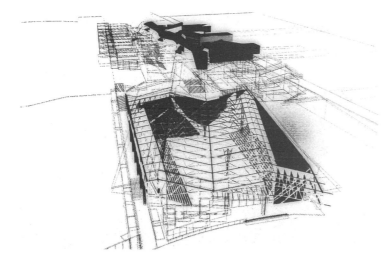

Computer perspective.

Diamond Ranch High School
Pomona, California, USA.
Perspectives.

Opposite
Aerial view of the model.

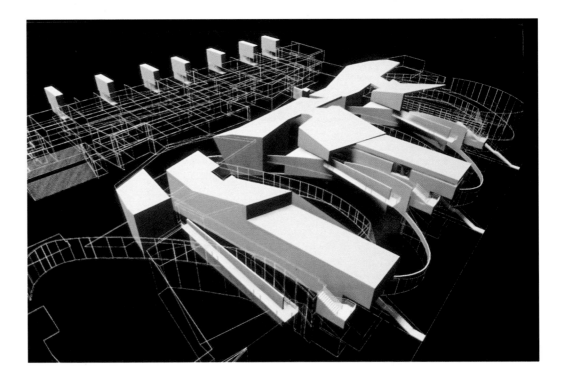

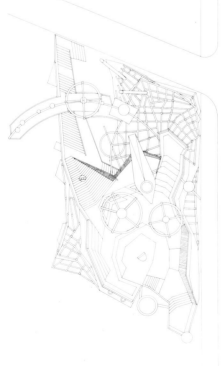

MASAHARU TAKASAKI

Tokyo, Japan

Masaharu Takasaki's response to the visual and structural chaos of Japanese cities is to invoke the power of nature, but without approaching anything like the ideas of the "organic" that are entertained in the west. His buildings are highly complex structures, executed in moulded metal and glass, with the occasional prominent timber element, which invites their colonisation by nature. He believes in architecture as a social art, "a form through which people are incited to realise their own visions of cosmos, nature and themselves."

Earth Architecture, Tokyo, Japan

For the Earth Architecture project, extensive psychological studies were undertaken. The architectural spaces created are the result of detailed consideration of how to combine and arrange "open domains" and "closed domains", meetings and partings, so as to facilitate and to keep a balance between the symbiosis and independence of individuals that will induce favourable personal relations and improve the quality of the activities performed there.

The site commands Mt. Fuji far to the west. The view of the mountain – the spiritual symbol of eternity – is incorporated into the architecture so that it can be shared by the residents and the neighbouring community; this also renforces awareness of the need for a symbiosis between them.

Earth Architecture is like a mountain, with its ground surface and its vegetation. The "Sky Plaza" is open to the community and embodies residents' willingness to share community spaces. There are no units with conventional floor plans: only free spaces with core facilities are proposed.

Earth Architecture
Tokyo, Japan.

Opposite
Above
Aerial view of the complex.
Below
Upper level circulation paths.
Left
Site plan.

Opposite
South elevation.

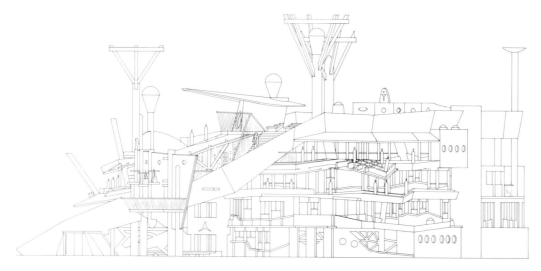

SIR RICHARD ROGERS

London, Great Britain
Tokyo, Japan

Since the revelation of the Pompidou Centre which he designed with Renzo Piano, Sir Richard Rogers' career has led him to construct major projects throughout Europe, the United States and Japan. He is the most flamboyant of all the so-called "high-tech" architects, as the Lloyd's Building in London, one of his masterpieces, testifies. But throughout his work, he has also consistently addressed underlying issues of urban planning. Over the last few years, Rogers has been particularly preoccupied with the question of how to control light and internal climate in his buildings, constantly on the look out for solutions that might be derived from the latest progress in automated information systems and new building materials.

The Architecture of the Future
Essay

I am searching for an architecture which will express and celebrate the ever-quickening speed of social, technical, political and economic change; an architecture of permanence and transformation where urban vitality and economic dynamics can take place, reflecting the changing and overlapping of functions; building as a form of controlled randomness which can respond to complex situations and relationships. Such architecture can be partially achieved by the zoning of buildings into long-life served and short-life servant activities.

The creation of an architecture which incorporates the new technologies entails breaking away from the platonic idea of a static world, expressed by the perfect finite object to which nothing can be added or taken away, a concept which has dominated architecture since its beginning. Instead of Schelling's description of architecture as frozen music, we are looking for an architecture more like some modern music, jazz or poetry, where improvisation plays a part, an indeterminate architecture containing both permanence and transformation.

The best buildings of the future, for example, will interact dynamically with the climate in order better to meet the users' needs and make optimum use of energy. More like robots than temples, these apparitions with their chameleon-like surfaces insist that we rethink yet again the art of building. Architecture will no longer be a question of mass and volume but of lightweight structures whose superimposed transparent layers will create form so that constructions will be effectively dematerialised.

To date – and here I include early Modernism – architectural concepts have been founded on linear, static, hierarchical and mechanical order. Today we know that design based on linear reasoning must be superseded by an open-ended architecture of overlapping systems. This systems approach allows us to appreciate the world as an indivisible whole. We are, in architecture as in other fields, approaching a holistic ecological view of the globe and how we live on it.

In architecture, invisible micro-electronics and bio-technology are replacing industrial mechanical systems. We shall soon be living in a world so non-mechanical that buildings such as Lloyds of London, which is generally considered too innovative, will seem outdated and look old-fashioned.

Buildings, the city and its citizens will be one inseparable organism sheltered by a perfectly fitting, ever-changing framework. Posts, beams, panels and other structural elements will be replaced by a seamless continuity. These mobile, changing robots will possess many of the characteristics of living systems, interacting and self-regulating, constantly adjusting through electronic and bio-technological self-programming.

Present day concern for single objects will be replaced by concern for relationships. Shelters will no longer be static objects, but dynamic frameworks. Accommodation will be responsive, ever-changing and ever-adjusting. Cities of the future will no longer be zoned as today in isolated single-activity ghettos; rather, they will resemble the more richly layered cities of the past. Living, work, shopping, learning and leisure will overlap and be housed in continuous, varied and changing structures.

In the case of architectural structures, responsive systems, acting much like muscles flexing in a body, will reduce mass to a minimum by sifting loads and forces with the aid of an electronic nervous system which will sense environmental changes and register individual needs.

Today, automatic pilots in aeroplanes can monitor all control functions and environmental parameters many times a second, continuously adapting and modifying the aircraft control systems to achieve optimal flight and passenger comfort. The future is here, but its impact on architecture is only just beginning to be felt.

Michael Davies, one of my partners, has described the experience of living in a responsive building of the future:

> "Look up at a spectrum-washed envelope, whose surface is a map of its instantaneous performance, stealing energy from the air with an irridescent shrug, rippling its photogrids as a cloud runs across the sun, a wall which, as the night chill falls, fluffs up its feathers and, turning white on its north face and blue on the south, closes its eyes but not without remembering to pump a little glow down to the night porter, clear a view patch for the lovers on the south side of level 22 and so turn 12 per cent silver just before dawn."

It is not popular to link the economy and consumption with culture, and to suggest that today it is the accounting system that dictates to the Arts. Yet I firmly believe that to achieve a new cultural enlightenment, one which includes architecture, it will be necessary to redefine the balance between capital, labour, the planet and its poor.

I confess my opposition to our present exploitative economic system and my faith and unshaken conviction that a global community in which art and science are harnessed to serve the common good would represent the most beautiful and enlightening achievement of the human spirit.

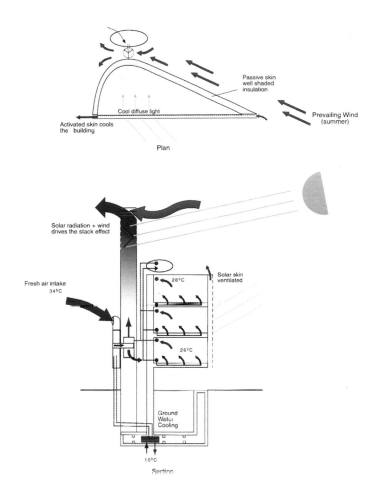

Passive skin
well shaded
insulation

Cool diffuse light

Prevailing Wind
(summer)

Activated skin cools
the building

Plan

Solar radiation + wind
drives the stack effect

Solar skin
ventilated

28°C

Fresh air intake
34°C

26°C

Ground
Water
Cooling

10°C

Section

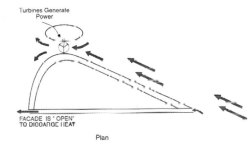

Turbines Generate
Power

FACADE IS "OPEN"
TO DISCHARGE HEAT

Plan

Wind Drives
Thermal Chimney

Exhaust fan bypassed
if reclaim not worthwhile

Ventilated skin
discharges heat

21°C

Building purged
with cool air

14°C

Ground
Water
Cooling
if neccessary

10°C   Section

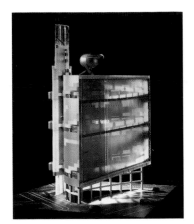

Turbine Tower
Tokyo, Japan
View of the model.

Left
Above
Plan and section
Operation on a summer day
Hot air is pre-cooled by the ground water
using a heat exchange system. Its
temperature is further reduced as it enters
the rooms by the chilled concrete slabs.
Used air is drawn out with the assistance
of sun and wind. As it passes through the
heat exchange system it reduces the
temperature and humidity of the air being
drawn in. The double skin cavity of the
southern facade traps the solar gain and
discharges it by way of ventilation top and
bottom

Below
Plan and section
Operation on a summer night
The concrete structure of the building is
chilled by flushing cool night air through it.
In mid-summer, the night air rises to a
temperature of 20ºC and needs to be
chilled by the cool ground water. When
necessary, off peak electricity is used to
control the temperature of the water in the
basement tank which will rise slightly
during peak summer. The turbines are used
to generate energy.

Turbine Tower, Tokyo, Japan

The brief for the Turbine Tower, Tokyo, was for a dynamic landmark building that would stand out above the surrounding urban sprawl. The climate is extreme, cold in winter and hot and uncomfortably humid in summer. The main circular road for Tokyo passes along the southern side of the site.

The building aims to blend simple principles with new technology to achieve a responsive architecture that is both brilliant and optimistic, and makes the most of the environment and our capacity to harness it. Wind tunnel simulation was used to study how to accelerate the wind as it passed through the core so it could be used to drive turbines and power the building. Computer predictions have helped to create a fluid and dynamic architecture that is, in addition, self-sufficient.

Inland Revenue Offices, Nottingham, Great Britain

The Inland Revenue's new offices in Nottingham is a low energy building and is designed to be naturally ventilated; exposed concrete is used to moderate internal temperatures and water is used to cool down even further during hot summers. Fountains provide a cool background noise within the open atrium. Energy consumption is less than thirty per cent that of a conventional building.

Masterplan for Parc Bit, Majorca, Spain

The Masterplan for Parc Bit creates three small sustainable communities. A balanced cycle of activities is maintained over the day, as well as throughout the week, to create a 24-hour urban community and permanent public activity throughout the year.

Opposite
Inland Revenue Offices, Nottingham
Great Britain.
Two views of the model.

Below
Section.

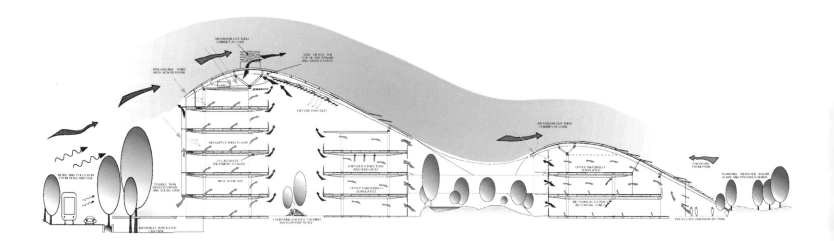

156

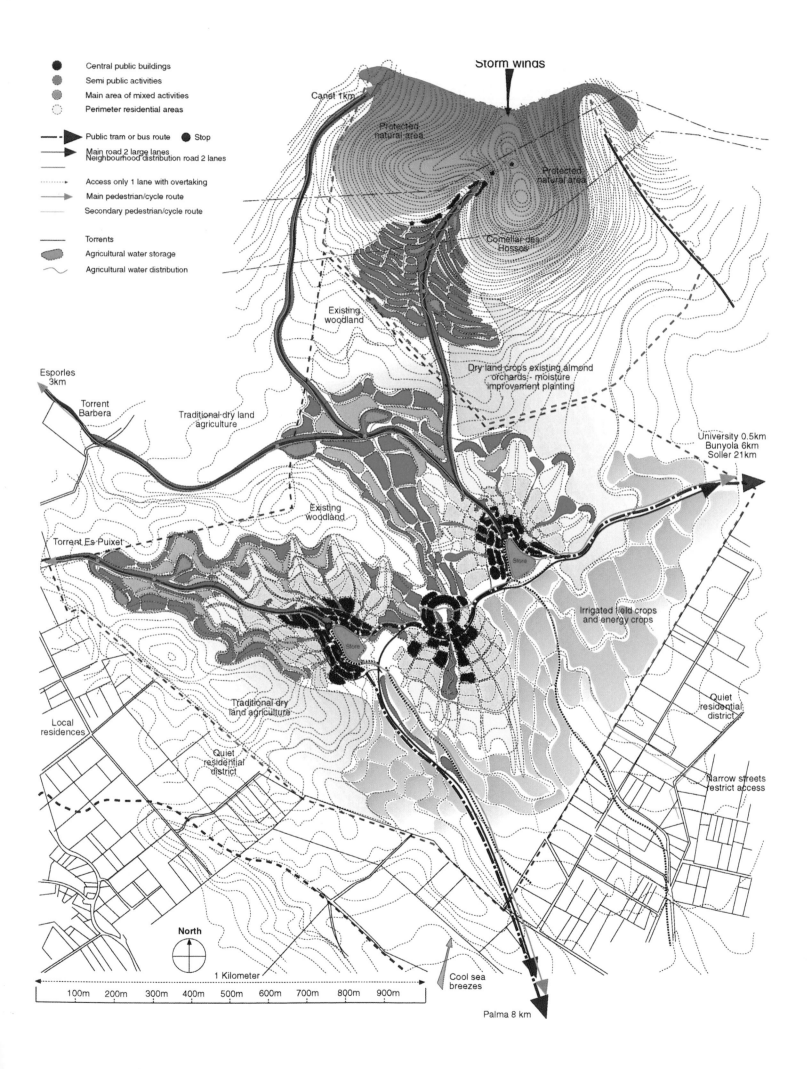

Storm winds

Canet 1km

Protected natural area

Protected natural area

Comellar des Hossos

Existing woodland

Dry land crops existing almond orchards:- moisture improvement planting

Esporles 3km

Torrent Barbera

Traditional dry land agriculture

University 0.5km
Bunyola 6km
Soller 21km

Existing woodland

Torrent Es Puixet

Store

Store

Irrigated field crops and energy crops

Quiet residential district

Traditional dry land agriculture

Local residences

Quiet residential district

Narrow streets restrict access

North

Cool sea breezes

1 Kilometer

100m 200m 300m 400m 500m 600m 700m 800m 900m

Palma 8 km

Central public buildings
Semi public activities
Main area of mixed activities
Perimeter residential areas

Public tram or bus route   Stop
Main road 2 large lanes
Neighbourhood distribution road 2 lanes

Access only 1 lane with overtaking
Main pedestrian/cycle route
Secondary pedestrian/cycle route

Torrents
Agricultural water storage
Agricultural water distribution

Masterplan for Parc Bit
Majorca, Spain.

Opposite
The urban matrix is assembled by
superimposing different elements. The aim
is to integrate the elements with each
other so that the systems for water,
agriculture, movement, social mix and the
strategy for energy work well together.
The size of each village is defined by the
limits of easy walking distance from the
centre to the furthest point. The mix of
uses and social activities is gradually
diffused from a vibrant publicly focused
centre to the more peaceful, residential
areas. Renewable sources of energy are
used to generate power locally.

Above
Model of an individual unit.
Below
Urban matrix.

ITSUKO HASEGAWA

Tokyo, Japan

After working with the Japanese architects Kiyonori Kikutake* (the central figure of the Japanese Metabolism movement) and Kazuo Shinohara, Itsuko Hasegawa has developed her own highly original work. Her vocabulary is masterful and "absolutely modern": complex, lightweight structures, sophisticated superimposition of perforated metal sheets to produce shimmering effects, translucent glass imitating paper partition walls, and a virtuosic use of lighting effects based on spectral decomposition. Itsuko Hasegawa is one of the most original figures in contemporary architecture. Her work poses in new (specifically Japanese?) terms the unresolved question of the relationship between nature and civilization.

Opening up Architecture through Communication
A feminine approach
Essay

As if to compensate for the massive destruction of nature and cities, the extremely consumer-oriented Japanese society has become increasingly dependent on the mass media to simulate a new artificial environment. Simulation with its dream-like imagery gives us the illusion of communicating with a self-fulfilling imagination. We continue to live in a fictional world, conscious that we can only have access to the beauty of nature through these media.

As this contrast becomes more and more obvious, people have started to ask questions: may not the simulated images themselves be in fact the cause of the deterioration of our quality of life? We have become aware of destruction on a global scale and have noticed that the nature that surrounds us does no longer sends out harmonious messages. Yet all man-made objects are ultimately derived from nature. Nature embraces every aspect of human existence. Man-made space merely provides different levels of environment and quality of life within nature. The state of that space is a reflection of the state of society.

Nowadays technical and scientific progress is too rapid for us even to notice the changes that take place. Whereas in the past we could evolve slowly in harmony with nature, the speed of present progress has accelerated the rate of its destruction. Architecture, on the other hand, from the eighteenth century to today, has aimed to homogenize the world, to make it transparent, and to deny gravity by achieving lightness of structure. How can architecture reorient itself as a life-supporting environment when we are all aware that we are living at the extremity of life? How can our imagination,

Opposite
Fruit Museum
Yamanashi, Japan.

shaped by the new technological society, influence the outcome of architectural development?

Nothing will come out of that mysticism that is based on the seductions of technological progress, such as virtual reality. When we think about the world as a long-term continuum, an environment which should last forever, we realize how poor it has become today. Technological progress may eventually help to reveal inherent human potential and sensitivity. It may help to transform unconsciousness into consciousness. But today the difference between the human body and the world of simulation is increasing. As technology develops, this situation may lead to the isolation of human beings from their environment.

In order to break out of this dilemma, it is necessary to harness both physical human vigour and the multiplicity of media-created information environments. In architecture, this means giving equal importance to both "hardware" and "software".

Through experience, I have come to understand that many people willingly recognize the importance of their own environment, express concern about the state of public facilities that affect their daily lives, and want to participate to regain control over them. It is not sufficient for architects and city planners to implement their own personal beliefs. I am trying to introduce a new flexible architectural system which will be receptive to the diversity of individuals.

S.T.M Building
Tokyo, Japan.

In the case of public buildings, the design normally follows the parameters outlined in an official programme. This kind of programme tends to be abstract and does not address the real needs of individual users. The resulting architectural design may be either mundane or monumental; in any case, it will not be responsive to reality. Like the city itself, public buildings must be able to accommodate the complexity and diversity of individual needs in order to attract people. In the past, public building projects were often used as an expression of the architect's ego, and their (lack of) social significance was hidden behind their supposed artistic values. In one sense, this approach can help to control the chaotic and unruly state of Japanese cities. But blind dependence on this approach can create an enormous rift between owners and users.

The current confusion of the Japanese urban environment is the result of the post-war interpretation of democracy, of a selfish possessiveness by individuals and corporations, and of the lack of communal consensus. The reason why large civil engineering, new-town and urban redevelopment projects, carried out by governments during periods of high economic stability and growth have been so uninspiring and of such low design quality, can be traced back to the political reality of Japan. A hierarchical decision-making process excludes anything that does not neatly fit the prototypes of national uniformity. Thus we encounter, everywhere in this country, what my English friend Peter Cook calls "garbage" urban landscapes.

Although the central government promoted the idea of urban diversity in the 1980s, it was only a modified centralism; and as the subservience of local communities to the central government became more concrete, the sense of local powerlessness grew stronger. However, some communities have embarked upon their own development plans in an entrepreneurial spirit. In those communities, the citizens cooperate with the authorities, and are critical of them too. We feel that this kind of communication could be used as a tool to alter drastically the way in which social architecture is planned. Both architects and individual citizens can experiment with mechanisms for assembling various materials and realize together a shared vision through the mutual experience of discord. Strategically speaking, we must create a process for returning public buildings to their users, involving them in decision-making and making them recognize their active involvement in the building process.

There are some architects who claim that architectural integrity bears no relationship to practicality and that architecture can be beautiful independently of any human involvement. Such narcissistic attitudes can only diminish the quality of architecture. They fully deserve the oft-heard criticism that architects do not have a social conscience.

One factor that led to the successful establishment of communication on the Shonandai Cultural Centre project was that we all shared a common sense of "architecture as second nature", which we used as the guiding principle for our design. Our cities are different from physically static European cities. Ours is an abstract form of nature, and their architecture retains a flexible relationship with natural phenomena such as the wind, water and topography. Architecture is a vessel for people's rich and ambiguous emotional responses, as well as for the changing seasons, climate, and the mysteries of the universe. We might call it a poetic machine.

In fact, I am more interested in creating a common dream through architecture than in regaining social acceptance for my profession. It is clear to me that my attitude towards architecture is not that of an exclusive dogma but consistently ad hoc, so that it is inclusive of many conflicting notions at the same time. My architectural reality is based on popular rationalism with a multipolar value system and is not the orthodox nationalism of a single value system. This attitude requires a change of architectural paradigm if we are to understand the unorganized forces of consciousness and embody the diversity of every group so that it can function as a constructive force.

Fruit Museum, Yamanashi, Japan

Three structures with differing characteristics are aligned on a shallow south-east slope offering a wonderful view of Mount Fuji. They are a tropical greenhouse, an atrium event space, and an educational workshop for teaching. The greenhouse is a shelter in the shape of a deformed globe, while the atrium is a saucer-shaped glass shelter with loose curves. The workshop is a transparent rectilinear building encased in a lopsided, egg-shaped pergola over which fruit-bearing lianas crawl freely.

House at Higashitamagawa Japan.

Exhibition Pavilion, Nagoya, Japan

Designed as a temporary structure that was to be demolished after four months, the Nagoya Exhibition Pavilion comprises a theatre with 270 seats and a hanging garden. The site appeared shrouded in a light mist, changing as one approached into a garden enveloped in clouds and trees.

The architect's objective was to create a space that would allow a sort of coexistence with nature by using lightweight, translucent materials and "membranes" that allow the light, wind and sound to penetrate through them into the space inside. The visitor could thus "experience all those emotions that rationalism has forgotten, the sense of well-being offered by nature and by the sublime music of the universe".

Exhibition Pavilion
Nagoya, Japan.

Shonandai Cultural Centre, Fujisawa, Japan

For the Shonandai Cultural Centre, Itsuko Hasegawa has tried to produce a concentration of latent allusions to nature, which function like human memories. These allusions have been recreated through a project for "architecture as latent nature", in the form of an artificial hill (architecture as topography). "Rethinking architecture means recreating it according to a new natural order, so that it is richer than the topography it replaces, and is also a memorial to the segment of nature that has been destroyed. The building expresses itself as a means Hot communication with nature, as a means also to pay homage to the continuity of life on its most primitive level. In practice, I tried to imagine architecture as a second nature, which could react both to contemporary technology and to the spirit of the age".

Exhibition pavilion
Nagoya, Japan.

Shonandai Cultural Centre
Fujisawa, Japan.

Above
Night view of the interior.
Below
View of the piazza from the north tower.

Opposite
Above
The piazza by day, general view.
Below
"Metal vegetation".

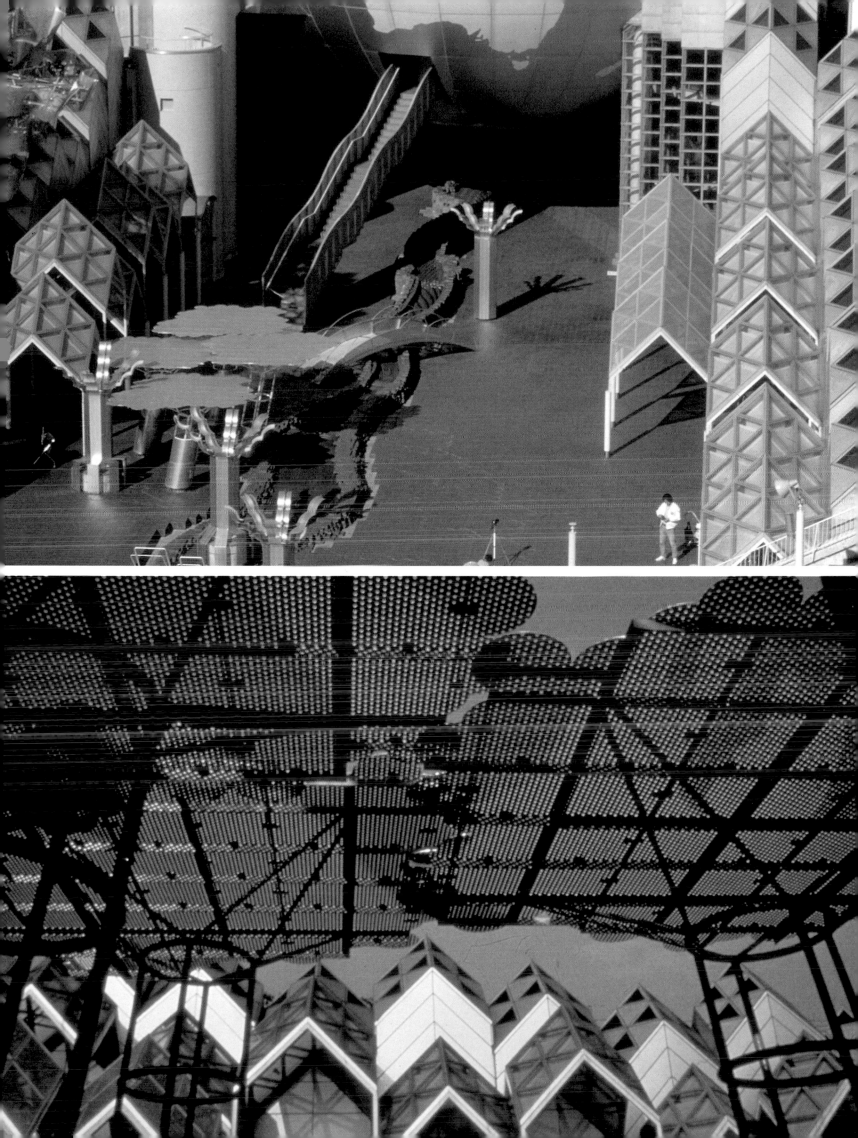

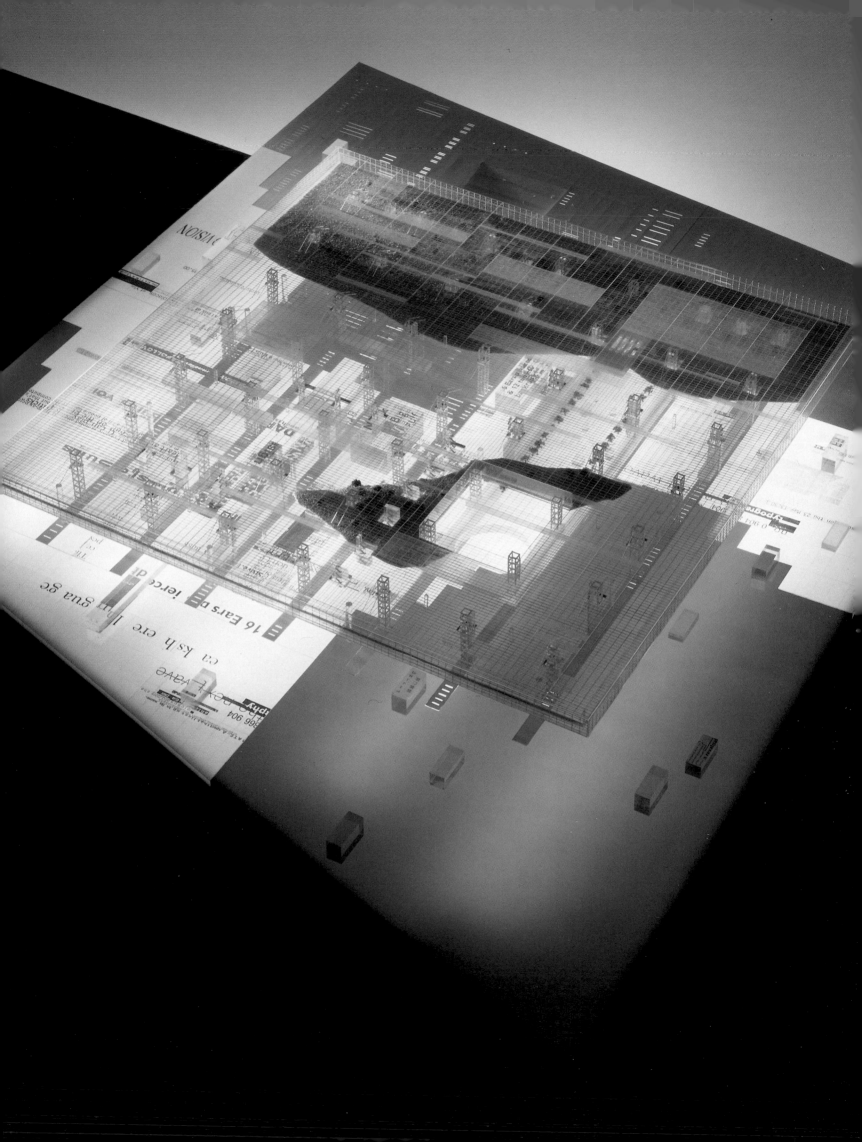

5. TOWARDS A PIXEL ARCHITECTURE

"C : \"
Bill Gates

Electricity and its scintillating effects had already given today's architects those brilliant and evocative tools of which Las Vegas and Shinjuku, Tokyo are the accepted icons. The development of the new media, the information networks (which boast their own architecture), the cathode tube and the profusion of images from every source (from micro to macrocosm) hold a double fascination for a whole generation of architects:

– the impact of the unique plasticity they create, revealing as yet unexplored possibilities for architecture;

– their less tangible impact on form (or rather the absence of form) which haunts the imagination, creating a ghostly aesthetic of disappearance.

Will architects know how to rise to the challenge of creating immaterial space? ■

Opposite
Crystal Monolith
Yokohama, Japan.
Shin Takamatsu
View of the model.

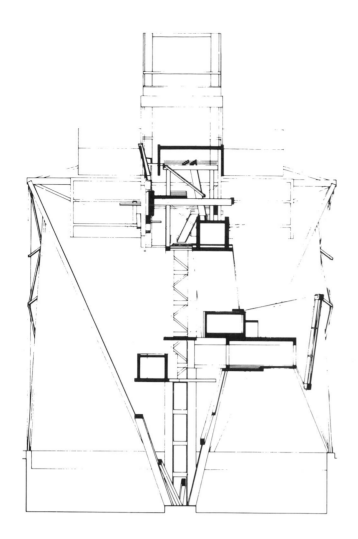

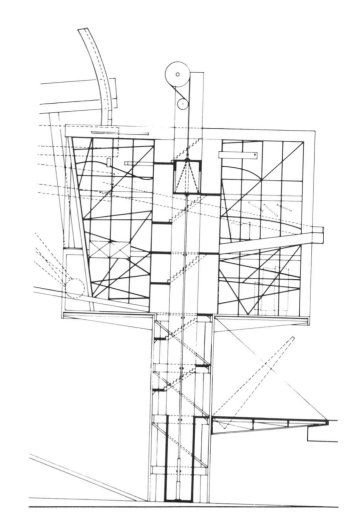

ASYMPTOTE ARCHITECTURE

New York, USA

Founded in 1987 in New York by Lise-Anne Couture and Hari Rashid, Asymptote Architecture set out to question the very basis of architecture, its methods and its goals, in a world whose traditional structures have been overturned by the information revolution. Asymptote projects, whatever form they take – systems (known as "optigraphs"), installations, or more traditional models and drawings – force us to confront modes of perception that have been modified by technology (and which are haunted by an obsession with surveillance). In their submissions to competitions for the Alexandria Library, the Moscow Theatre, the Groningen Court House, or the Spreebogen district of Berlin, Lise-Anne Couture and Hari Rashid address problems that are crucial for the future of architecture: the adequation of the traditional order of preoccupations with the environment, behaviour, functionality and even perfection, faced with the influence of new technologies. "Today, architectural forms emerge from a space of flux and fluidity".

Steel Cloud, Los Angeles, Californie, USA

The Steel Cloud or Los Angeles West Coast Gateway is typical of Los Angeles, a place construed of grand fictions and utopian fantasies. Inspired by optical machinery, flight simulation, and the technologies of surveillance, this episodic architecture seeks to reconfigure information, speed and the instantaneous into a new city-space. Here an anticipatory monument reveals an invisible site directly above the Hollywood Freeway as a place where "the super-rapid position of rest" of a closing millennium can be felt. This space for the post-information age, made up of infinitely oscillating fields devoid of perspective or depth, forms an architecture of ambiguity and anonymity amidst the noise and distraction of Los Angeles.

The Steel Cloud is not a monument to some militaristic conquest or political authority, rather it is a device to be filled and conquered by the human spirit, a living monument, accommodating galleries, libraries, theatres, cinemas, parks and plazas, each intersected by the fluid and transient city. Here aquariums and suspended landscapes oscillate to the arcane rhythms of the freeway. The Cloud itself, held together by cables, steel girders, harnesses and weights, counters the precarious shifting plates beneath it. This strange and disparate architecture is constantly being unfinished and resituated.

Steel Cloud
Los Angeles, California, USA.
Views of the model.

Opposite

Above
Sections of the library, the galleries and the Immigration Museum.
Below
View of the model.

Overleaf

Above
Longitudinal section and cross section of the Museum of Time.
Below
View of the model.

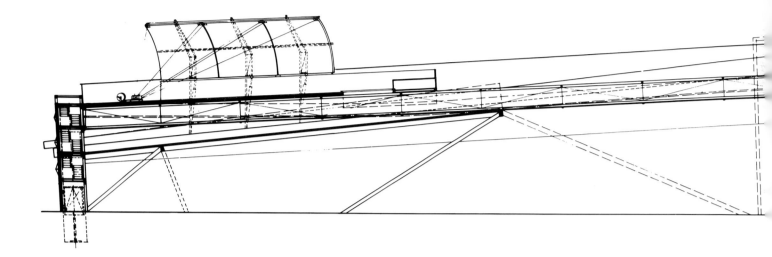

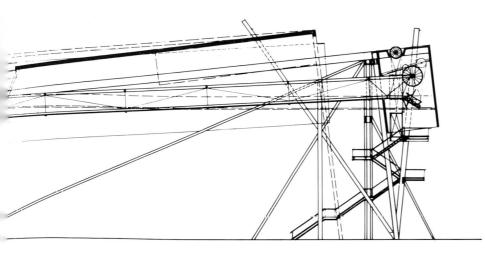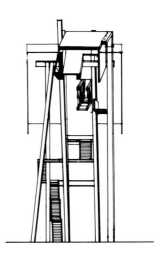

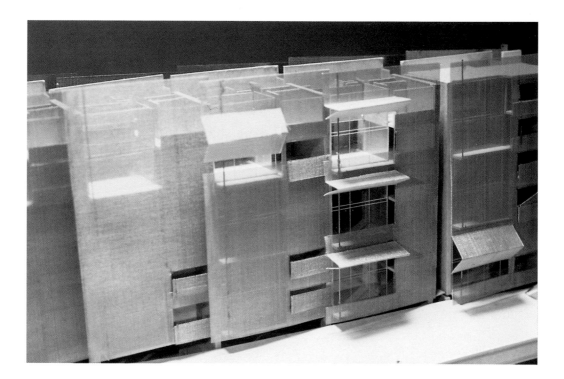

DILLER & SCOFIDIO

New York, USA

Elizabeth Diller and Paul Scofido trained in New York in the late seventies, in the poetic and polemical atmosphere of John Hedjuk's* Cooper Union. They have since developed their own very particular approach: their projects and installations are intended to decipher and interpret the rituals, institutions and discouse which maintain society in its current state of cohesion, but also to reveal the ideology underlying the events and assumptions that make up contemporary life.

The Gifu Housing Project, Gifu, Japan

Diller and Scofidio believe that the rhetoric of "variety" that accompanied the introduction of standardization in European Modernism was an illusion, which delivered anonymity instead. The economic constraints and inevitability of repetition, which come with standardization in social housing, however, need not lead to the erasure of the individual dwelling. Their Gifu Housing Project, Japan, articulates distinctly in plan, and positions uniquely in section, each of its one hundred units.

The "reptilian" building is made up of rectangular stacks that interlock leaving a discrepancy of 1.5 degrees which accumulates into a shallow curve. Each unit is offset from the next by one metre to leave space for the entry door, a surface always approached frontally, in keeping with tradition. The outermost skin of diaphanous overlapping "scales" of perforated metal is mobile to the south. To the North, it serves to privatize the ramping system along which each unit is placed at a unique elevation.

The Tower of Babel, New York, USA

The Tower of Babel addresses the question of the fate of cultural diversity in our progressively mono-cultural world. It is a permanent installation planned for the corner of 42nd Street and Eighth Avenue, comprising a stack of video screens which feature giant speaking mouths, each reciting a sequence of adages on the theme of language in the most prominent languages spoken in the United States. The conglomeration of voices will be audible as an indistinct blur, except for the voice closest to the street. After each adage is spoken, the images in the stack will drop one interval from the top. The tower inverts the proposition of the biblical Tower of Babel in which language is used as a weapon against the earliest mono-culture in order to secure the heavens from the common people. Rather, the project aestheticizes the very sound of babel and through the successive de-lamination of voices, the rich complexities of communication are emphasized.

Jump Cuts, San Jose, California, USA

Jump Cuts will be a permanent facade for the world's largest Cineplex theatre planned for San Jose, California, composed of sculptural, electronic and video components which will broadcast images and texts, both informative and contemplative, to the street. Using liquid crystal technology, the facade will intermittently exchange the view of the activity in the lobby seen from the street with video views of the street taken from within the building – thus turning the building inside-out like a glove, electronically. Film extracts, trailers and adverts will also be used.

The Tower of Babel
New York, USA.
Temporary installation.

Right
View of the model.

Opposite
Jump Cuts
San Jose, California, USA.
Video facades.

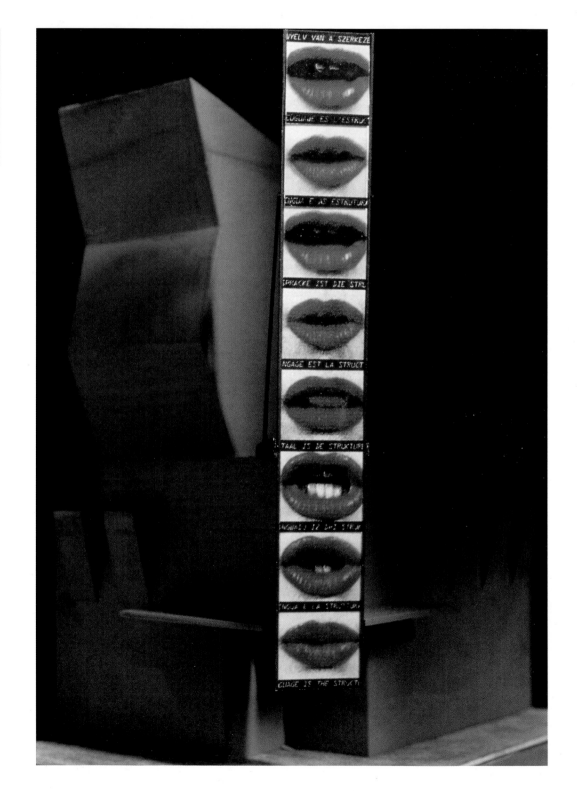

176

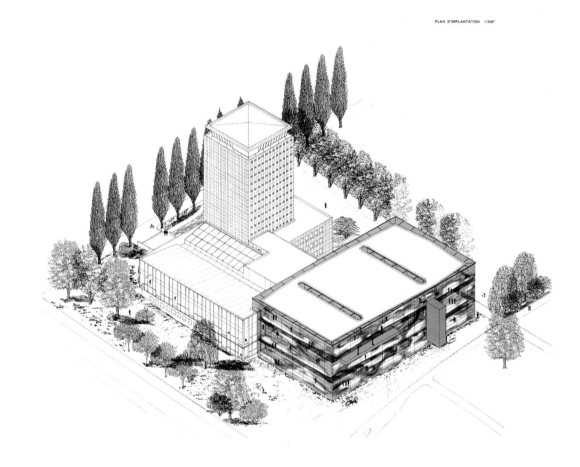

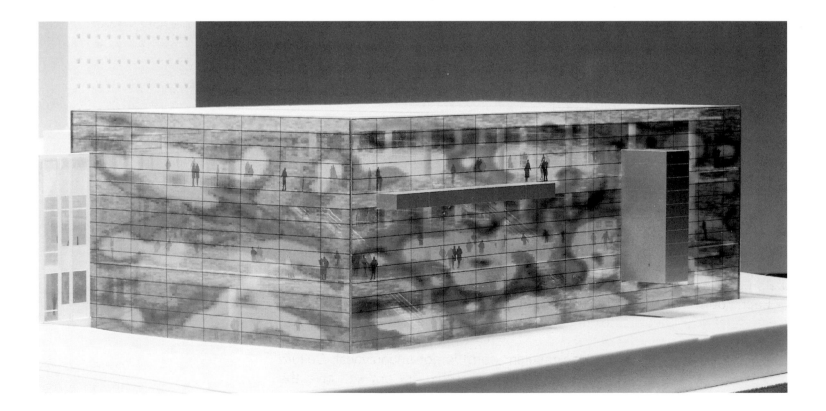

DU BESSET AND LYON

Paris, France

From their apprenticeship with their prestigious elders, Jean Nouvel and Frank Gehry, Pierre Du Besset and Dominique Lyon learned the discipline of an approach that explores all the possibilities of the programme and the site and a great liberty of form without loss of control. Since they established their own practice in 1984 they have worked on several modest but difficult projects (the restoration of the Rotonde des Vétérinaires in the Parc de La Villette, and the Le Monde newspaper building, both in Paris) and competition entries (the Jussieu libraries, the Dijon University Campus, etc.)

The Mediatheque in Orleans (1994) reveals their sound grasp of urban projects and their ability to transform a banal programme into a subtle building endowed with a moving fragility.

Extension to the University Library, Dijon, France

A library gathers information and organizes access to it. The pleasure it gives lies in the perception of this accumulation.

The extension to the University Library in Dijon places the user at the heart of this system. He can see all that is on offer at a glance and without being overwhelmed: on the facade he can see monochrome motifs that are free, mobile, translucid or transparent; the floors and the ceilings float within this fluid skin. The continuity of the coloured motifs is visible beneath the floors and the activities taking place on other levels can be guessed at.

Mediatheque, Orleans, France

A mediatheque is a place where people find for themselves the means by which to increase their knowledge. The Orleans Mediatheque seeks to clarify the idea of this process which cannot take place unless the user demonstrates his curiosity. Thus he must proceed in stages. The architectural process corresponds to the intellectual process: each functional space in the programme (lending room, reading room, periodicals room, cafeteria, etc.) is identified by very simple means: a symmetrical plan, a single colour. Each space is treated as a room. There are as many rooms as there are elements in the programme.

Each room has its raison d'être and at the same time integrates the presence of its immediate neighbours. They form a whole to which nothing can be added and from which nothing can be taken away, resulting in a simple form that binds them together. But the resulting form is not unequivocal. Culture cannot be grasped globally. The various rooms rebel, jut out and give the building a monumental dimension.

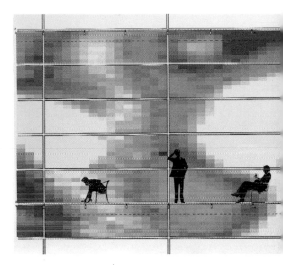

Extension to the University Library Dijon, France.

Above
Facade in screenprinted glass
(distorted vision)

Opposite
Above
General axonometric.
Below
Model of the library.

Mediatheque, Orleans
France.

Above
The Mediatheque in context.
Below
Perforated metal sunshades to filter light
and vision.

Opposite
View over the cityscape from inside

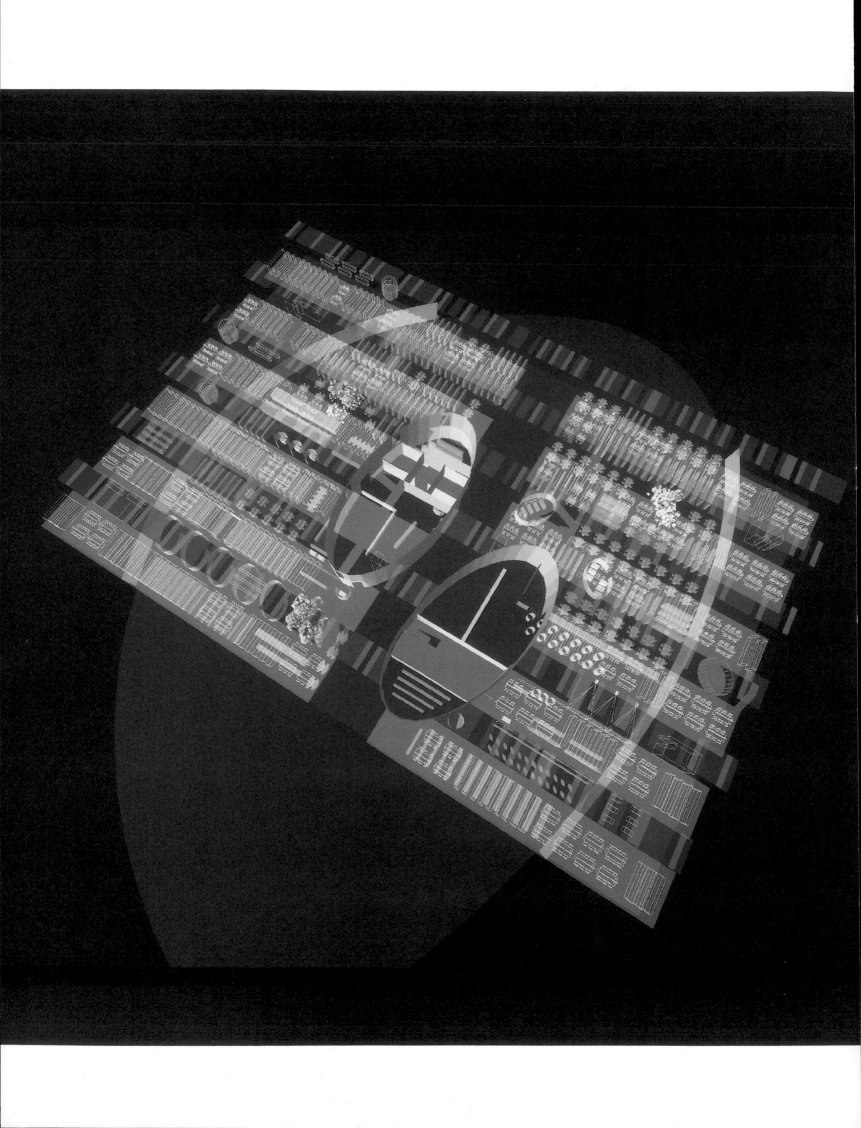

TOYO ITO

Tokyo, Japan

Since the 1970s, Toyo Ito has been exploring a number of questions that have never received a definitive answer: how to define an introverted domestic space (his U-shaped house), how to re-read modernity (how to *build* Le Corbusier's Domino House), etc. Today, he is working against a homogenized society in which life is entirely simulated and has thus lost its meaning. How can we create real architecture in a universe in which objects are losing their reality? How can we create a permanent space appropriate to a society in perpetual flux? Ito tries to answer these questions by emphasizing the ephemeral and the fictional. His idea of "nirvana" is situated at the furthest limits of technological control. The result is a fluctuating immaterial architecture, sensitive to the elements, and integrating modern methods of producing images and sounds.

Sendai Mediatheque, Japan

The Mediatheque at Sendai is a place where the primitive body and the virtual body reacting to electronic flux can be combined and organized. The design does not emphasize architectural form, but highlights the structure as a natural flux as well as an electronic matching.

The building consists of seven layers one on top of the other, each matching a different communication situation, using different media. There are twelve tubes controlling and organizing the layers. They are flexible structures, at the same time providing vertical circulation and flow space for all kinds of energy and information, light and sound. The building is surrounded by a skin that controls the interior environment.

The artist Laurie Anderson says: "The body of a modern human being consists of an electronic flux". Since ancient times, our body has been linked to nature as a fluid consisting of water and air. Now the body as electronic flux is changing the forms of communication, but our primitive body still seeks after beautiful light or a cool breeze.

Tower of the Winds, Yokohama, Japan

The Tower of the Winds in Yokohama is a remodelling of an existing tower built for ventilation and water storage twenty years ago. It is sheathed in perforated aluminium and the external walls are covered with acrylic mirror plates. More than two thousand electric light bulbs are controlled by computer to respond to the wind, noise, and temperature. During the day, the aluminium panels reflect light and accentuate the simple form of the cylindrical structure. As the lamps are lit at dusk, a kaleidoscopic effect is created. The aluminium panels become an almost transparent film and the tower loses its physical form and is changed into a virtual image. It has no specific architectural form and may be compared to visual background music.

JEAN NOUVEL

Paris, France

Jean Nouvel achieved recognition in the 1980s with a series of buildings each of which differed in their form and connotations. Nouvel sees himself as an architect of the specific: a specific programme and project conditions are matched by a specific response. This principled stance is accompanied by a clear-cut belief that architecture, rather than being an autonomous discipline, is permeated by, and ought to mirror, social realities.

Architects must try to take into account the free flow of images, miniaturisation, automation, speed, the conquest of space, and the emerging symptoms of a new popular culture (rap music, sport, etc.)

Nouvel's architecture emphasises material and light over the interplay of volume and space. It tends to dissolve the materiality of the world in a subtle combination of reflections, refractions, superimpositions, dilutions, flashing signs and moving colours.

Mutations
Essay

The concept of architecture is going through a process of massive change, barely discernible amidst the haze and dust clouds raised by the urban cataclysm that has struck our planet. Population explosion, industrial revolution and its direct consequences, urban encroachment of rural areas, the global market and global communication with their burgeoning networks: these are some of the reasons which explain why, in the 20th century, four or five times more buildings have been built than in the entire previous course of human history.

The transformation is profound, and the scope of architecture has been considerably extended. Today, the built fabric, which has grown up despite appalling conditions, is the visible consequence of an accelerated sedimentation. The facts stare us in the face: the inevitable has become reality. Once again, *topos* has taken precedence over *logos* . New building has been designed in difficult conditions, with barely a thought; the definitive criterion has been above all sheer urgency.

Much has been built, and in an utterly haphazard way. Conscientious architects have repeatedly criticised this state of affairs. But what have they proposed instead? Solutions which are either clinical, like Le Corbusier's Cité radieuse (Radiant City)[*], ecological, like Frank Lloyd Wright's Broadacre City[*], or plastic, like De Stijl's [*] colour and form chart.

In fact, since the 15th-century invention of the city as an architectural object, History has repeatedly demonstrated that the city lends itself less and

189

less to an overall plan; that, on the contrary, it is the result of economic forces operating on a given territory, forces which brook no resistance, least of all that of aesthetic or humanist *a priori* theories. Besides, the tangible consequences of such theories are not always devoid of ambiguity.

Thus, in a roundabout, haphazard, expedient way, forms have emerged. These forms are often chaotic, yet still at times decipherable: it is even possible to attempt to link them to a secret order from which a fatal beauty occasionally wells up, often as the direct result of a given geographical context.

The new image of the world which has taken shape before our eyes is simultaneously fascinating, disturbing, occasionally disconcerting and sometimes even disgusting and repellent; yet it is difficult to deny it those qualities usually reserved for veritable "concretion-creations".

What is clear today, and inevitably concerns us as regards the future of our discipline, is that the *tabula* is no longer *rasa* . The early years of the century were swept along on the euphoric wave of industrial expansion and burgeoning modernity. Today we are no longer faced with inventing the city of tomorrow on the basis of aesthetic, cultural and ethical criteria that are shared by a generation for whom progress is a driving force with boundless possibilities. We have to face the fundamental truth that modern cities have been invented without us, at times, in spite of us. They are the outcome of evolution, a new layer on the planet's crust, perhaps signifying the dawn of a new era – the urban age.

The architectural vision of the city is in need of radical rethinking. It is high time to admit that, in the present historical conjuncture, a typological and morphological approach to cities merely leads to archaism, to the building of pre-urban-age cities. It can no longer serve as a serious conceptual basis. More than ever, it is the architect's duty to be aware of life, to form an opinion as to its direction and evolution. And for the architect, for whom 'doing' is as important as 'knowing', who has to translate a project into brick and mortar, and who is confronted with the contradiction between the rapidly evolving city and the lethargic pace of the architectural process itself, this is a complex and extremely awkward problem. The founding texts by Alberti[*] and More[*] still have a certain mystique for us: the former grounded architecture as an autonomous discipline, the latter as a prophetic, humanist, libertarian vision. How can an increasingly wide and fragmented knowledge be reconciled with a more and more pervasive praxis? No one is expected to achieve the impossible. The architect cannot simultaneously be philosopher, scientist, and artist; nor perform the role of one-man-band – planner, designer, engineer, economist, lawyer, site manager – that architectural practice implies. Yet Alberti's gamble of renouncing a global vision in favour of a restricted, autonomous, purely professional approach has had to yield to historical fact. Alberti's doctrine held sway for half a millenium. How is the architect to respond today?

Any contemporary definition of architecture would have to start by stating what architecture does not involve. Emergent modern architecture sought to create a new world; overreaching its capacities, it failed in this ambition, unable to grasp that the world does not belong to the architect but that, on the contrary, the architect belongs to the world. Architecture is a modification and an extension of the world, a victory over chaos, an involuntary adventure. Each era has to reinvent its own means of evolution and harness related knowledge. To succeed in such an adventure, one must draw upon all the resources for knowledge of contemporary thought.

Conference Centre
Tours, France.

190

Obviously, for the architect, who is necessarily grounded in reality, science is useful in its everyday applications. Technological and technical progress, and the introduction of new materials with revolutionary properties represent, if it may be put this way, grounds for calling what he knows into question. In its relationships with pure and applied science, architecture tends towards a performative synergy.

At this stage, a new factor intervenes in the evolution of our discipline, a factor rarely taken into consideration on a historical or critical level: although architecture has taken on board this performative synergy, it no longer stands in awe of modernity. The fascination which technical prowess, revered as a symbol, inspired in the pioneering modern architects has had its day. Nowadays, although the role of the engineer has lost none of its power, nobility, or prestige, the technical effort involved need no longer be revealed. Architecture is expected to be self-evident, to be guided by something other than sheer contingency or harsh constructional realities.

The very concept of the city has exploded. The city has become a cosmos, a galaxy of innumerable individual units, where things are in a perpetual flux of formation and disintegration. We have to invent its evolutionary processes, to assess change, to go along with this change or act against it. I sense today that the evolution of these galaxies is at a standstill and that, in the future, they will only develop through a process of iteration, alteration, or revelation. This implies an end to long-term planning, to standard blueprints, to zoning. It means that each urban decision will be the result of a binary choice between integration and differentiation.

The notions of integration and differentiation in turn imply a very special kind of commitment on the part of the architects called upon to choose between them. Only "conceptual" architects who as a matter of principle have conducted the most detailed analyses and imagined the widest range of possibilities will be capable of choosing with complete lucidity.

If we ponder the future of architecture, we must also pose the awkward question of the relationship between History and modernity. The very definition of modernity is of necessity subject to perpetual change. Today, I would readily propose as an initial definition of modernity that it is the best possible way of making the most of our memory – a permanently updated diagnosis.

A second definition might run as follows: modernity is knowing, then choosing the right course and the swiftest possible implementation to take us in the direction of our evolving knowledge, within a framework of analysis and diagnosis.

An attempt may be made to define the criteria of evolution, to discuss the paradigms of modernity.

One of the first things to be noted is that space and form play an ever-diminishing role and that, on the other hand, light and material are assuming increasing importance. Simplicity and complexity are further paradigms. As form and space have been simplified and smoothed out, only a new level of interpretation will enable us to say to what extent an object, which may appear simple, is in fact more complex than we may have ever actually conceived. Or consider the paradigms of density and lightness. Things will be increasingly condensed: here, one could point to the tendency to miniaturisation and heightened performance, or again, to mechanisation and passive systems.

This leads me to the notions of "support" and "contribution": in a building, we have to determine which are the fixed and which the mobile elements.

Euralille
Station triangle, Lille, France
Façade with screenprints and holographs.

The current trend is towards an increasingly clear-cut dissociation: in other words, "supporting" features include everything intended to last, while "contributing" features cover all those that are subject to rapid change.

More than ever today, architecture is political. Architects are, in their own way, politicians. At the same time, this democratic dimension should be kept distinct from the cultural dimension.

We will only change through a process of giving. Film-maker Wim Wenders has said that the most important and most under-estimated word of all is "kindness". I believe this to be true, I believe in the value of giving, I believe that architects today should not only be level-headed, but big-hearted at the same time.

Endless Tower, la Défense, Paris, France

The aesthetic of a double disappearance: an endless tower.

The human mind is obsessed and fascinated by infinity, eternally raising metaphysical questions: where does it begin? where does it end?

The tower is a metaphysical object. It calls the idea of a limit into question.

The tower vanishes into the ground, and springs out of it. The conditions governing the construction of an extremely high building reside in this twin dynamic of burial and emergence.

The building disappears into the firmament. The materials employed – opaque granite, polished, perforated aluminium, and clear, reflective glass – invest it with an immaterial, unreal aspect. Soaring higher and higher, it slowly fades from sight. The successive use of different materials emphasises the natural, graduated effect.

Floor by floor, the building dematerialises until the simple transparent wall at its very tip melts into the background of the sky.

The Cartier Foundation, Paris

The ghost of a park. Transparent. Inclusive. Behind the tall, glazed enclosure that has replaced the former uninterrupted wall, the trees emerge, part of the twenty-five-foot high shell against which they gently brush.

Cartier Foundation
Paris, France.
Day view

Chateaubriand's cedar stands alone, framed by two screens that mark the entrance. Passing under the cedar, visitors discover the trees surrounding the exhibition hall, another twenty-five-foot glazed building, as they take in the full depth of the site.

In summer, the large sliding windows are opened, transforming the hall into an extension of the gardens.

The sky itself appears transparent. From the boulevard, the building seems like a shimmering halo against the backdrop of the sky, superimposed on which are real or virtual trees, as reflected and refracted by the glazed screens.

The architecture, with its finely woven glazing and steel, has an all-pervasive lightness, blurring the tangible limits of the building, eclipsing the impression of a solid volume in a poetically evanescent haze, and once again opening out the pleasant prospect of a fine garden long tucked away from sight. It is an architecture which deliberately adopts a clear stance in relation to the notion of transparency and its allegedly supine neutrality. When virtuality confronts reality, it is architecture's duty to courageously assume the image of contradiction.

Lyons Opera House, France

The modernisation of this 19th-century opera house, built in the very centre of town, provided the pretext for an architectural *tour de force*. The neo classical facades were retained, preserving the building's integration with the surrounding urban fabric. The new theatre has tripled the original volume: part of the programme involved the provision of new spaces under the old building, while a semi-cylindrical luminous vault has been installed above. The cantilevered Italian auditorium and the public areas play on a register combining both familiar and novel sensations: the ritual dignity associated with the colours deployed – deep blacks, gold and red; the shimmering reflections of the suspended shell evoking the sleek refinement of a grand piano; the vertiginous escalators that run the full height of the building. The new Lyons opera house, with its striking silhouette, is intended to be a significant landmark in the urban centre and at the same time a refined and highly efficient working space.

Cartier Foundation
Paris, France.
Night view.

Cartier Foundation
Paris, France.

Above
The town seen from inside.
Below
Entrance to the building.

Opposite
Endless Tower
La Défense, Paris, France.
View of the model.

Page 196
Lyons Opera House,
France.

Above left
The building in the city.
Below left
The entrance hall.
Above right
The stalls.
Below right
Access areas.

Page 197
View of the building from the City Hall.

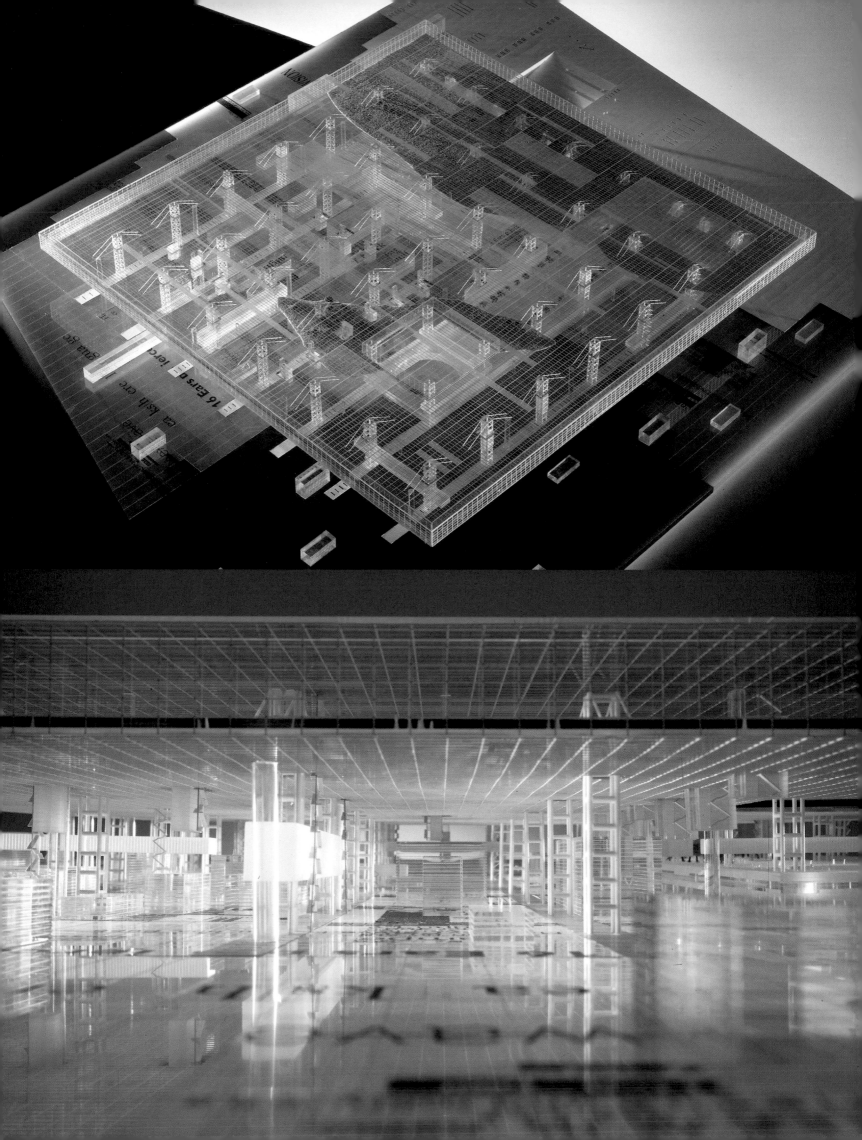

SHIN TAKAMATSU

Kyoto, Japan

Shin Takamatsu was educated in Kyoto, where he studied architecture, founding his own practice in 1980. He developed a highly personal style that was inspired by the heavy, massive and impressive machinery created by 19th-century engineering, as well as by mediaeval armour. His buildings were menacing forms, which evoked both Fritz Lang's film, *Metropolis*, and samurai masks. In them, he tried to offer a spatial summary of "the symptoms of what is wrong with the city".

More recently, influenced by "the volatile character of society and the consequent transformation of architecture", he has redirected his work towards the search for a "space of marginal activity", that is, a space that might escape from the strict confines of the programme. In the process, his work has grown lighter in material and in form, and acquired a new, almost evanescent geometrical simplicity.

Crystal Monolith, Yokohama, Japan

The Crystal Monolith is an architectural project which works to reinforce the collective memory. It is a design for an amusement park on an abandoned crude oil tank yard for the Yokohama Design Forum. The concept is to create an artificial sea in a 450 x 450 x 15 m (492 x 492 x 16 yds) glass box which floats 30 m (33 yds) above the ground.

A few decades from now, there may no longer be any unpolluted seas, and people may not even remember that there once was unpolluted sea.

Future Port City

Future Port City is a design for an airport and a Utopian city for the year 2050. The design meets the brief of satisfying the demand for the proper accommodation of new technologies, as extrapolated into the next millennium. The architect has tried to anticipate probable changes in the perception of space and time that may be generated by the revolution in speed.

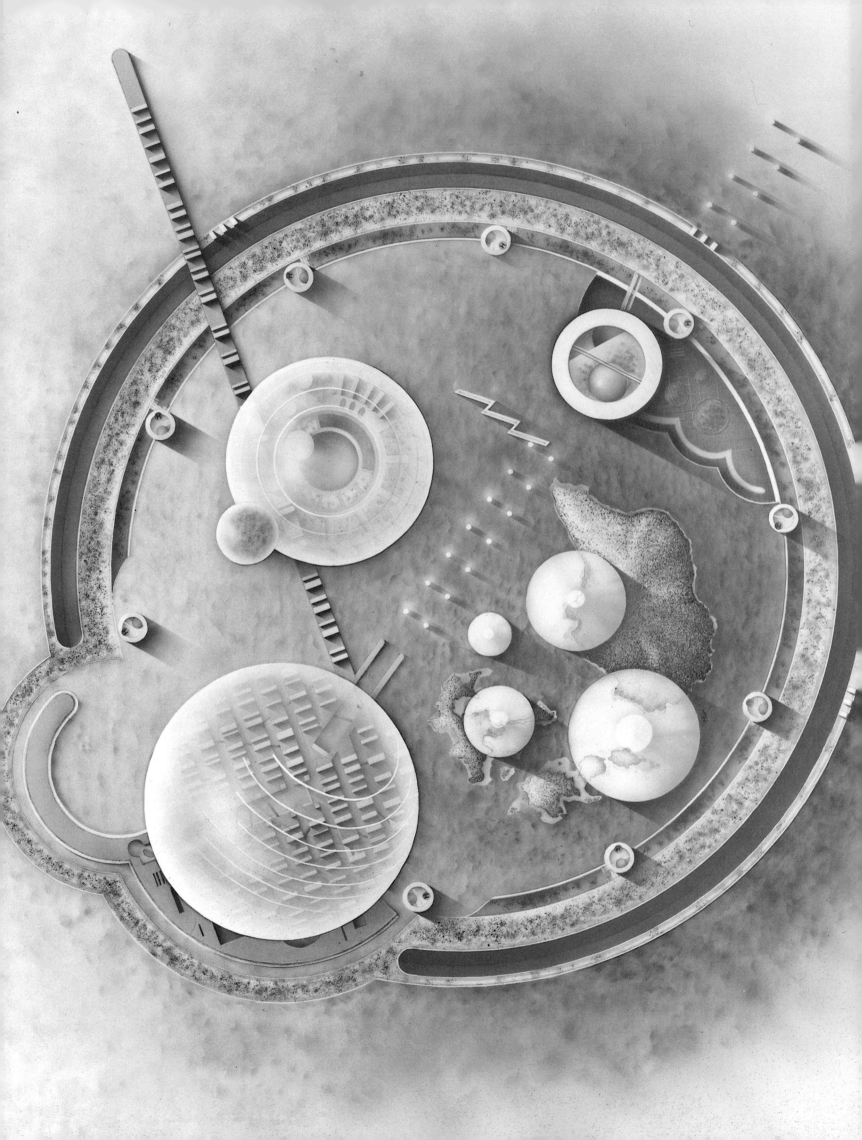

BIOGRAPHIES

ALSOP & STÖRMER

WILLIAM ALSOP

Born in 1947 in Northampton, Great Britain.
1969: Architectural Association Diploma, London.
1973-77: works with Cedric Price.
1979: creation of Alsop & Lyall.
1990: creation of Alsop & Störmer
Member of the Royal Institute of British Architects; fellow of the Royal Society of Arts; William Van Allen Medal for Architecture, New York.
Has taught at St-Martin's School of Art, at the Architectural Association, at Ball State University, Indiana, and at the University of Vienna.

JAN STÖRMER

Born in 1942 in Berlin, Germany.
1962: Diploma in Architecture and Engineering, Bremen, Germany.
1969: Founder member of Me-di-um Architecten, Hamburg.
1990: joins William Alsop.

Selected buildings and projects: Cardiff Bay Visitors' Centre, (1990); North Greenwich Museum, London; CrossRail Station, Paddington, London (1992).

EMILIO AMBASZ

Born in 1943 in Argentina.
1965: MA in architecture from Princeton University.
1970-76: Curator of Design at the Museum of Modern Art, New York. Exhibitions: *Italy: The New Domestic Landscape* (1972); *The Architecture of Luis Barragan* (1974), *The Taxi Project* (1976).
He has taught at Princeton University and at the Hochschule für Gestaltung, Ulm.
Selected buildings and projects: Mycal Sanda Cultural Centre, Japan; Museum of American Folk Art, New York; Conservatory, San Antonio Botanical Center, Texas (1988).

ARAKAWA AND MADELINE GINS

ARAKAWA

Born in 1936 in Japan.
1961: moves to New York.
1987: created Containers of Mind Foundation with Madeline Gins.
1994: inauguration of an «Arakawa» room at the Nordrhein-Westphalen Museum, Düsseldorf.
Chevalier of the Order of Arts and Letters (1986); John Simon Guggenheim Fellowship (1987-88); Belgian Critics' prize (1988).

MADELINE GINS

Born in 1941 in New York, USA.
1962: graduated Barnard College, New York.
1963: collaboration with Arakawa on the «Mechanism of Meaning» research project.
Has exhibited with Arakawa since 1972 in Europe, the USA and Japan.

Constructions: Ubiquitous Site "Nagi Ryoanji" Heart (Permanent Installation) Nagi MOCA, Japan (1994); Site of Reversible Destiny (theme park and house), Gifu, Japan (1995).

ASYMPTOTE ARCHITECTURE

LISE ANNE COUTURE

Born in 1959.
1986: M. Arch. from Yale University, USA.

1988-89: Muschenheim fellowship from the University of Michigan.
Has taught at the Frankfurt Städelschule, at the University of Michigan at Ann Arbor, at Barnard College, New York, at Harvard Graduate School of Design and at Parsons School of Design, New York.

HANI RASHID

Born in 1958.
1985: M.Arch from Cranbrook Academy of Art.
Has taught at the Royal Danish Academy of Copenhagen, at the Southern California Institute of Architecture at Los Angeles, at Harvard University and at Columbia University.
1987: creation of Asymptote Architecture in New York.

Selected projects and buildings: urban plan for city of Lanciano, Italy (1987); Steel Cloud, Los Angeles (winning competition entry, 1988); Alexandria Library, Egypt (competition entry 1989); Berlin Spreebogen, Germany (competition entry 1993).

PETER COOK

Born in 1936 at Southend-on-Sea, Great Britain.
1953-56: Bournemouth College of Art, Department of Architecture.
1960: Architectural Association Diploma, London.
1961: first *Archigram* magazine, followed by eight more published annually.
1962: joined Taylor Woodrow Design Group.
1968-76: Archigram Architects, loosely formed in 1962, is formalised as a group.
He is professor of architecture at the Bartlett School of the Built Environment, University College, University of London.
Selected buildings and projects: Arcadia (1976-78); Langen Glass Museum, Germany, (with C. Hawley, 1986); Way Out West, Berlin (1988); Housing at Lutzowplatz, Berlin (1989); Canteen block, HbK, Frankfurt (1989-92).

COOP HIMMELBLAU

WOLF PRIX

Born in 1942 in Vienna, Austria.
Studied at the University of Vienna and at SCI-Arc in Los Angeles, USA.
Teaches at the School of Applied Arts in Vienna, at SCI-Arc, at the Architectural Association in London and at Harvard University, USA.

HELMUT SWICZINSKY

Born in 1944 in Poznan, Poland.
Studied at the University of Vienna and at SCI-Arc.
1968: Coop Himmelblau founded in Vienna.

Selected buildings and projects: Reiss Bar, Vienna (1977); Rote Engel, Vienna (1981); Groningen Museum, Netherlands (1994).

DECQ AND CORNETTE

ODILE DECQ

Born in 1955 at Laval, France.
1978: Architecture diploma, Paris.
1979: Diploma of Urbanism and Urban planning, École des sciences politiques, Paris.

BENOIT CORNETTE

Born in 1953 at La Guerche de Bretagne, France.
1978: Graduated in Medicine, Rennes.
1985: Graduated in Architecture, Paris.

Selected buildings and projects: Banque populaire de l'Ouest, Rennes, France (1990); Control Tower, Bordeaux Airport (1993 competition).

DILLER & SCOFIDIO

ELISABETH DILLER

Born in 1954 in Lodz, Poland.
1979: graduated from the Cooper Union School of Architecture, New York.
Teaches at Princeton University.

RICARDO SCOFIDIO

Born in 1935 in New York, USA.
1960: graduated in Architecture from the Columbia University, New York.
Teaches at the Cooper Union School of Architecture, New York.

Buildings and projects: Para-Site, video installation, New York (1991); SuitCase Studies, installation, New York (1992); Permanent "marquee" for largest movie theatre in the world, San José, California (1995).

GÜNTHER DOMENIG

Born in 1934 in Klagenfurt, Germany.
International Urbanism and Architecture prize, Cannes (1969); European prize for building in metal (1975).
Professor, University of Technology, Graz, Austria.
Selected buildings and projects: swimming pool and restaurant, Olympic Games, Munich (1975); Savings Bank, Vienna (1979); Stone House, Steindorf (1986); Power Station, Unzmarkt (1988); RESOWI, Graz University (1994-96).

DU BESSET AND LYON

PIERRE DU BESSET

Born in 1949 in Paris, France.
1974: Diploma from the École des Beaux-Arts, Paris.
1977-85: worked with Jean Nouvel.

DOMINIQUE LYON

Born in 1954 in Paris, France.
1979: Diploma from the École des Beaux-Arts, Paris.
1979-85: worked with Jean Nouvel, then with Frank O. Gehry.
1986: creation of Du Besset and Lyon.

Selected buildings and projects: maison de La Villette, parc de La Villette, Paris, (1987); offices for *Le Monde* newspaper, Paris (1990); French pavilion at Expo'92, Seville, (competition entry 1992); University Library at Jussieu, Paris, (competition entry 1992).

SIR NORMAN FOSTER

Born in 1935 in Manchester, Great Britain.
1961: BA in architecture and city planning from Manchester University.
1962: M.Arch. from Yale University, USA.
1967: creation of Foster Associates, now Sir Norman Foster & Partners.
Knighted by H.M. the Queen in 1990; Gold Medal, American Institute of Architects, 1994.
Selected buildings and projects: Sainsbury Centre for the Visual Arts, East Anglia, Great Britain (1974-78); Hong Kong & Shanghai Bank, Hong Kong (1979); Sackler Galleries at the Royal Academy of Arts, London (1979); Stansted international airport (1991); Commerzbank headquarters, Frankfurt (1991); Chek Lap Kok Airport, Hong Kong (1992); Nîmes Arts Centre (1993).

MASSIMILIANO FUKSAS

Born in 1944 in Rome, Italy.
1967: set up his practice in Rome.
1969: Architecture diploma from La Sapienza University, Rome.
Has taught at the University of La Sapienza in Rome, at the Fine Arts Academy in Stuttgart, at the École spéciale d'architecture, Paris and at Columbia University, New York.
Selected buildings and projects: Paliano Gymnasium, Italy (1985); Orvieto Cemetery, Italy (1990); restructuring of the banks of the Seine at Clichy, France (winning competition entry, 1991); the old harbour in Hamburg, Germany (winning competition entry, 1991); mediatheque, Rezé, France (1991).

FRANK O. GEHRY

Born in 1929 in Toronto, Canada.
1954: architecture diploma from the University of Southern California, USA.
1960: town planning diploma from Harvard University, USA.
Worked with Victor Gruen, Pereira & Luckman in Los Angeles, and with André Rémondet in Paris.
1962: founded Frank O. Gehry & Associates.
Pritzker Prize (1989); Lilian Gish prize (1994).
Selected buildings and projects: studio for Ron Davis, Malibu (1972); Gehry's house additions, Santa Monica (1978); Loyola Law School, Los Angeles (1982), Winton House, Minneapolis (1987); Vitra Museum, Weil am Rhein (1989); Eurodisney Leisure Centre, France (1990); concert hall, Los Angeles (winning competition entry, 1991); American Center, Paris (1993).

NICHOLAS GRIMSHAW

Born in 1939 in Hove, Great Britain.
1965: Architectural Association Diploma, London.
1980: founded Nicholas Grimshaw & Partners.
Fellow of the Chartered Society of Designers (1988); Hon. Doctorate of Letters from the University of the South Bank, London (1993); C.B.E. (1993); Mies Van der Rohe Pavilion prize (1995).
Selected buildings and projects: Oxford Ice Rink (1982); Financial Times printing works, London (1988); Combined Operations Centre for British Airways, Heathrow (1993); British Pavilion at Expo'92, Seville (1992).

ZAHA HADID

Born in 1950 in Bagdad, Iraq.
1977: Architectural Association Diploma, London.
Has taught at the Architectural Association, Columbia University, Harvard University and the University of Graz in Austria.
Architectural Design Gold Medal, London (1982).
Selected buildings and projects: The Peak, Hong Kong (winning competition entry 1983); Video Pavilion, Groningen, Netherlands (1990); Mansoon Restaurant, Sapporo, Japan (1990).

ITSUKO HASEGAWA

Born in 1941 in Shizuoka, Japan
1964: graduated from the department of architecture, Kanto Gakuin University, Japan.
1964-69: worked with Kiyonori Kikutake.
1969-78: assistant to Kazuo Shinohara at the Institute of Technology, Tokyo.
1979: established Itsuko Hasegawa Atelier.
Japan Architecture Institute Prize (1986); Aron Arts prize (1990).

Teaches at Tokyo Denki University and at Harvard University, USA.
Selected buildings and projects: Atelier at Tomigaya, Japan (1986); Shiranui Hospital, Japan (1990); Cona Village, Japan (1990); Footwork Computer Centre, Japan (1992).

JACQUES HONDELATTE

Born in 1942 at L'Absie, France.
1967: founded Duprat, Fagart, Hondelatte.
1969: Architecture Diploma from the École d'architecture, Bordeaux.
1978: established his own practice in Bordeaux.
Teaches at the École d'architecture, Bordeaux.
Selected buildings and projects: council housing, Castres, France (1979); housing, Angoulême, France (1983); school at Pessac, France (with Jean Nouvel; competition entry, 1984); University library, Jussieu, France, (competition entry, 1992); Lalanne building, Messanges, France (1995).

FRANKLIN D. ISRAEL

Born in 1945, New York, USA. Died June 1996.
1967: BA from the University of Pennsylvania.
1968: Yale University.
1971: MA from Columbia University, New York.
1975-77: senior architect at Llewelyn-Davies.
1977: established Franklin D. Israel Design Associates
Rome Prize in architecture (1973).
Professor at the School of Art and Architecture at the University of California at Los Angeles.
Selected buildings and projects: corporate headquarters for Limelight Productions, Hollywood (1991) and Virgin Records, Beverly Hills (1991); Dan House, Malibu (1995).

TOYO ITO

Born in 1941 in Seoul, Korea.
1965: architecture diploma from the University of Tokyo.
1971: establishment of Urban Robot (URBOT), Tokyo, now Toyo Ito & Associates Architects.
Mainichi Art Prize for the Yatsushiro Municipal Museum, Japan (1992).
Selected buildings and projects: Yatsushiro Municipal Museum, Kumamoto (1991); Shimosuwa Municipal Museum, Nagano (1993); Aged People's Home in Yatsushiro, Kumamoto (1994); Yatsushiro Fire Station, Kumamoto (1995).

DANIEL LIBESKIND

Born in 1945 in Lodz, Poland.
1970: architecture diploma from the Cooper Union School of Architecture, New York.
1972: postgraduate course in the history and theory of architecture, University of Essex, Great Britain.
Head of the Department of Architecture at the Cranbrook Academy of Art
Selected buildings and projects: Yatai Pavilion World Design Exhibition, Japan (1989); "Symbol for the City", urban design construction, Groningen, Netherlands (1993).

ENRIC MIRALLES MOYA

Born in 1955 in Spain.
1978: diploma in architecture from ETSAB, Barcelona.
1984: establishment of the Miralles and Carme Pinós practice, now Enric Miralles Moya.
Teaches at ETSAB, Barcelona and has an architecture Master Class at the Städelschule in Frankfurt.
Selected buildings and projects: Social Centre

for Circulo de Lectores, Madrid (1992); La Mina Civic Centre, Barcelona (1993); Ramblas in Reus, Tarragona (1993); National Rhythmic Gymnastics Centre, Alicante (1994).

MORPHOSIS

THOM MAYNE

Born in 1944, at Waterbury, Connecticut, USA.
1968: BA in architecture from the University of Southern California.
1978: MA in architecture from Harvard University.
1972: Co-founder of the Southern Californian Institute of Architecture (SCI-Arc).
1975: establishment of Morphosis with Michael Rotondi.
Teaches at Harvard, Yale and SCI-Arc.
Rome Prize (1977); architecture prize of the American Academy of Arts and Letters (1992).

Selected buildings and projects: Cedars Sinai Comprehensive Cancer Centre, Los Angeles (1987); AGB Library, Berlin (1988); MTV Studios, Potsdamer Platz, Berlin (1990).

ERIC OWEN MOSS

Born in 1943 in Los Angeles, USA.
1965: BA from the University of California at Los Angeles (UCLA)
1968: MA from the University of Berkeley.
1974: architecture diploma from Harvard University.
1974: establishment of Eric Owen Moss Architects.
Teaches at the Southern California Institute of Architecture (SCI-Arc).
Selected buildings and projects: Lindblade Tower, Culver City (1989); the Lawson/Western House, Los Angeles (1993); Ince Theatre, Culver City (1994).

JEAN NOUVEL

Born in 1945 in Fumel, France.
1970: establishment of his first office, now called Architectures Jean Nouvel.
1972: Diploma of the École des Beaux-Arts, Paris.
Chevalier of the Order of Arts and Letters (1983); chevalier of the Order of Merit (1987); Architecture Grand Prix (1987).
Selected buildings and projects: Institute of the Arab World, Paris, with G. Lezenes, P. Soria, Architecture Studio (1987); Agence CLMBBDO, île Saint-Germain (1993); Conference Centre, Tours (1993); social housing, Bezons (1993).

OFFICE OF METROPOLITAN ARCHITECTURE

REM KOOLHAAS

Born in 1944 in Rotterdam, Netherlands.
1972: Architectural Association Diploma, London.
1974: establishment of OMA in London and New York with Madelon Vriesendorp, and Zoe and Elia Zenghelis.
1978: publication of «Delirious New York».
1980: establishment of OMA in Rotterdam.
Selected buildings and projects: Dance Theatre, The Hague (1987); Byzantium, Amsterdam (1990); Nexus housing, Fukuoka (1991); Konsthal, Rotterdam (1992); Lille Grand Palais, Lille, France (1994).

RENZO PIANO

Born in 1937 in Genoa, Italy.
1964: diploma from Milan Polytechnic.
1965-70: worked with Louis Kahn in Philadelphia and Z.S. Malowski in London.

1971-80: collaboration with Richard Rogers, Peter Rice and Richard Fitzgerald.
1981: establishment of Building Workshop in Genoa and Paris.
Selected buildings and projects: Pompidou Centre, Paris (1977); De Ménil Foundation, Houston, Texas (1989); *Crown Princess* liner (1989); Bercy commercial centre, Paris (1990).

CHRISTIAN DE PORTZAMPARC

Born in 1944 in Brittany, France.
1969: Diploma from the École des Beaux-Arts, Paris.
1971: established his own practice.
Taught at the École spéciale d'architecture, Paris and at the Paris-Nanterre Architecture School.
Commander of the Order of Arts and Letters; Architecture Grand Prix (1992); Pritzker Prize (1994).
Selected buildings and projects: Les Hautes Formes housing, Paris (1975); Opera Dance Academy, Nanterre (1983), Bourdelle Museum, Paris (1992).

FRANÇOIS ROCHE

Born in 1961 in Paris, France.
1987: Architecture Diploma.
1993: demonstration at the Institut français d'architecture.
Villa des Médicis external fellowship.
Selected buildings and projects: House of Japan, Paris (competition entry 1990); film storage building, Bois d'Arcy (1991); Art and Media Museum (competition entry, 1991); Spreebogen, Berlin (competition entry, 1993); renovation of the Deligny swimming pool, Paris (1993).

SIR RICHARD ROGERS

Born in 1933 in Florence, Italy.
1959: Architectural Association Diploma, London.
1961: Architecture Diploma from Yale University, USA.
1963: establishment of Team 4 with Sue Rogers and Norman and Wendy Foster.
1971: establishment of Piano & Rogers, now Sir Richard Rogers & Partners in London and Tokyo.
Légion d'honneur (1986); Royal Gold Medal for Architecture (London, 1985); knighted by H.M. the Queen in 1991; Chevalier of the Order of Arts and Letters (1995).
Taught at the Universities of California, Princeton, Harvard and Berkeley.
Selected buildings and projects: Pompidou Centre, Paris (1977); Lloyds Building,
London (1986); INMOS factory, Newport, Great Britain (1982); headquarters building for Channel 4 television, London (1991).

SHIN TAKAMATSU

Born in 1948 in Shimana, Japan.
1971: graduated in architecture from Kyoto University.
1974: MA in architecture from Kyoto University.
1980: doctorate from Kyoto University. Establishment of Shin Takamatsu Architects & Associates in Kyoto.
1992: established Takamatsu & Lahyani Architects in Berlin
Fuchi Bikan Prize (1983); International Interior Design prize (1987); Grand Prix of the Osaka Architects' Association (1987).
Selected buildings and projects: Wako Building, Tokyo (1990); Sand Museum, Nima (1990); Syntax, Kyoto (1990); Solaris Building, Awagasa (1990); Earthtecture, Tokyo, (1991).

MASAHARU TAKASAKI

Born in 1953, in Kagoshima, Japan.
1976: graduated from the Meijo University School of Architecture.
1982: founded Takasaki Manobito Institute.
1990: founded Masaharu Takasaki Architects.
First prize in *The Japan Architect* International House Design Competition.
Teaches at Stuttgart Technological University and the University of Graz.
Selected buildings and projects: Crystal Light, Tokyo (1987); Tamana City Observatory Museum, Kumamoto (1992); Kuju National Park Restaurant, Oita (1994); Kihoku-cho Astronomical Museum, Kagoshima (1995); Shomyo Kindergarten, Kagoshima (1995).

KIYOSHI SEY TAKEYAMA

Born in 1954 in Osaka, Japan.
1977: graduated from Kyoto University School of Architecture.
1979: graduated from Tokyo University Graduate School of Architecture.
Associate Professor at Kyoto University School of Architecture
Selected buildings and projects: OXY Nogizaka, Tokyo (1987); D-Hôtel, Osaka (1989); house in Modorigaoka, Tokyo (1989); TERRAZA, Tokyo (1991); Blue Screen House, Osaka (1993).

BERNARD TSCHUMI

Born in 1944 in Lausanne, Switzerland.
1969: degree in architecture from the Federal Institute of Technology (ETH), Zurich.
Dean of Columbia University Graduate School of Architecture.
Selected buildings and projects: Chief Architect for the Parc de La Villette project, Paris (1983); city-bridges, Lausanne (1988); video gallery, Groningen, Netherlands (1989); Chartres master plan, France (winning competition entry, 1991).

LEBBEUS WOODS

Born in 1940 in Lansing, Michigan, USA.
Graduated from Purdue University School of Engineering and the University of Illinois School of Architecture.
Has been Visiting Professor at SCI-Arc, Harvard and Columbia Universities; and is now Visiting Professor of Architecture at the Cooper Union School of Architecture, New York, and at the University of Innsbruck, Austria.
Selected buildings and projects: Zagreb-Free-Zone (1991); War and Architecture (1992-93); apartment blocks Electroprivrede Building, Unis Towers, Sarajevo (1994); Havana Projects (1995).

SHOEI YOH

Born in 1940 in Kumamoto, Japan.
1962: graduated in economics from Keio Gijuku University, Tokyo.
1964: foreign student grant in aid, majored in Fine and Applied Arts at Wittenberg University, Springfield, Ohio, USA.
1970: Shoei Yoh & Associates Fukuoka.
Visiting Professor at Columbia University Graduate School of Architecture, New York and lecturer at Kyushi University,Japan.
Japan Institute of Architecture Prize (1983 and 1989); IAKS prize Cologne, gold medal (1993).
Selected buildings and projects: stainless steel house with light grille (1981); glass house between sea and sky (1991); Galaxie, Toyama and gymnasium (1992); community centre and kindergarten, Naiju (1994); centre for children and old people (1995).

GLOSSARY

ARCHITECTS

Alberti Leon Battista (1404-72)
Painter, musician, scientist, architect, Alberti is a Renaissance man. His treatise «De re aedificatoria» defines a building as a whole where all the parts are in harmony, and architecture as an autonomous discipline.

Baumgarten Paul
Modernist Berlin architect who carried out interesting research during the thirties with Eternit. He built the station at Müllverlade on the Spree Canal (1950) and an elegant building in the Hansaviertel district (1957).
His restructuring of the Reichstag during the sixties is being destroyed to make way for Sir Norman Foster's new project.

Bayer Herbert
Bayer was born in Austria at the beginning of the century and was a pupil of the Bauhaus at Weimar before becoming a teacher of typography and advertizing at Dessau. After 1938 he continued his career in the United States.

Behrens Peter (1868-1940)
Heir to Schinkel and the classical tradition, Behrens is also the architect who, at the beginning of the century, instituted new relations with industry. His collaboration with A.E.G. led to the advent of industrial design. Three young architects worked in his office around 1910: Walter Gropius, Le Corbusier and Mies Van der Rohe.

Gropius Walter (1883-1969)
Influenced by Behrens and industrial rationalism, Gropius established the Bauhaus teaching, and then went into exile, first in England, then in the United States where he was very influential through his teaching at Harvard. He advised Emery Roth & Sons on the Pan Am Building in New York (1964).

Hejduk John (1929-)
This American architect and poet was among the first to introduce fiction into architectural thinking. His influence springs from his role as head of the Cooper Union School of Architecture (since 1964) and as theoretician and member of the New York Five (with Peter Eisenman, Michael Graves, Charles Gwathmey and Richard Meier).

Isozaki Arata (1931-)
A disciple of Kenzo Tange, and member of the Metabolist Movement, steeped in western culture (Duchamp and Marilyn Monroe), Isozaki's oeuvre is both brilliant and eclectic.

Johnson Philip (1906-)
First curator of the department of architecture at the Museum of Modern Art in New York, Johnson became an architect in 1940. After facilitating the exile of Mies Van der Rohe in the United States in 1938 he was his most assiduous pupil until he embraced post-modernism of which he became the most cynical promoter.

Kahn Louis I. (1901-1975)
Educated in Philadelphia, Kahn received late recognition for his building for the Yale Gallery (1954) before becoming the archetypal modern with buildings such as the Salk Institute, La Jolla (1965), the Kimbell Museum, Dallas and the Dacca Parliament in Bangladesh (1974).

Kikutake Kiyonori (1928-)
Creator and leader of the Japanese Metabolists, Kikutake's work consists of large utopian projects and megastructures, aerial and underwater cities of a kind that proliferated in Japan in the sixties.

Kleihues Josef Paul (1933-)
German architect whose work melds Italian rationalism with Prussian classicism. From 1979 on he was the influential director of the International Building Exhibition (IBA) in Berlin.

Laprade Albert
French architect who, with L. Bazin, built the Marbeuf Garage (1929) – now destroyed – and played an active role in the 1937 Paris Exposition.

Le Corbusier Charles Edouard Jeanneret called (1887-1966)
One of the great figures of the twentieth century whose theoretical work leading to certain questionable architectural and urban principles sometimes camouflages an oeuvre that is both innovative and infinitely variable. His masterpieces: the Villas Savoye at Poissy and Stein at Garches, the Salvation Army Hostel, Paris, the Unité d'habitation in Marseille, the monastery of la Tourette, the chapel at Ronchamp, and Chandigarh in India are among the most important works of this century.

Lissitzky El (1890-1941)
A founder member and proselyte of Russian Constructivism in the twenties.
His « Proun », indebted to Malevich and Suprematism, advocated a new state of art between painting and architecture.

Loos Adolf (1870-1933)
Viennese but fiercely opposed to the Secession, Loos travelled in America where he discovered Sullivan and the Chicago school which inspired his famous polemical essay "Ornament and Crime." The Steiner House in Vienna (1910) is the first concrete house. His rigorously classical buildings have an elegant refinement.

Meier Richard (1934-)
The American architect Richard Meier has perfected the architecture of Le Corbusier's «white villas».

Mendelsohn Eric (1887-1953)
German Expressionnist and architect of a cult building of its time: the Einstein Tower in Potsdam (1924). Mendelsohn built some of the most remarkable commercial buildings (shops and offices) in Germany during the thirties. From 1933 he pursued his career in England and then in the United States.

Mies Van der Rohe Ludwig (1886-1969)
One of the great masters of twentieth-century architecture, the most classical and the most influential of the «pure» modernists. His master-pieces include: the Barcelona pavilion (1927), the apartment blocks on Lake Shore Drive, Chicago (1951), the Seagram Building, New York (1958) and the Berlin National Gallery (1968).

Mozuna Kiko (1941-)
Japanese architect who reconciles the traditions of east and west in strongly symbolic objects.

Neutra Richard (1892-1970)
Viennese architect in exile in the United States where he practised in Chicago before settling in Los Angeles. He built the Lovell House there in 1929. It remains one of the models of modern heroic architecture. He greatly influenced a whole generation of young Californian architects.

Piñon & Viaplana
Architects belonging to the new Barcelona School.

Piños Carmen
Spanish architect, partner of Enric Miralles Moya.

Poelzig Hans (1869-1936)
German Expressionist architect influential during the twenties (Grosses Schauspielhaus, Berlin, 1919). His work was discredited by the rationalists, but is now once again attracting interest.

Price Cedric
British architect, dandy and eminence grise for a whole generation, Price brilliantly synthesizes high tech, ecology and recycling in his theoretical projects (Potteries Thinkbelt, Fun Palace) and his temporary installations. A key work is the InterAction Centre, London (1977). Teaches at the Architectural Association.

Scharoun Hans (1893-1972)
One of the first Expressionists, member of Bruno Taut's «glass chain», Hans Scharoun was Chief Architect for the reconstruction of Berlin and was reponsible for the Berlin-capital plan in 1957 and some apartment blocks (Romeo & Juliet, Stuttgart). He built his master piece, the Berlin Philharmonic Hall, in 1964.

Schinkel Karl Friedrich (1781-1841)
The purest of the Berlin classicists, Schinkel influenced both Peter Behrens and Mies Van der Rohe.

Schindler Rudolf (1887-1953)
Viennese architect, an admirer of Adolf Loos, Schindler emigrated to the United States in the second decade of the century and worked with Frank Lloyd Wright before setting up his own practice in Los Angeles. He had a brilliant but uneven career leaving two undisputed masterpieces: his own house in King's Road and Dr. Lovell's Beach House at Newport (1926). He was influenced by De Stijl. His subtle sensitivity to the Southern Californian setting and the appropriateness of his buildings to that environment is increasingly appreciated today.

Shinohara Kazuo (1925-)
Japanese architect of very elegant houses in Japanese style that are subtly symbolic. But his later works are vidently high tech and express the chaos inherent in the Japanese city.

Stirling Sir James (1926-1992)
First recognized as an orthodox modernist, Stirling was influenced by the historicists and at the end of his career built curious structures in which Egyptian, classical and baroque play an

ironic role. The Staatsgalerie in Stuttgart is his masterpiece.

Taut Bruno (1880-1938)
His Glass Pavilion at the Werkbund exhibition in Cologne (1914) was the prelude to the Glass Architecture which he developed with the Expressionists of the Novembergruppe. He built two remarkable «Siedlungen» in Berlin: the Britz complex (with Martin Wagner, 1930) and «Uncle Tom's Cabin» (1931). He left Germany in 1933, going first to Japan and then to Turkey.

Tusquets Oscar (1941-)
A Barcelona architect who puts the anecdotal above theory, the particular above the general, ambiguity above clarity and the figurative aove the abstract. He is closest to Venturi of all the Europeans.

Van Doesburg Theo (1883-1931)
Painter and founder (with J.J. Oud) of the De Stijl movement that applies Mondrian's ideas to architecture and to design. He was their most energetic promoter. His only buildings are a café in Strasbourg, l'Aubette (with Jean Arp), and his own studio/house at Meudon.

Venturi Robert
American architect whose two books «Complexity and contradiction in architecture» and «Learning from Las Vegas» have made him the most influential theoretician of the Post-Modern movement.

Webb Michael (1937-)
British architect, member of Archigram.

Wright Frank Lloyd (1867-1959)
The great master of American architecture whose career covers a large part of the twentieth century. It began in Chicago with Sullivan, continued in Japan, then in the United States. Wright built more than four hundred buildings including: the Unity Temple, Oak Park (1906), Frederick C. Robie House (1909), the Miniaturan, Pasadena, Fallingwater (1936), Johnson's Wax Company Administration Building (1936), the Luckland Campus, and the Solomon R. Guggenheim Museum (1956).

BUILDINGS

Broadacre City
Frank Lloyd Wright's plan for a democratic city with no hierarcy and no city centre.

Crystal Palace
Built for the 1851 Great Exhibition in London, the Crystal Palace was an immediate success because of its size, its audacity and its prefabricated iron and glass structure. It was taken down at the end of the Exhibition and erected again in Sydenham but was destroyed by fire in 1936.

Garden City
Inspired by the socialist Utopians of the nineteenth century, Ebenezer Howard's garden cities reconcile the city-dweller with nature and create a self-sufficient community life away from the turpitude of the city. The first one was Letchworth (1903).

Glass Pavilion
Built in 1914 for the Deutscher Werkbund exhibition, Bruno Taut's Glass Pavilion is an

example of a Modern architecture whose constructional rigour does not exclude formal preoccupations.

National Gallery, Berlin
The last building by Mies Van der Rohe (1968). The architecture of this large-scale pavilion lies somewhere between Prussian classicism and Japanese minimalism.

Pompidou Centre
The most extreme example of a high-tech monument, the architects of which - Piano and Rogers - have stressed its artisanal charcter on innumerable occasions.

Radiant City
The ideal city according to Le Corbusier (1935).

Ronchamp
The most convoluted of Le Corbusier's works, built towards the end of his career at the same time as he wrote the poem to the right angle.

Siedlungen
Between the wars Germany produced a series of apartment blocks inspired by Modern architects. The growth of social housing was spectacular and often of very good quality for the time. May in Frankfurt, Gropius, Taut, Scharoun, and Mies Van der Rohe in Berlin were among those who contributed to this development.

GROUPS

Archigram
The first issue of *Archigram* was published in 1961. It was a kind of magazine put together by a group of young London architects (Warren Chalk, Peter Cook, Denis Crompton, David Greene, Ron Herron, Michael Webb). Eight issues were published in which the group developed an architecture inspired by the consumer society and Pop images and which, once rationalized, would constitute the basis for British high-tech.

Graz, School of
In the sixties, Raimund Abram and Günther Domenig founded a movement in violent reaction to the International Style. It continued in the seventies with such young architects as Enfried Huth, Szyskowitz & Kowalsky, Klaus Kada and Gerngross & Richter. The monument to this period is the refectory of the Ursuline nuns at Graz, a zoomorphic building in concrete, designed by Domenig and Huth (1976).

Haus Rücker Co
Founded in Vienna at the beginning of the seventies by Laurids Ortner, Günther Zamp and Klaus Pinter, Haus Rücker Co has organized various demonstrations that question our use of the city and the introduction of communications technologies into the urban environment.

Independent Group
Formed in London in 1952, the I.G. included artists Richard Hamilton and Eduardo Paolozzi, critics Reyner Banham and Lawrence Alloway and architects Peter and Alison Smithson. The «Parallel of Life and Art» exhibition at the Institute of Contemporary Art in 1953,

punctuated with advertisements, popular magazines and science fiction images prefigures Pop Art and the more romantic side of high-tech architecture.

Missing Link Productions
Space capsules and inflatable structures constitute the weapons of this Viennese group of the seventies for the transformation of the city. Later, Missing Link came back to earth to study the Viennese Siedlungen of the thirties from a historicist rather than futurist viewpoint.

Novembergruppe
For a short period from 1918 to 1920, the Novembergruppe comprised all the young architectural activists in Berlin, from Gropius to Mendelsohn and from Taut to Mies Van der Rohe in an expressionist movement. The group was dissolved following the repression of the Spartakist revolt. Bruno Taut continued its Expressionist vein in his «chain of glass», while Gropius went on to found the Bauhaus.

ENGINEERS

Arup Ove (1895-1993)
A Scandinavian who emigrated to London, Ove Arup played a role in almost every great adventure in contemporary architecture and collaborated with architects as diverse as Lubetkin, the Smithsons, Jorn Utzon and Piano & Rogers.

Brunel Isambard Kingdom (1806-1859)
One of the great British engineers of the nineteenth century. His structures include the Clifton Suspension Bridge at Bristol and the liners *Great Western* and *Great Eastern*. He was also the inventor of the first portable hospital designed for the Crimean War.

Candela Felix (1910-1994)
A Spaniard who emigrated to Mexico, Candela specialised in curtains of thin concrete (Church of Our Lady of the Miracles in Mexico, 1955).

Fitzpatrick Antony (1955-)
A British engineer, part of the brilliant Ove Arup team. Has worked with leading international architects including Sir Norman Foster (the Hong Kong & Shanghai Bank).

Freyssinet Eugène (1879-1962)
A French engineer who designed bridges and the magnificent hangar at Orly Airport (1916).

Fuller Richard Buckminster (1895-1989)
The self-taught Fuller was one of the most brilliant engineers of the twentieth century. Inspired by car production, he designed an industrialised house, the Dymaxion in 1927. Later his research was concerned with reticular structures which led to the invention of the geodesic dome.

Morandi Riccardo (1902-)
An Italian engineer famous for his structures in prestressed concrete: the Arno bridge (1956), the Polcevera viaduct (1965) and the A6 motorway in France.

Nervi Pier Luigi (1891-1979)
Italian engineer who developed a technique called ferrocemento in which a series of steel meshes make concrete more tensile. His major work is the Turin Exhibition Hall (1949).

Paxton Joseph (1803-1865)
A British gardener, Paxton was self-taught and built innovative glasshouses before his masterpiece, the Crystal Palace, in 1851.

Prouvé Jean (1901-1984)
This French engineer perfected the curtain wall: from the Maison du Peuple in Clichy (with Beaudoin and Lods, 1939) to the first tower at La Défense in Paris, and from his metal house in Meudon to his basic housing for the Abbé Pierre, his work is the fruit of a stubborn and generous perfectionism.

Rice Peter (1935-1992)
A senior engineer at Ove Arup, Peter Rice's career was both brilliant and tumultuous: he was the structural engineer for the Sydney Opera House and for the Pompidou Centre. Renzo Piano has said of him that he solved technical problems like a virtuoso pianist playing with his eyes closed.

INSTITUTIONS

Deutscher Werkbund
Founded in 1907 by Muthesius to bring about a fusion of the arts, architecture and the applied arts, the Werkbund was responsible for three important exhibitions: Cologne in 1914, which brought together the pioneers of the alliance of the arts and industry including Van de Velde, Gropius, Behrens, Hoffman and Taut; Weissenhof in 1927, a development built by the best European architects of the time; and the 1930 Paris exposition which revealed, through Gropius, the work of Herbert Bayer, Moholy Nagy and Breuer, all refugees from the Bauhaus.

I.A.U.S (Institute of Architecture and Urban Studies)
The Institute of Architecture and Urban Studies was founded in New York by Peter Eisenman. It acts as a theoretical laboratory and exhibition space.

I.B.A.
The Internationale Bauausstellung (international building exhibition) follows in the footsteps of Weissenhof (an exhibition held in Stuttgart in 1927 that presented models of contemporary housing). In the course of reconstruction work on the city, a first exhibition on the theme of housing was held in Berlin, leading to the building of the Hansaviertel district in 1957, on which an impressive number of talented European architects worked. The success of this operation led to the institutionalization of the I.B.A.

Architecture Schools mentioned in the text

Architectural Association, London;
School of Architecture and Conservation, Columbia University, New York, USA;
Cooper Union School of Architecture, New York;
École des Beaux-Arts, Paris;
School of Architecture and Urbanism, Harvard University, Cambridge, Mass., USA;
Illinois Institue of Technology (IIT), University of Chicago, Ill., USA;
Istituto Politécnico, Milan, Italy;
Southern California Institute of Architecture (SCI-Arc), Los Angeles, Ca, USA ;
School of Architecture at the University of California at Los Angeles (UCLA), USA;
School of Architecture at the University of Southern California (USC), Los Angeles, USA;
School of Art and Architecture at Yale University, New Haven, Connecticut, USA.

Bauhaus (1919-1933)
Founded in Weimar by Walter Gropius, the Bauhaus remains the most famous school of the century both for its innovative teaching programme, the reputation of its faculty - which included Johannes Itten, Vassily Kandinsky, Paul Klee, Moholy Nagy, Josef Albers, Marcel Breuer, Herbert Bayer - and for its troubled history. It was transferred from Weimar to Dessau in 1925. Gropius resigned in 1928 and was succeeded by Hannes Meyer, then Mies Van der Rohe. The school closed in Berlin in 1933 but the teaching of the Bauhaus was continued in the United States by Gropius at Harvard and Moholy Nagy at Chicago.

Hochschule für Gestaltung, Ulm.
Established by Max Bill in 1951, the Ulm School was intended as a continuation of the Bauhaus. It too had a troubled existence. Max Bill resigned in 1956 and was succeeded by Herbert Ohl. Teaching emphasised strict methodology but was gradually radicalised under the influence of Maldonado, Schnaidt and Bonsiepe and had to close down in 1968. The Ulm school remains synonymous with «Gute Form».

Vkhutemas
The Vkhutemas were created in 1918 in Moscow to combine the teaching of the arts, the applied arts and architecture. Directed by the constructivists Ladovsky, Tatlin, Rodchenko and others, who greatly influenced Soviet architecture of the twenties and were at the origin of the Bauhaus.

PHOTO CREDITS

Cover and pages 188, 190, 191, 192, 193, 194, 196, 197: photos Philippe Ruault.
Pages 2, 162, 164, 165: photos Mitsumasa Fujitsuaka.
Page 6: photo André Morain.
Page 8: photo Matsumoto Norihiko.
Page 9: photo Rivière, musée d'Orsay.
Page 10: photo CNACGP.
Page 11 right: photo Barch-Reisinger Museum, Harvard University ; left: document 1937 Exposition.
Pages 14, 16, 17, 18, 19: documents P. Cook / Ch. Hawley.
Pages 20, 22, 23, 24, 25: documents Arakawa and Madeline Gins.
Pages 26, 31, 33 bottom: photos Udo Hesse.
Page 29: city of Cologne.
Page 30: Art Institute of Chicago.
Page 33 top: photo Elisabeth Govan.
Pages 12, 34, 37, 38, 39: documents Bernard Tschumi Architects.
Page 38 top: photo Dan Cornish.
Pages 40, 42, 43: documents Lebbeus Woods.
Pages 44, 46, 47: documents François Roche.
Pages 48, 60: photos Xavier Basiana Vers.
Page 50 bottom: photo Kanji Hiwatashi.
Page 52 left: Yutaka Kinumaki.
Page 52 right: Toshimaru Kitajima.
Page 53: photo Yutaka Kinumaki.
Pages 54-55: photos Yoshio Hata.

Pages 56-57: documents Nicholas Grimshaw and Partners.
Pages 58-59: photos John Edward Linden.
Page 63: photo Richard Davies.
Page 64: document Alsop / Störmer.
Pages 66-67: photo P. Raffery.
Pages 68, 70, 71: documents Jacques Hondelatte.
Pages 72, 136, 137: photos Joshua White.
Page 74: photo Fujita.
Pages 75, 76, 77, 78: photos Nicolas Borel.
Page 79: infographics J.C. Chaulet.
Pages 80, 83: documents Agence Takeyama.
Pages 85, 86, 87: photo Satoshi Asakawa.
Page 88: photo Kozlowski.
Pages 90, 91: photos Aki Furudate.
Page 92: infographics Christophe Valtin.
Pages 94, 95: documents Decq / Cornette.
Pages 96, 98, 99: photo Gert von Bassewitz.
Pages 100, 102, 103, 104, 105: documents OMA.
Pages 106, 108, 110, 111: documents Zaha Hadid
Page 109: photos Richard Bryant
Pages 112, 116, 117, 118, 119: photos Margherita Spiluttini.
Pages 114, 115, 130, 131: photos Tom Bonner.
Pages 120, 122, 123: photos Hisao Suzuki.
Pages 124, 125: photos Christopher Yates.

Pages 126, 127: photos Grant Mudford.
Pages 128, 129: photos Paul Groh.
Pages 132, 134, 135: photos Don F. Wong.
Page 138: photo Takashi Miyamoto.
Pages 140, 144 bottom, 145 bottom: documents Emilio Ambasz.
Pages 143, 144 top, 145 top: photos Ryuzo Masunaga.
Pages 146, 149: photos Eui-Sung Vi.
Pages 147, 148: documents Morphosis.
Pages 150, 151: documents Takasaki.
Pages 152, 155, 157, 159: photos Eamonn O'Mahony.
Page 160: photo Itsuko Hasegawa.
Page 163: photo Katsuaki Furudate.
Pages 166, 167: photos Shuji Yamada.
Pages 168, 198: documents Nacasa and Partners.
Pages 170, 172, 173: documents Asymptote Architecture.
Pages 174, 175, 176, 177: documents Diller / Scofidio.
Pages 178-179: documents Du Besset and Lyon.
Pages 180-181: photos Denance Archipress.
Pages 182, 184, 185: documents Toyo Ito.
Pages 186, 187: photos Shinkendiku-Sho
Page 201: photo Retoria.

Printed in France by Groupe Horizon
Parc d'activités de la plaine de Jouques - 200, avenue de Coulin - 13420 Gémenos
Printer N° 0411-013